Best of
International
Cooking

HPBooks®

A World of Good Foods

Here it is, the first large, fully illustrated cookbook of authentic and easy-to-make specialties from 64 countries. It is the result of many years' work and testing. This superb book will provide you new and delicious suggestions for everyday meals. It's also great for celebrations, simple suppers with friends or family and gourmet meals for special occasions.

Each recipe has a color photo so you can see how the finished dish will look. All recipe ingredients should be readily available in your supermarket or gourmet-food store.

In our search for recipes, we kept mainly to dishes that are well known and popular in the respective countries. We have chosen recipes that are representative of the national cuisine of the people and not merely those that appear on restaurant menus. In addition to well-known dishes, we have selected some unusual ones. We hope they will meet with your approval.

We have included a number of basic recipes that are referred to throughout the book. One of these is puff-pastry dough. Puff pastry is not easy to make, but in some areas may not be available. Where it is available, it is found in the frozen-food department. We suggest you call several supermarkets and specialty stores in your community to see if it is available before making your own.

We believe this book is unique in allowing you to enjoy culinary delights from around the world. We know you will enjoy preparing the recipes and wish you every success, as well as many compliments from your guests!

Annette Wolter and Christian Teubner

ANOTHER BEST-SELLING VOLUME FROM HPBooks®

Executive Editor: Rick Bailey
Editorial Director: Retha M. Davis
Editor: Carroll Latham
Art Director: Don Burton
Photography: Christian Teubner, George deGennaro Studios and Ray Manley Studios
Typography: Cindy Coatsworth, Michelle Claridge

Published by HPBooks®, P.O. Box 5367, Tucson, AZ 85703
602/888-2150
ISBN 0-89586-278-6
Library of Congress Catalog Number 83-82993
© 1984 Fisher Publishing, Inc. Printed in the U.S.A.
Cover photo: Array of International Foods

First published under the title *Spezialitäten der Welt köstlich wie noch nie* © Gräfe und Unzer GmbH, Munchen 1982

English edition published by The Hamlyn Publishing Group Limited, 1984

Contents

Kitchen Equipment from Around the World

Much of the kitchen equipment in daily use in other countries can be bought from kitchen-specialty stores. Many speciality dishes are easier to make if you use the correct equipment, but you can often use what you already have in your kitchen. However, if this book inspires you to do so, invest in some of the kitchen equipment described below.

Wok

The wok is a traditional Oriental cooking pan. Use it for stir-frying, steaming and for making soups. In the Orient, it is used over an open fire so the center of the rounded base comes into direct contact with the flame. Thus the temperature is lower around the edges, which is important for those dishes where the ingredients are added and fried at different times. As ingredients are cooked, they are pushed to the cooler rim of the wok to keep warm. Other raw ingredients are added and cooked in the center of the pan. Woks may have a round or flat base. The round base is placed on a metal ring on the stove top. Those with a flat base can be placed directly on an electric or gas stove burner. Electric woks have built-in thermostats and can be set at a range of temperatures. Before using a new wok, *season it.* First, soak the wok in hot soapy water for one hour, adding boiling water periodically. Scour thoroughly inside and outside to remove any machine-oil coating. Rinse thoroughly, then dry over medium heat. Leaving the wok over heat, add 2 teaspoons peanut oil. Using tongs to hold a paper or cloth towel, rub the oil over the hot wok. Repeat 2 or 3 times, then wipe with a dry towel. After using your wok, wash it in hot soapy water. Season again if the wok begins to rust.

Most woks come with a metal rack. With boiling water in the bottom of the wok, other containers can be placed on the rack for steaming vegetables, meats and breads. Metal and wooden tools can be used to stir and remove food from the wok.

Mortar and Pestle

In many African and Asian countries, a mortar and pestle is an essential item of kitchen equipment. Use these to grind dried ingredients and to puree and blend both raw and cooked ingredients. Mortars and pestles are available in various sizes and may be made of metal, wood, porcelain or glass.

Mortars and pestles are available in various shapes and sizes.

A paellera is the traditional pan for cooking Spanish paella.

Paella Pan

Usually made from cast iron, this large pan is fairly deep and has handles on both sides. In Spain it is known as a *paellera*. Gourmets maintain that paella, the famous Spanish dish which originated in the Levant, only tastes right made in this type pan. Traditionally, paella is eaten with wooden spoons, straight from the pan.

Stovetop Casserole

Stovetop casseroles may be iron, aluminum or glass ovenware. They can be used on top of the stove and in the oven without fear of breaking. Several recipes call for stovetop casseroles. If unavailable, use saucepans to do as much cooking as possible, then transfer ingredients to ovenware for baking.

Stovetop casseroles are made of iron, aluminum, ceramic or glass.

Springform pans have straight removable sides.

Molds

Molds used in this book may be decorative or plain. Some foods to be cooked are poured into a mold and suspended over boiling water while others are lowered into the water. This may be done in a double boiler or as shown below.

Springform Pan

Springform pans have removable sides that fasten tightly to a flat or tube-pan center. The side is straight and is held in place with a clamp. They are traditionally used for cheesecakes, and other cakes and breads that need a straight-sided pan.

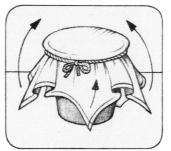

The wide rim or flaired top of some molds lets you fasten a cloth over the mold.

Knot the ends of the cloth above the mold. The mixture in the mold cooks by hanging in simmering water.

Basic Recipes

Light Meat Stock

2 lbs. beef or veal bones, chopped
Water
1 lb. meaty beef shanks
1/8 teaspoon salt
2 leeks or 1/2 onion, chopped
1 carrot, chopped
1 celery stalk, chopped
1 onion
4 black peppercorns
1 bay leaf

Place beef or veal bones in a large pot; add cold water to cover. Bring to a boil, then drain; rinse bones and pan thoroughly. In pan, combine blanched bones, beef shanks, salt and cold water to cover. Bring to a boil; skim foam from surface until clear. Partially cover pan; simmer 1-1/2 hours. Add remaining ingredients; simmer uncovered 1-1/2 hours longer. To remove fat from surface, skim with a spoon; use paper towels to soak up remaining fat that rises to surface. Set stock aside to cool; when cool, remove any remaining fat. Strain stock through a fine sieve. Makes about 1 quart.

Variation

Chicken Stock: Substitute chicken bones and meat for beef bones and meat.

Coconut Milk

Coconut milk can be made at home. Grate 3-1/2 cups fresh coconut or use unsweetened packaged coconut. In a medium saucepan, combine coconut and 2 cups milk. Bring to a boil. Let stand 30 minutes. Strain mixture through muslin or cheesecloth into a bowl, squeezing well to remove all milk. Discard coconut. Makes about 2 cups.

Vanilla Sugar

1-1/2 cups sugar
1 vanilla bean

Make your own vanilla sugar by placing sugar and vanilla bean in a pint jar with a tight-fitting lid. Let stand 1 to 2 weeks before using. Shake jar periodically. As flavored sugar is used, add more sugar. Makes 1-1/2 cups.

Puff Pastry

2/3 cup chilled unsalted butter
1-1/3 cups all-purpose flour
2/3 cup cake flour
1 teaspoon salt
1 teaspoon lemon juice
1/2 to 2/3 cup ice water

Melt 1 tablespoon butter; refrigerate remaining butter. Sift flours onto a cool marble slab or board; make a large well in center. Place salt, lemon juice, 1/2 cup water and 1 tablespoon melted butter in center of well. Blend ingredients in well, together, using your fingertips. Using fingertips of both your hands, gradually work in flour to form coarse crumbs. If crumbs are dry, add more water, a few drops at a time. Cut dough several times with a metal spatula to be sure ingredients are blended. Do not knead. Press dough into a ball. Dough will be soft. Wrap in waxed paper or plastic wrap; refrigerate 15 minutes.

Lightly flour remaining chilled butter. Place floured butter between 2 sheets of waxed paper; flatten with a rolling pin. Remove top sheet of waxed paper. Fold butter in half; replace between waxed paper. Continue flattening and folding until butter is pliable but not sticky. Butter should have same consistency as dough. Shape butter into a 6-inch square; lightly sprinkle with flour.

On a cool surface, roll out dough to a 12-inch square slightly thicker in center than at sides. Set butter in center of dough. Fold corners of dough toward center of butter, then fold sides of dough over butter, like an envelope. Place dough, with seams down, on a floured surface. Press down on top with a rolling pin to slightly flatten dough. Roll out dough to a rectangle 7 to 8 inches wide and 18 to 20 inches long. Fold in thirds like a business letter. Gently press seams with rolling pin to seal. Turn dough to bring seam side to your left so dough opens like a book. This is called a *turn*. Again roll dough to a large rectangle and fold in thirds. This is the second *turn*. Wrap dough in waxed paper; refrigerate 15 minutes. Repeat rolling process, giving dough a total of 6 turns. Refrigerate at least 1 hour after last turn. Makes 1 pound.

Cook's Tips

- Let frozen puff-pastry dough thaw at room temperature about 1 hour.
- Roll out puff-pastry dough on a lightly floured surface. During rolling, it is important to roll dough in two directions, from top to bottom and from left to right. If rolled in only one direction, it will not rise evenly during baking.
- Cut puff-pastry dough with a very sharp knife to prevent edges from sticking together. If using a pastry cutter, dip it in cold water before cutting out dough.
- When brushing puff-pastry dough with egg yolk, avoid cut edges or the coating will prevent pastry from rising evenly during baking.
- Dough trimmings can be laid one on top of another, pressed firmly together and rolled out again. Use small pieces and strips for decoration.
- Always place puff-pastry dough on a baking sheet or in a pan that has been sprinkled lightly with cold water. Steam from the water helps the pastry to rise.
- Refrigerate puff-pastry dough 15 minutes before baking.

Flaky Pie Pastry

2 cups all-purpose flour
1/2 teaspoon salt
2/3 cup vegetable shortening, chilled
7 to 8 tablespoons cold water

In a medium bowl, stir together flour and salt. Use a pastry blender or fork to cut in shortening until mixture resembles coarse crumbs. Sprinkle with 7 tablespoons water. Stir until mixture forms a ball and leaves side of bowl. Add more water if needed. Turn out dough onto a lightly floured surface. Knead 10 to 15 times. Divide dough into 2 equal portions. Roll 1 portion to a 12-inch circle. Fold in half, then in half again. Place in a 9-inch pie pan with folded corner in middle of pan. Unfold dough; gently ease into pan. Trim edge 1/2 inch larger than pan. Fill with prepared pie filling. Roll out and fold remaining dough as directed above. Cut small slashes about 1-1/2 inches from point. Place folded dough over filling with folded corner at center. Gently unfold dough; trim edge 1 inch larger than pan. Fold upper crust under lower crust to make a raised edge. Flute edge. Makes pastry for 1 (9-inch) double-crust pie.

Blender Hollandaise Sauce

4 egg yolks
2 tablespoons lemon juice
1/4 teaspoon salt
Pinch of red (cayenne) pepper
1 cup butter, melted

In a blender or food processor fitted with a metal blade, process egg yolks, lemon juice, salt and red pepper until blended. With machine running, gradually pour in butter. Process a few seconds longer until smooth and thick. Makes about 1-1/4 cups.

Variations

Sauce Maltaise: Substitute orange juice for lemon juice.
Béarnaise Sauce: Add 3 tablespoons chopped onion, 1 teaspoon chopped tarragon, 1 teaspoon chopped parsley and 1 tablespoon white-wine vinegar.
Mousseline Sauce: Carefully fold 1 cup whipped cream into 1 cup Blender Hollandaise Sauce.

Cook's Tip

Hollandaise Sauce makes even the plainest dishes special. Use with vegetables, fish, poultry and broiled or roasted meats.

Swedish Mayonnaise

1/3 cup mayonnaise
1/3 cup apple puree
About 3 tablespoons grated fresh horseradish

In a small bowl, combine mayonnaise, apple puree and 3 tablespoons horseradish. Add more horseradish, if desired. Refrigerate at least 1 hour; stir before serving. Serve with cold fish or meat. Makes about 2/3 cup.

Potato Dumplings

6 medium potatoes
Water
Salt
1 tablespoon butter
2 bread slices, cut in cubes
About 1 cup all-purpose flour
2 eggs
1/8 teaspoon ground nutmeg

Cook unpeeled potatoes in lightly salted water until tender. While potatoes cook, melt butter in a medium skillet; add bread cubes. Sauté until golden brown; set aside. Drain and peel cooked potatoes. Press peeled potatoes through a sieve or ricer into a large bowl. Sprinkle 3/4 cup flour over top. In a small bowl, beat eggs; stir in 1/2 teaspoon salt and nutmeg. Pour over potatoes and flour. Using a scraper or your hands, quickly combine ingredients into a light dough. Work quickly or dough will become sticky. Gradually work in more flour to make a somewhat dry dough. Shape dough into a roll 3 inches in diameter. Bring 3 quarts water to a boil; add 2 teaspoons salt. Cut potato roll into 3/4-inch slices. Flour your hands; use your hands to shape each slice into a ball, enclosing 2 or 3 browned bread cubes in each. Carefully drop dumplings into boiling water; bring water back to a boil. Simmer gently about 20 minutes. Dumplings will float to surface when done. Use a slotted spoon to remove cooked dumplings from water. Makes 10 to 12 dumplings.

Bread Dumplings

8 small day-old French-bread rolls, thinly sliced
Salt
1-1/2 cups warm milk (110F, 45C)
1 tablespoon butter
1/2 onion, finely chopped
1 tablespoon finely chopped parsley
3-1/2 qts. water
2 eggs, slightly beaten
1/8 teaspoon dried leaf marjoram
1/2 teaspoon white pepper
Fresh breadcrumbs, if needed

Place bread in a large bowl; sprinkle with salt. Pour in milk; cover and soak 1 hour. Melt butter in a medium skillet. Add onion and parsley; sauté until onion is transparent. Set aside to cool. In a large pot, bring water to a boil; stir in 2 teaspoons salt. Meanwhile, stir eggs, marjoram, white pepper and sautéed-onion mixture into bread mixture. Use your hands to press mixture into bottom of bowl. Shape about 2 tablespoons bread mixture into a dumpling. Carefully drop into boiling water. If dumpling falls apart, stir a few tablespoons fresh breadcrumbs into mixture. Shape remaining mixture into balls. Add dumplings, a few at a time, to boiling water. Bring back to a boil; simmer gently about 20 minutes, uncovered. Dumplings will float to surface when done. Use a slotted spoon to remove cooked dumplings from water. Makes 8 to 10 dumplings.

Aioli Sauce

5 garlic cloves, crushed
1 egg yolk
1/8 teaspoon salt
Pinch of white pepper
1 cup olive oil
1 teaspoon lemon juice
1/2 teaspoon water

In a small bowl, beat garlic and egg yolk until thoroughly blended. Stir in salt and white pepper. Using a whisk or electric beater, beat in oil, a few drops at a time, until about half of oil has been added. Then slowly pour in remaining oil. Beat in lemon juice and water. Makes about 1 cup.

Rémoulade Sauce

2 cups mayonnaise
2 tablespoons finely chopped dill pickle
1 tablespoon Dijon-style mustard
2 tablespoons mixed finely chopped tarragon, chervil, parsley and chives
1 tablespoons chopped drained capers, if desired

In a medium bowl, combine all ingredients. Blend well. Refrigerate until used. Serve with fish, meat, poultry and vegetables. Makes about 1-1/3 cups.

Greek White Sauce

1/4 cup butter
1/3 cup all-purpose flour
1-1/2 cups milk
3 eggs
Salt and white pepper

Melt butter in a medium saucepan. Stir in flour; cook 1 to 2 minutes. Gradually stir in milk; continue stirring until slightly thickened. In a small bowl, beat together eggs, salt and white pepper. Stir in about 1/4 cup hot milk mixture. Stir egg mixture into remaining milk mixture. Stirring constantly, cook until slightly thickened. Makes about 2 cups.

Clarified Butter

Melt 1 cup butter in a small saucepan. Simmer until butter separates; do not brown. Let butter cool slightly. Strain separated butter through a muslin cloth or several layers of cheesecloth. Discard milky solids. Store in refrigerator. Makes about 3/4 cup.

Ham Kariba

2 large avocados
Juice of 1/2 lemon
3 medium tomatoes
1 small head lettuce
1 small onion, finely chopped
1 hard-cooked egg, chopped
1/4 cup chopped peanuts
1/4 cup mayonnaise
1/2 teaspoon salt
1/8 teaspoon red (cayenne) pepper
4 large ham slices
Parsley

Cut avocados in thin strips; sprinkle with lemon juice. Peel tomatoes; remove and discard seeds. Chop tomatoes. Separate lettuce into leaves. Shred tender inner leaves; reserve outer leaves. In a large bowl, combine avocado strips, chopped tomatoes, shredded lettuce, onion, egg and peanuts. In a small bowl, combine mayonnaise, salt and red pepper. Pour over vegetable mixture. Toss to distribute. Spread mixture evenly over ham slices. Loosely roll ham and filling into cones. Arrange reserved lettuce leaves on a platter. Place ham rolls on lettuce. Garnish with parsley. Makes 4 servings.

Noodle Stew

1 tablespoon vegetable oil
1 lb. boneless pork, cut in 3/4-inch cubes
3 onions, finely chopped
3 medium tomatoes, peeled, chopped
1 garlic clove
Salt
1 fresh red chili
Pepper
2 teaspoons lemon juice
2 teaspoons sugar
1 tablespoon Worcestershire sauce
Water
12 oz. uncooked flat noodles
1-1/4 cups shredded Cheddar cheese (5 oz.)

Heat oil in a large saucepan. Add pork, onions and tomatoes. Crush garlic with a pinch of salt; add to pork mixture. To handle fresh chilies, cover your hands with rubber or plastic gloves. After handling chilies, do not touch your face or eyes. Cut chili in half; remove seeds and pith. Cut in thin slices. Add to pork mixture. Season with salt, pepper, lemon juice, sugar and Worcestershire sauce. Cover and cook over low heat 30 minutes. Meanwhile, bring salted water to a boil; add noodles. Cook 10 minutes or until tender; drain. Stir drained noodles and cheese into pork mixture. Serve in a large bowl or platter. Makes 6 servings.

Passion-Fruit Cream
GRENADILLA CREAM

1 (1/4-oz.) envelope unflavored gelatin (1 tablespoon)
Water
6 tablespoons sugar
1 cup passion-fruit or other tropical-fruit juice
1 cup fresh orange juice
1 cup whipping cream

Decoration:
Whipped cream
12 maraschino cherries
2 tablespoons chopped nuts
Crystalized-ginger pieces

In a 1-1/2-quart bowl, soften gelatin in 1 tablespoon cold water, 3 to 5 minutes. Stir in 1/2 cup boiling water until gelatin dissolves. Add sugar and juices; stir until sugar dissolves. Refrigerate until center is syrupy and outer portion has begun to set, 30 to 40 minutes. In a small bowl, whip 1 cup cream until stiff; fold into partially set gelatin. Spoon mixture into 4 dessert dishes; refrigerate 1 hour or until set. Decorate each serving with a dollop of whipped cream, cherries and chopped nuts. Makes 4 servings.

Apricot Roll
WATERBUL

Pastry & Filling:
1/2 (1-1/4-lb.) pkg. frozen puff pastry, thawed
3/4 cup apricot jam
1-1/2 cups ground almonds
1 egg yolk, beaten

Glaze:
1 tablespoon cornstarch
1 cup sugar
1 cup orange juice
Piece of orange peel
1 tablespoon butter
6 tablespoons sherry

To make pastry and filling, preheat oven to 475F (245C). On a lightly floured board, roll out pastry to a 14'' x 11'' rectangle. In a small bowl, combine jam and almonds; spread over pastry, leaving a 1/2-inch strip on 1 long side uncovered. Brush uncovered pastry strip with egg yolk. Beginning with jam-covered long side, roll up jelly-roll fashion. Pinch edge to roll to seal; press ends together to seal. With seam-side down, score top of rolled pastry at 1/4 to 1/2-inch intervals. Rinse a large baking sheet in cold water; place roll on wet baking sheet. Bake in center of oven 30 minutes or until golden brown.
To make glaze, in a medium saucepan, combine cornstarch and sugar. Gradually stir in orange juice. Add orange peel, butter and sherry. Place over medium heat. Stirring occasionally, bring to a boil. Continue stirring until thickened. Remove orange peel. Brush hot glaze over baked apricot roll; serve warm. Makes 6 to 8 servings.

Chicken in Peanut Sauce

NIKATSE NKWA

1 (3-lb.) chicken, cut in pieces
Water
Salt
4 bay leaves
6 medium tomatoes, peeled, cut in quarters
1 (6-oz.) can tomato paste
3 onions, cut in quarters
1 cup smooth-style peanut butter
Pepper

In a large saucepan, cover chicken with water. Add 2 teaspoons salt and bay leaves. Bring to a boil; reduce heat and simmer 30 to 45 minutes or until tender. In a blender, puree tomatoes, tomato paste and onions. Remove cooked chicken from pan; keep warm. Strain cooking liquid, discarding bay leaves. Pour 2-1/2 cups strained cooking liquid back into pan. Add pureed mixture; simmer 10 minutes. Remove from heat; whisk in peanut butter, 1 tablespoon at a time. Cover and simmer 10 minutes longer. Season with salt and pepper. Place chicken in a large bowl; pour sauce over chicken. Serve with cooked rice. Makes 4 servings.

Chicken with Yoloff Rice

2/3 cup dried black beans
Water
1 (3-lb.) chicken, cut in pieces
Salt
1 cup uncooked long-grain white rice
1/2 cup vegetable oil
4 onions, cut in rings
6 medium tomatoes, peeled, chopped
1 (6-oz.) can tomato paste
Pinch of red (cayenne) pepper
3 tablespoons all-purpose flour
2 eggs, beaten
3 tablespoons dry breadcrumbs
Black pepper

Soak beans in cold water to cover 12 hours. Boil beans in soaking water 40 to 50 minutes or until soft. In a large saucepan, cover chicken with water. Add 1 teaspoon salt. Bring to a boil; reduce heat and simmer 10 minutes. Drain well; set aside. Bring 2 cups water and 1 teaspoon salt to a boil. Add rice; cover and simmer 20 minutes or until tender. Meanwhile, heat 6 tablespoons oil in a large saucepan. Add onion rings; sauté until transparent. Add tomatoes, tomato paste, red pepper and a pinch of salt. Boil until reduced to a thick sauce; stir in cooked rice. Drain cooked beans. In a large serving bowl, layer cooked beans and rice mixture; keep warm. Season boiled chicken pieces with salt and black pepper. Dip each piece in flour, then in egg, and then in breadcrumbs. Heat remaining 2 tablespoons oil in a large skillet. Add coated chicken; cook until browned and crisp. Serve with rice-and-bean casserole. Makes 4 to 6 servings.

Spinach Stew
KONTO-MIRE

1 lb. mixed beef and pork for stew
1 bay leaf
Water
6 tablespoons vegetable oil
2 onions, finely chopped
4 medium tomatoes, peeled,
 pureed
6 to 8 lean bacon slices, diced
1/2 cup ground pumpkin seeds, if
 desired
1 bunch spinach, chopped (12 oz.)
Salt and pepper

Put meat in a medium saucepan; add bay leaf and water to cover. Bring to a boil; reduce heat and simmer 1 hour or until tender. Discard bay leaf. Heat oil in a medium saucepan. Add onions; sauté until transparent. Add tomatoes; simmer a few minutes, stirring constantly. Add bacon; simmer 5 minutes. Stir in pumpkin seeds, if desired; simmer 5 minutes longer. Add spinach; simmer 10 minutes, gradually adding cooking liquid from meat. Add meat; cook 2 minutes longer. Season with salt and pepper. Makes 4 servings.

Variation

Cook meat in a pressure cooker using 2 cups water. Reduce cooking time from 1 hour to 15 minutes. Complete as above.

Sweet Meat

LAHM LHALOU

2 lbs. boneless lamb, cut in 3/4-inch cubes
1/2 teaspoon salt
2 tablespoons vegetable oil
1/3 cup blanched whole almonds
2/3 cup sugar
1 (3-inch) cinnamon stick
1 cup water
2 tablespoons orange juice or orange-flavored liqueur
1-1/2 cups pitted prunes

Sprinkle lamb with salt. Heat oil in a medium saucepan. Stirring constantly, cook lamb, 1/2 at a time, until lightly browned. Remove browned lamb from pan. Add almonds, sugar and cinnamon stick to pan drippings. Stir well; add water and orange juice or liqueur. Bring to a boil, stirring constantly. Add browned lamb and any drippings. Cover and simmer 1 hour or until tender. Stir in prunes 15 minutes before end of cooking time. Remove cinnamon stick before serving. Makes 6 servings.

Cook's Tip

In Algeria, this hearty stew is served as part of a meal with several other dishes. If you want to serve it as a main course, serve with Couscous, page 191.

Chicken with Cheese Croquettes

SFERIA

2 tablespoons butter
1 (3-lb.) chicken, cut in pieces
1 onion, finely chopped
1 teaspoon salt
1/2 teaspoon ground cinnamon
Pinch of pepper
1 cup drained canned chick peas or garbanzo beans
1 cup water
1 egg yolk
1 tablespoon lemon juice

Croquettes:
6 to 8 white-bread slices, crusts removed, torn in pieces
6 tablespoons milk
1 egg, slightly beaten
1/4 teaspoon ground cinnamon
1/4 teaspoon salt
1 cup grated Emmentaler cheese (4 oz.)
1 teaspoon orange juice or orange-flavored liqueur
1 cup vegetable oil

Melt butter in a large skillet. Add chicken and onion; fry until golden brown. Add salt, cinnamon, pepper, peas or beans and water. Bring to a boil. Reduce heat. Cover and simmer 1 hour.
To make croquettes, soak bread in milk. Squeeze dry; discard milk. Combine soaked bread, egg, cinnamon, salt, cheese and orange juice or liqueur. Shape into small balls; flatten slightly. Heat oil in a medium saucepan. Fry balls until golden.
To complete, strain chicken and peas or beans, reserving liquid. Place cooked chicken and croquettes in a dish. Pour drained peas or beans over top; keep warm. In a small saucepan, combine egg yolk, lemon juice and 6 tablespoons strained cooking liquid. Stir over medium heat until slightly thickened. Do not boil. Pour hot sauce over chicken. Makes 8 servings.

Date Cake
DJAMILAH

1 cup blanched almonds
1 cup sugar
4 eggs, separated
1/2 teaspoon vanilla extract
3 tablespoons cornstarch
1-1/2 cups finely chopped dates (7 oz.)
3 tablespoons butter, melted
1 tablespoon orange juice or orange-flavored liqueur

Butter a round 10-inch cake pan; line with waxed paper. Butter waxed paper; set pan aside. Preheat oven to 400F (205C). In a blender, process almonds with 3/4 cup sugar until finely ground. Beat egg yolks with remaining sugar and vanilla. Stir in almond mixture, cornstarch, dates, butter and orange juice or liqueur. In a medium bowl, beat egg whites until stiff; fold into date mixture. Pour batter into prepared pan. Bake in center of oven 30 to 40 minutes or until center springs back when pressed with your fingers. Invert onto a rack; remove pan. Cool on rack. Makes 1 single-layer cake.

Variation

When cool, drizzle cake with icing and decorate with chopped dried dates.

Almond Macaroons
MAKROUL EL LOUSE

4 cups ground almonds (1-1/2 lbs.)
1-1/4 cups plus 2 tablespoons granulated sugar
Grated peel of 1 lemon
2 large eggs, slightly beaten
All-purpose flour
1 cup water
2 teaspoons orange juice or orange-flavored liqueur
2 cups powdered sugar

Preheat oven to 350F (175C). In a large bowl, combine almonds, 1-1/4 cups granulated sugar and lemon peel. Beat in eggs. Divide almond mixture in half. Dust your hands with flour. With floured hands, shape each half of almond mixture into a roll, 1-1/2 inches in diameter. Cut each roll into 18 slices. With floured hands, shape each slice into a ball; sprinkle with flour. Place balls on an ungreased baking sheet; bake 15 minutes or until lightly browned. Cool on a rack. In a small saucepan, combine remaining granulated sugar and water. Bring to a boil, stirring constantly. Boil until a light syrup forms, 15 to 20 minutes; do not let syrup brown. Pour syrup into a shallow bowl. Cool, then stir in orange juice or liqueur. Dip baked macaroons in syrup, then roll in powdered sugar; set aside to dry. Makes 36 macaroons.

Cook's Tip

These macaroons will keep for several weeks in a well-sealed tin.

Lamb & Tomato Soup

MEZZA BISHURBA

2 lbs. lamb bones
Water
1/2 lb. boneless lamb
9 medium tomatoes (3 lbs.)
2 onions, finely chopped
2 teaspoons salt
1/8 teaspoon ground nutmeg
1/8 teaspoon pepper
1/2 teaspoon sugar
1/2 cup uncooked long-grain white rice
2 tablespoons chopped fresh basil or 1 tablespoon dried leaf basil

In a large saucepan, cover bones with water; boil 10 minutes. Rinse immediately with cold water; rinse pan. Place lamb and blanched bones in saucepan. Add 7 cups water; bring to a boil. Reduce heat and simmer 1 hour; remove and discard bones. Simmer lamb 30 minutes longer or until tender, skimming foam from surface until surface is clear. Peel tomatoes; remove and discard seeds. Chop tomatoes. Add chopped tomatoes, onions, salt, nutmeg, pepper and sugar to lamb. Simmer 10 minutes. Stir rice into soup. Cover and simmer 20 minutes or until rice is tender. Remove lamb from soup; cut into strips. Stir lamb strips and basil into soup. Pour soup into a tureen or serve in individual bowls. Serve immediately. Makes 6 servings.

Fish with Sesame Sauce

SAMAKAH HARRAH

3 lbs. whole perch, pike, sea bream or sunfish
Salt
3/4 cup olive oil
3 onions, chopped
1 large green bell pepper, chopped
1/4 cup chopped walnuts
3 tablespoons chopped parsley
1/2 cup seedless green grapes, cut in halves, or
**   3 tablespoons pomegranate seeds**
Black pepper

Sesame Sauce:
4 garlic cloves, crushed
1 cup sesame-seed paste (tahini)
About 1/2 cup water
6 tablespoons lemon juice
1 teaspoon salt

Rub fish inside and out with 2 teaspoons salt. Pour 1/2 cup oil into a shallow baking dish. Add fish, turning to cover lightly with oil. Let stand 15 minutes. Preheat oven to 400F (205C). Heat remaining oil in a large skillet. Add onions; sauté until golden brown. Add green pepper and nuts; sauté 5 minutes. Stir in 2 tablespoons parsley and 1/3 cup grape halves or 2 tablespoons pomegranate seeds. Season with salt and black pepper. Stuff fish with onion mixture; secure with wooden picks. Bake fish, uncovered, 40 to 50 minutes, basting frequently with pan drippings. Cooked fish will flake easily when pierced with a fork.
To make sauce, combine garlic, sesame-seed paste, water, lemon juice and salt; mix well. Sprinkle baked fish with remaining parsley and grape halves or pomegranate seeds. Spoon sauce over fish or serve separately. Makes 6 servings.

Tabbouleh
TABBOULEH

1 cup fine bulgur
Water
2 medium tomatoes, finely chopped
1 onion, finely chopped
1 cup finely chopped parsley
Juice of 2 lemons
1 teaspoon salt
Pepper
2 tablespoons chopped fresh mint
1/3 cup olive oil
Lettuce leaves
Mint sprigs

Place bulgur in a large bowl; add water to cover. Let stand 1 hour or until bulgur has doubled in size and most of the water is absorbed. Drain well; squeeze dry. Add tomatoes, onion, parsley, lemon juice, salt and pepper. Combine chopped mint and oil; stir into bulgur mixture. Line a salad bowl with lettuce leaves; spoon in bulgur mixture. Garnish with mint sprigs. Serve with Stuffed Yeast Rolls, opposite. Makes 4 servings.

Stuffed Yeast Rolls
SFEEHA

1-1/4 cups warm water (110F, 45C)
1 (1/4-oz.) pkg. active dry yeast (1 tablespoon)
1 teaspoon sugar
4 to 4-1/2 cups all-purpose flour
1 teaspoon salt
3 tablespoons olive oil
1 egg yolk, slightly beaten

Savory Filling:
2 cups chopped onion
1 tablespoons salt
2 tablespoons pine nuts
3/4 lb. ground lamb
1 small tomato, diced
1/2 green bell pepper, finely chopped
3 tablespoons chopped parsley
3 tablespoons lemon juice
2 tablespoons wine vinegar
1 tablespoon tomato paste
1/8 teaspoon red (cayenne) pepper
1/8 teaspoon ground allspice

In a large bowl, stir together water, yeast and sugar. Beat in 2 cups flour, salt and oil; let stand 10 minutes. Stir in enough of remaining flour to make a soft dough. Knead until smooth and elastic. Let rise in a warm place until doubled in bulk. Punch down dough; shape into 16 balls. Let rise until doubled.
To make filling, sprinkle onions with salt; let stand 30 minutes, then puree. Stir in remaining filling ingredients.
To complete, roll raised dough balls into 4-inch circles; brush edges with egg yolk. Spoon 3 tablespoons filling onto each circle. Pinch edges together over filling. Let rise 30 minutes on a greased baking sheet. Preheat oven to 425F (220C). Bake 30 minutes. Makes 16 rolls.

Argentina

Stuffed Beef Roll

MATAMBRE

2 (16" x 8") slices boneless beef sirloin or top round,
   about 1 inch thick (4-1/2 lbs.)
1/2 garlic clove
1 cup red-wine vinegar
1 teaspoon dried leaf thyme
6 large carrots
Water
Salt
1 bunch spinach (12 oz.)
4 hard-cooked eggs, cut in wedges
1 large onion, cut in rings
3 tablespoons chopped parsley
1 teaspoon red (cayenne) pepper
1/4 cup vegetable oil
About 2-1/2 cups hot beef stock or broth
Pepper

Beginning on a long side, cut horizontally through each beef piece to within 3/4 inch of the opposite side. Each piece will flatten to about 16" x 15". Open each and press flat; place in a large shallow dish, 1 on top of the other. Crush garlic; blend with vinegar and thyme. Sprinkle seasoned vinegar over each beef rectangle. Cover and refrigerate 6 hours. Quarter carrots lengthwise. Cook in a pot of boiling salted water 20 minutes or until nearly tender. Clean spinach. Preheat oven to 400F (205C). Remove beef from marinade; pat dry with paper towels. Place beef cut-side up on a flat surface, with a long side of each overlapping about 2 inches. With a meat mallet, pound overlapping edges together. Spread spinach over entire beef surface. Arrange cooked carrots crosswise over spinach. Sprinkle egg wedges and onion rings over carrots and spinach. Sprinkle with parsley, 1 teaspoon salt and red pepper. Beginning on a short side, roll beef and filling. Tie with kitchen string at 2- to 3-inch intervals. Place in a large roasting pan. Pour oil over top; bake, uncovered, about 10 minutes. Pour about 2 cups stock or broth around beef. Cover and roast 1 hour, adding more stock or broth as needed. At end of cooking time, turn off oven. Open door slightly; let beef stand in oven 10 minutes. Remove string; slice beef and arrange on a warm platter. Strain cooking liquid; season with salt and pepper. Serve over beef roll or in a separate bowl. Makes 8 to 12 servings.

Cook's Tips

Place the uncooked beef in the freezer 30 to 60 minutes before cutting. The cold meat holds its shape and is easy to cut.

In Argentina, this rolled beef is usually served cold. Before carving, it is refrigerated several hours with a weight on top to press out all the moisture.

Mulligatoni Soup

1/2 (3-lb.) stewing chicken
Salt
1 bay leaf
1 onion, chopped
1 carrot, chopped
1 parsnip, chopped
7 cups water
3 tablespoons butter
6 to 8 bacon slices, diced
4 medium tomatoes, peeled, chopped
1 garlic clove, crushed
1/2 cup all-purpose flour
Pinch of red (cayenne) pepper
Pinch of ground nutmeg
2 white-bread slices

In a large pot, combine chicken, 2 teaspoons salt, bay leaf, onion, carrot, parsnip and water. Bring to a boil; reduce heat. Cover and simmer 1-1/2 to 2 hours. Melt 1 tablespoon butter in a medium skillet. Add bacon; sauté 1 to 2 minutes. Add tomatoes and garlic; simmer 2 minutes. Sprinkle flour over tomato mixture; stir over low heat until flour is golden brown. Strain chicken, reserving 3-1/2 cups cooking liquid. Stir a little reserved cooking liquid into tomato mixture to make a smooth sauce. Stir in remaining reserved cooking liquid. Season with salt, red pepper and nutmeg. Add strained vegetables to soup. Remove and discard skin and bones from chicken. Cut meat into strips; add to soup. Heat soup through. Remove and discard bay leaf. Cut bread into cubes. Melt remaining 2 tablespoons butter in a skillet. Add bread cubes; sauté until crisp. Pour soup into a tureen or serve in individual bowls. Top with sautéed bread cubes. Makes 4 servings.

Spicy Lamb Roast

1 (2-1/4-lb.) boneless lamb-leg roast
1/2 teaspoon ground nutmeg
1/2 teaspoon ground cinnamon
1 onion, cut in thin rings
2 garlic cloves, crushed
3 whole cloves
1 bay leaf
1-1/2 cups packed brown sugar
2 cups wine vinegar
1 cup water
2-1/2 cups hot meat stock or broth
1/4 teaspoon salt
1/8 teaspoon white pepper

Rub lamb with nutmeg and cinnamon. Sprinkle 1/3 of the onion rings into a large bowl. Top with lamb, garlic, whole cloves and bay leaf. Cover with remaining onion rings. In a small bowl, dissolve brown sugar in vinegar; pour over lamb mixture. Cover and refrigerate 24 hours, occasionally turning lamb and other ingredients. Preheat oven to 375F (190C). Remove lamb from marinade; reserve marinade. Place lamb in a baking pan. Add water to reserved marinade; pour over lamb. Cover and bake 2 to 2-1/2 hours or until tender, occasionally adding stock or broth. Place cooked lamb on a platter. Slice to serve. Strain pan juices; remove and discard bay leaf. Add remaining stock or broth. Season with salt and white pepper. Serve over lamb or in a separate bowl. Makes 4 to 6 servings.

Australia

Banana Crescents

2-3/4 cups all-purpose flour
Grated peel and juice of 1 lemon
1/2 cup sugar
1 egg, beaten
1/2 cup butter, chilled
1 to 2 tablespoons milk, if needed
8 small ripe bananas
1 egg, separated
6 tablespoons apricot jam
2 tablespoons sliced almonds

Sift flour into a bowl; stir in lemon peel, sugar and 1 beaten egg. Use a pastry cutter or fork to cut in butter. With your fingertips, quickly press ingredients together, adding milk, 1 teaspoon at a time, as needed. Wrap dough to prevent drying; refrigerate 1 hour. Preheat oven to 400F (205C). Grease a large baking sheet; set aside. Peel bananas; sprinkle with lemon juice. On a lightly floured surface, roll out dough to 20" x 10". Cut into 8 (5-inch) squares. Brush edges of dough squares with egg white. Place 1 banana diagonally across each square. Fold dough over banana as shown; press edges together to seal. Beat egg yolk; brush over dough. Arrange on greased baking sheet. Bake 20 minutes or until lightly browned. Place on a cooling rack. Heat jam until fluid; brush over warm crescents. Sprinkle with sliced almonds. Makes 8 crescents.

Pavlova Cake

5 egg whites
2 tablespoons vanilla sugar or 2 tablespoons granulated sugar and
   1/4 teaspoon vanilla extract
3/4 cup granulated sugar
3/4 cup powdered sugar
Scant 1/2 cup cornstarch

Filling:
2 cups fresh whole strawberries
1/4 cup powdered sugar
1-1/2 cups whipping cream
1 tablespoon cherry brandy

Line a baking sheet with waxed or brown paper. Draw a 9-1/2-inch-diameter circle on center of paper. Preheat oven to 225F (105C). In a large bowl, beat egg whites until soft peaks form. Beat in vanilla sugar or 2 tablespoons granulated sugar and vanilla extract until stiff peaks form. Sprinkle 3/4 cup granulated sugar and powdered sugar over beaten egg whites. Beat in until sugars dissolve. Sift cornstarch over top; fold in. Spoon into a pastry bag. Using a large tip, pipe egg-white mixture in a long spiral to completely fill circle. Pipe small balls around edge to make a raised side, as shown. Bake 1-1/2 hours or until firm. Turn off oven; do not open oven door. Let meringue stand 15 minutes in closed oven.

To make filling, puree 1 cup strawberries in a blender or food processor; pour into a medium bowl. Stir in 2 tablespoons powdered sugar. In a medium bowl, beat whipping cream with remaining 2 tablespoons powdered sugar until stiff. Fold in brandy. Spread cream mixture in baked meringue. Arrange reserved whole strawberries over cream mixture; spoon pureed berries over top. Refrigerate until chilled, about 2 hours. Makes 8 to 10 servings.

Liver-Dumpling Soup
LEBERKNÖDELSUPPE

8 or 9 day-old bread rolls, cut in thin slices
Salt
3/4 cup warm milk (110F, 45C)
1 tablespoon butter
1/2 onion, finely chopped
2 tablespoons chopped parsley
3/4 lb. beef liver, ground
2 eggs, slightly beaten
1/8 teaspoon dried leaf marjoram
1/8 teaspoon white pepper
2 qts. water
Dry breadcrumbs, if needed
3-1/2 cups beef stock or broth
Chopped parsley

Place bread in a large bowl; sprinkle with 1 teaspoon salt. Pour warm milk over top. Cover and let stand 1 hour. Melt butter in a medium skillet. Add onion and 2 tablespoons parsley; sauté until limp. Set aside to cool. Stir cooled sautéed onion, liver, eggs, marjoram and white pepper into soaked-bread mixture. Blend thoroughly. In a large pot, bring water and 1/2 teaspoon salt to a gentle boil. Press 1 tablespoon liver mixture into a ball. Drop into gently boiling water. If dumpling falls apart, work a few tablespoons of breadcrumbs into remaining liver mixture. Shape mixture into 8 dumplings; add to gently boiling water. Simmer 20 minutes uncovered; dumplings will float to surface when done. Use a slotted spoon to remove cooked dumplings from water; keep hot. Heat stock or broth; serve hot dumplings in hot stock or broth. Garnish with chopped parsley. Makes 4 servings.

Steak with Onions
ZWIEBELROSTBRATEN

4 beef top-loin or tenderloin steaks
2 tablespoons lard
1 teaspoon salt
1/2 teaspoon white pepper
4 onions, cut in rings
2 tablespoons butter
1 cup beef stock or broth
Few drops wine vinegar, if desired

Slash fat edges of beef at 2-inch intervals. In a large skillet over medium-high heat, melt lard. Add beef; sear 2 to 3 minutes on each side or until browned on the outside but still slightly red inside. Season with salt and white pepper. Set seared beef on a platter; keep warm. Add onions to skillet; sauté until golden. Place onions in a bowl. Use paper towels to wipe any remaining lard from skillet; melt butter in skillet. Add sautéed onion rings; stir to coat with butter. Add stock or broth; bring to a boil. Add vinegar, if desired. Pour onion sauce over cooked beef. Serve hot with pickled cucumbers or French-style green beans and baked potatoes. Makes 4 servings.

Styrian Pork & Vegetable Stew
STEIRISCHES WURZELFLEISCH

1 garlic clove
Salt
1-3/4 lbs. boneless pork, cut in 1-1/4-inch cubes
1 large onion, finely chopped
2 carrots, cut in thin sticks
1/4 celeriac or 2 celery stalks, thickly sliced
1 rutabaga, cut in wedges
White pepper
2 whole cloves
1/2 bay leaf
Water
4 large potatoes, peeled, cut in quarters
1 tablespoon vinegar
1 tablespoon grated fresh horseradish or 1 teaspoon prepared
  horseradish
2 tablespoons chopped parsley

Crush garlic with 1 teaspoon salt. In a large saucepan, combine pork cubes, garlic-salt mixture, onion, carrots, celeriac or celery, rutabaga, 1/8 teaspoon white pepper, cloves and bay leaf. Cover with water; bring to a boil. Cover and simmer 30 minutes. Add potatoes to pork mixture; cook 20 minutes longer or until potatoes are tender. Remove bay leaf. Season with vinegar, horseradish, salt and white pepper. Cover and continue cooking until pork is tender. Pour stew into a tureen or serve in individual bowls. Sprinkle chopped parsley over stew. Makes 4 to 6 servings.

Vienna Boiled Beef
WIENER TAFELSPITZ

Water
1 teaspoon salt
1 (2-1/4- to 3-lb.) beef brisket
2 leeks, white part only
1 onion, cut in rings
2 large carrots, cut in thin sticks
1/2 celeriac or 4 celery stalks, cut in thin sticks
2 gherkins, if desired
Parsley
Swedish Mayonnaise, page 8

In a large pot, heat 2 quarts water with salt. Add beef; bring to a boil. Skim foam from surface until surface is clear. Partially cover pot; simmer 1-1/2 hours. Cut leeks in 2-inch pieces, then cut into halves lengthwise. Add leeks, onion, carrots and celeriac or celery to beef. Cook until beef and vegetables are tender. Cut beef into 1/2-inch slices; arrange on a platter. Cut gherkins lengthwise in thin slices, leaving 1 end uncut. Spread out slices like a fan; garnish beef with gherkins, if desired. Serve vegetables in a separate dish with 3 to 4 tablespoons cooking liquid spooned over top. Garnish with parsley. Serve with Swedish Mayonnaise. Makes 6 to 8 servings.

Sweet Yeast Buns
BUCHTELN

1/4 cup warm water (110F, 45C)
1 (1/4-oz.) pkg. active dry yeast (1 tablespoon)
1/4 cup granulated sugar
3/4 cup warm milk (110F, 45C)
2 eggs, slightly beaten
1/2 teaspoon salt
Grated peel of 1 lemon
1/2 cup plus 1 tablespoon butter, melted
4-1/4 to 4-1/2 cups all-purpose flour
Powdered sugar

In a large bowl, combine water, yeast and 1 teaspoon granulated sugar. Let stand 5 minutes to soften. Stir in remaining granulated sugar, milk, eggs, salt, lemon peel and 3 tablespoons butter. Beat in 2 cups flour; let stand 10 minutes. Stir in enough remaining flour to make a soft dough. Turn out dough onto a lightly floured surface. Clean and grease bowl. Knead dough 8 to 10 minutes or until smooth and elastic. Place dough in greased bowl, turning to coat all sides. Cover; let rise in a warm place, free from drafts, until doubled in bulk, 30 to 40 minutes. Melt remaining butter in a 9-inch-square baking pan. Punch down dough; shape into 16 balls. Roll balls in melted butter; arrange in pan. Cover and let rise 20 to 30 minutes or until almost doubled in bulk. Preheat oven to 425F (220C). Bake 20 to 25 minutes or until golden brown. Before serving, sprinkle with powdered sugar. Makes 16 buns.

Cook's Tip
These buns can be served as a sweet roll, hot from the oven, with custard. Or, cool and serve with coffee or tea.

Apple Strudel
APFELSTRUDEL

1 (1-lb.) pkg. frozen filo dough
1/2 cup butter, melted
1/4 cup powdered sugar

Filling:
1/3 cup raisins
1 tablespoon rum
2-1/4 lbs. cooking apples (4 medium)
Juice of 1 lemon
2/3 cup sugar
1/2 cup grated hazelnuts
6 tablespoons dairy sour cream
1/2 teaspoon ground cinnamon

Thaw filo dough in container. Prepare filling. Preheat oven to 400F (205C). Grease a large baking sheet; set aside. When working with 1 sheet of filo dough, keep other sheets covered with a damp cloth or plastic wrap. Place 1 sheet of thawed filo dough on a damp towel. Brush with some of the melted butter. Place another sheet on top; again brush with butter. Top with a third sheet of filo dough. Spread 1/3 of the filling along 1 long edge of dough, about 1 inch from edge. Using towel to help lift and roll, roll up filo dough and filling jelly-roll fashion. Pinch edges to seal. Place roll seam-side down on greased baking sheet. Repeat with remaining filo sheets and filling, making 3 rolls. Brush tops with butter. Bake 40 minutes or until golden brown and apples are tender. Cool on a rack; serve cold. To serve, dust with powdered sugar; cut in slices. Makes 3 strudels.
To make filling, soak raisins in rum 2 to 3 hours. Peel and finely slice apples. Sprinkle with lemon juice. In a small bowl, combine soaked raisins, sugar, nuts, sour cream and cinnamon. Add to apples; carefully toss to distribute.

Austria

Kaiser Pancake
KAISERSCHMARRN

2 teaspoons rum
1/4 cup raisins
2 cups all-purpose flour
1/4 teaspoon salt
1/4 cup plus 2 tablespoons sugar
4 eggs, separated
1/2 to 1 cup cold milk
1/4 cup butter
Powdered sugar

Sprinkle rum over raisins; set aside 30 minutes. Sift flour, salt and 2 tablespoons sugar into a large bowl. Beat egg yolks; add to flour mixture with enough milk to make a thick batter. In a medium bowl, beat egg whites until soft peaks form. Beat in remaining 1/4 cup sugar until stiff; fold into batter. Melt 2 tablespoons butter in a 10- to 12-inch skillet. Sprinkle half the soaked raisins into skillet. Spoon 1/2 of the batter evenly over raisins. Cook until bottom is browned and crisp; turn and brown other side. Use 2 forks to break pancake into 1-1/2-inch pieces. Let pieces dry in skillet 10 to 15 seconds, then place on a warm platter. Sprinkle with powdered sugar. Repeat with remaining butter, soaked raisins and batter. Makes 2 (10-inch) pancakes.

Cook's Tip

In Austria, Kaiser Pancake is eaten with stewed plums. *To stew plums,* halve and stone 2-1/4 pounds ripe plums. In a large saucepan, combine stoned plums, 5 tablespoons white wine, 5 tablespoons water, sugar to taste and a pinch of ground cinnamon. Stirring occasionally, cook over low heat until plums are soft. Serve warm.

Apricot Dumplings
MARILLENKNÖDEL

5 tablespoons butter, melted
1 cup drained, sieved cottage cheese (8 oz.)
Salt
2 eggs, slightly beaten
1-1/2 to 2 cups all-purpose flour
1 to 1-1/2 lbs. fresh apricots or plums
12 to 14 sugar cubes
2-1/2 qts. water
1/3 cup butter or margarine
1 cup fine dry breadcrumbs
3 tablespoons granulated sugar

In a large bowl, combine 5 tablespoons melted butter, cottage cheese, pinch of salt, eggs and enough flour to make a soft dough. Shape dough into a roll; cover and let stand 30 minutes. Wash and dry apricots or plums. Cut in halves; remove and discard stones. Place 1 sugar cube between each pair of apricot or plum halves; set aside. Bring water to a gentle boil; add 1 teaspoon salt. On a lightly floured board, press or roll out dough until about 1/2 inch thick. Cut into 2-inch squares. Place a stuffed apricot or plum in center of each. Press dough around fruit, covering completely. Add to gently boiling water; cook 8 to 10 minutes. Drain on paper towels; arrange on a platter. Melt 1/3 cup butter or margarine in a medium skillet. Add breadcrumbs and 3 tablespoons granulated sugar; sauté until golden brown. Sprinkle caramelized breadcrumbs over dumplings. Makes about 8 servings.

Stuffed Crepes
TOPFEN-PALATSCHINKEN

Crepes:
2/3 cup milk
2 eggs, slightly beaten
Pinch of salt
1 teaspoon plus 1 tablespoon granulated sugar
About 1 cup all-purpose flour
About 1/4 cup butter
Powdered sugar, if desired

Filling:
1/3 cup butter
1/2 cup sugar
Pinch of salt
Grated peel of 1/4 lemon
3 eggs, separated
1-1/2 cups ricotta cheese (12 oz.)
1/3 cup half and half
1/4 cup raisins

To make crepes, in a bowl, combine 1/3 cup milk, 1 egg, salt, 1 teaspoon sugar and enough flour to make a thin batter. Melt some butter in an 8-inch skillet. Pour a thin layer of batter into skillet. Cook crepe on both sides until crisp and lightly browned; keep warm. Repeat with remaining batter.
To make filling, beat together butter, 1/4 cup sugar, salt, lemon peel and egg yolks until light and fluffy. Stir in cheese, half and half and raisins. Beat egg whites until stiff; beat in remaining 1/4 cup sugar. Fold into cheese mixture. Butter a baking dish. Spread some filling on each crepe; roll up and arrange in buttered dish.
To complete, preheat oven to 350F (175C). Beat together 1 egg, 1/3 cup milk and 1 tablespoon sugar. Pour over rolled crepes. Bake 20 minutes. Sprinkle with powdered sugar, if desired. Serve warm. Makes 6 servings.

Salzburg Dumpling
SALZBURGER NOCKERLN

6 eggs, separated
1/2 cup granulated sugar
1/4 teaspoon vanilla extract
1/3 cup all-purpose flour
3 tablespoons unsalted butter
Powdered sugar

Preheat oven to 425F (220C). In a medium bowl, beat egg whites until soft peaks form. Gradually beat in granulated sugar until stiff but not dry. In a small bowl, beat egg yolks; stir in vanilla and 2 tablespoons beaten egg whites. Pour egg-yolk mixture over remaining beaten egg whites; do not stir. Sift flour over egg mixture. Fold egg-yolk mixture and flour into egg whites, quickly but carefully. Place butter in a shallow baking dish; place in oven until butter melts. Spoon egg mixture into hot dish. Using 2 tablespoons, shape egg mixture into 3 to 6 equal rolls or mounds. Place dish in center of oven. Bake 8 to 10 minutes or until golden brown. Sprinkle with powdered sugar. Serve immediately. Makes 3 to 6 servings.

Cook's Tip

Salzburg Dumpling is a type of soufflé. Place away from drafts when removed from the oven or dumpling may collapse.

Flemish Cream of Chicken Soup
WATERZOOI À LA GANTOISE

1 (3-lb.) stewing chicken with giblets
1/2 lb. beef cubes for stew
Water
2 onions, cut in wedges
1 celery stalk, chopped
2 leeks, white part only, chopped
1 carrot, cut in lengthwise quarters
1 teaspoon salt
2 egg yolks
6 tablespoons half and half
1/8 teaspoon white pepper
Juice of 1/2 lemon

Cut chicken into 4 pieces. Place chicken pieces, giblets and beef in a large pot. Cover with water; bring to a boil. Skim foam from surface until surface is clear. Add onions, celery, leeks, carrot and salt. Cover and simmer about 2 hours. Remove beef from cooking liquid; reserve beef for another purpose. Remove and discard skin and bones from cooked chicken. Cut chicken into small pieces. Strain cooking liquid, squeezing all liquid from vegetables; discard cooked vegetables. Boil cooking liquid until reduced to about 1 quart. In a small bowl, beat egg yolks with half and half and white pepper. Stir in about 1/3 cup cooking liquid; stir egg-yolk mixture into remaining cooking liquid. Simmer over low heat, stirring constantly, until thickened. Stir in lemon juice; add chicken pieces. Heat through. Pour into a tureen or serve in individual bowls. Serve immediately. Makes 4 servings.

Ardennes Chicory Soup
SOUPE À L'ARDENNAISE

1 lb. Belgian endive or chicory
2 leeks, white part only
1/4 cup butter
2 small potatoes, peeled, finely chopped
2-1/2 cups milk
Salt and white pepper
2 egg yolks
1/3 cup half and half
2 tablespoons finely chopped chives

Remove and discard core from each endive or chicory head; cut in 1/4-inch slices. Cut leeks in 1/4-inch pieces. Melt butter in a large saucepan. Add sliced endive or chicory and leeks; sauté 2 to 3 minutes. Add potatoes and milk. Season to taste with salt and white pepper. Bring to a gentle boil, stirring occasionally. Cover and simmer 45 minutes or until potatoes are tender. In a small bowl, beat egg yolks with half and half. Stir in 1/4 cup hot milk mixture. Stir egg-yolk mixture into remaining milk mixture. Stirring constantly, cook until slightly thickened. Pour into a tureen or serve in individual bowls. Garnish with chives. Serve immediately. Makes 4 servings.

Variation

Add 1/4 to 1/2 pound cooked-ham strips. Heat before serving.

Cook's Tip

In Belgium, endive is called *chicorée de Bruxelles* or *barbe-de-bouc* which means "goat's beard."

Stuffed Chicory
CHICORÉE ET VOLAILLE À LA BRUXELLOISE

4 heads Belgian endive or chicory
Salt
2 tablespoons lemon juice
6 tablespoons butter
1 chicken breast, boned, diced
2 tablespoons all-purpose flour
1/2 cup chicken stock or broth
1/2 cup half and half
Pinch of grated nutmeg
White pepper
4 cooked-ham slices
1 egg yolk
1/4 cup grated Gouda or Edam cheese (1 oz.)

Preheat oven to 350F (175C). Butter a shallow baking dish. Remove and discard core from each endive or chicory head. Place endive or chicory in buttered dish. Sprinkle with a little salt, lemon juice and 2 tablespoons butter. Cover and bake 1 hour. Melt 2 tablespoons butter in a large skillet. Add chicken; sauté 10 minutes. Melt remaining 2 tablespoons butter in a small saucepan; stir in flour. Continue stirring 1 to 2 minutes. Stir in stock or broth; simmer 5 minutes. Stir in half and half, nutmeg, pinch of salt and white pepper. Stir in sautéed chicken and any juices that have formed. Cut baked endive or chicory heads in halves lengthwise. Spoon about 1/3 of the sauce on 4 halves; top with remaining halves. Wrap a ham slice around each filled endive or chicory head; place in baking dish. Stir egg yolk and cheese into remaining sauce; spoon over filled heads. Bake until lightly browned. Serve hot. Makes 4 servings.

Flemish Beer Stew
CARBONNADE À LA FLAMANDE

1-3/4 lbs. beef top round
6 to 8 bacon slices
1 tablespoon lard
2 onions, cut in rings
1/2 garlic clove
1/2 teaspoon salt
1 tablespoon all-purpose flour
1/2 cup dark beer
1/2 to 1 cup beef stock or broth
1 parsley sprig
1/2 bay leaf
Pinch of dried leaf thyme
Pinch of sugar
Red-wine vinegar

Keeping separate, cut beef and bacon into thin 1-1/2-inch strips. Melt lard in a stovetop casserole; add beef strips. Brown over high heat; remove from pan and set aside. In same casserole, fry bacon strips until crisp. Remove from dish; set aside. Add onions to casserole; sauté 10 minutes. Preheat oven to 350F (175C). Crush garlic with salt. Add garlic-salt mixture and flour to sautéed onions. Stirring constantly, cook 2 to 3 minutes. Stir in beer and 1/2 cup stock or broth; bring to a boil. Stir in parsley, bay leaf, thyme, sugar and a little vinegar. Add cooked beef and bacon to casserole; add enough stock or broth to cover meat. Cover and bake 1 hour or until beef is tender. Remove bay leaf. Serve with parsleyed new potatoes. Makes 4 servings.

Apple Fritters
BEIGNETS AUX POMMES

3/4 cup all-purpose flour
1/8 teaspoon salt
1 egg, slightly beaten
1 tablespoon vegetable oil
1 teaspoon rum
1/2 cup light beer
Vegetable oil for deep-frying
2 egg whites
4 medium apples
1/2 cup powdered sugar

Sift flour and salt into a large bowl. Stir in egg, 1 tablespoon oil and rum. Gradually beat in enough beer to make a medium-thick batter similar to thickness of whipping cream. Cover bowl; let stand 1 hour. Heat oil for deep frying to 350F (175C) or until a 1-inch cube of bread turns golden brown in 50 seconds. Immediately before cooking fritters, beat egg whites until stiff and glossy. Use a wooden spoon to fold beaten egg whites into batter. Peel and core apples. Cut into 1/4-inch crosswise slices. Dip apple slices in batter, 2 or 3 at a time, covering completely. Carefully lower into hot oil. Fry apple slices until golden brown on both sides. Drain on paper towels; keep warm. Repeat until all apple slices are fried. To serve, generously sprinkle fritters with powdered sugar. Apple fritters are best served hot. Makes about 24 fritters.

Ghent Cheesecake
PLATTEKAASTARTE

Crusts:
2 teaspoons active dry yeast
1 tablespoon sugar
1/4 cup warm water (110F, 45C)
3/4 cup warm milk (110F, 45C)
1 egg, slightly beaten
Pinch of salt
1/4 cup butter, melted, cooled
2-1/4 to 2-1/2 cups all-purpose flour
5 tablespoons applesauce

Filling:
2 eggs, separated
1 cup cottage cheese (8 oz.)
1/2 cup crushed macaroons
2/3 cup sugar
1/4 cup ground almonds
1/4 cup vanilla sugar or 1/4 cup sugar and 1 teaspoon vanilla extract

To make crust, in a large bowl, stir yeast and sugar into water until dissolved. Stir in milk, egg, salt and butter. Beat in 1 cup flour until smooth. Cover and let stand 10 minutes. Stir in enough remaining flour to make a medium-stiff dough. Cover and let rise in a warm place, free from drafts, until doubled in bulk, about 1 hour. Butter a 9-inch springform pan; set aside. Roll out dough to a 14-inch circle. Fit into buttered pan. Spread applesauce over bottom. Preheat oven to 350F (175C).
To make filling, beat egg whites until stiff; set aside. In a medium bowl, beat together egg yolks and cottage cheese; beat in macaroons, 2/3 cup sugar, almonds and vanilla sugar or 1/4 cup sugar and vanilla extract. Fold in beaten egg whites. Spread mixture over applesauce. Bake 50 to 60 minutes or until golden. Makes 1 (9-inch) cake.

Stuffed Avocados
PALTA RELLENOS

4 oz. fresh or frozen, peeled, cooked shrimp
2 avocados
1/2 banana
2 teaspoons lemon juice
1/4 cup mayonnaise
1 tablespoon half and half
Salt and pepper
Pinch of paprika
Pinch of sugar
1-1/2 cups diced cooked chicken
5 or 6 lettuce leaves, shredded

If using frozen shrimp, thaw completely. Cut avocados in halves; remove stones. Use a teaspoon or melon baller to remove flesh from avocado skins; reserve avocado skins and 4 avocado balls. Dice remaining avocado flesh. Slice banana. In a medium bowl, combine diced avocado and sliced banana. Sprinkle with lemon juice. In a medium bowl, combine mayonnaise, half and half, salt, pepper, paprika and sugar. Fold in banana mixture, chicken and lettuce. Spoon mixture into reserved avocado skins; top with shrimp and reserved avocado balls. Makes 4 servings.

Variation

Substitute cooked fish for chicken.

Spicy Chicken
PICANTE DE GALLINA

1/4 cup olive oil
3 onions, cut in rings
1 (2-1/2-lb.) chicken, cut in pieces
1 cup hot chicken stock or broth
1/8 teaspoon black pepper
1 teaspoon red (cayenne) pepper
1 garlic clove
1 teaspoon salt
6 medium tomatoes
1/2 teaspoon dried leaf oregano
1 teaspoon caraway seeds
1 red bell pepper, cut in thin strips
2 tablespoons dry breadcrumbs
1 hard-cooked egg, sliced
12 pimiento-stuffed green olives

Heat oil in a saucepan. Add 2/3 of the onion rings; sauté until transparent. Add chicken pieces; fry until evenly browned. Add 1/2 cup stock or broth. Season with black and cayenne pepper. Cover and simmer 1 hour. Crush garlic with salt. Peel tomatoes; remove and discard seeds. Chop tomatoes. In a large saucepan, combine garlic-salt mixture, chopped tomatoes, remaining onion rings, remaining 1/2 cup stock or broth, oregano, caraway seeds and red bell pepper. Cover and simmer 20 minutes. Stir in breadcrumbs. Place chicken mixture on a platter. Spoon tomato mixture over top. Garnish with egg and olives. Makes 6 to 8 servings.

Beans with Tongue & Sausage

FEIJOÃDA

1-2/3 cups dried black beans or kidney beans
Water
1 (1-1/2-lb.) beef tongue
4 whole peppercorns
1 onion, cut in half
2 carrots, cut in sticks
1 large or 4 small boiling sausages

Vegetable Sauce:
5 medium tomatoes
3 tablespoons lard
1 onion, chopped
1 garlic clove, finely chopped
1/4 head cabbage, shredded
2 green bell peppers, finely chopped
Salt

Soak beans in cold water to cover 12 hours. Place beef tongue in a large saucepan. Add soaked beans with soaking water, peppercorns, onion and additional water to cover. Bring to a boil. Skim foam from surface until surface is clear. Reduce heat and simmer 4 hours. Add carrots and sausages. Simmer 1 hour longer or until tongue is tender.

To make sauce, peel tomatoes; remove and discard seeds. Coarsely chop tomatoes. Melt lard in a large saucepan. Add onion; sauté until transparent. Add chopped tomatoes, garlic, cabbage and green peppers. Cook 2 to 3 minutes, stirring constantly. Cover and simmer 20 minutes. Season with salt.

To complete, peel and slice cooked tongue. Remove and discard onion from bean mixture. Arrange sliced tongue, carrots and sausages on a platter. Serve hot with beans and vegetable sauce. Makes 8 to 10 servings.

Cook's Tip

Feijoãda can include as many different kinds of meat as you like. A really good feijoãda might have a dozen or more varieties. In addition to tongue and sausage, add salted dried bacon and fresh pork or beef. If you are using a combination of fresh and dried or salted meats, serve fresh meats on one side of a platter and salted or dried meats on the other side. Beans and vegetable sauce are served separately, accompanied by other side dishes, such as sliced oranges and a hot chili sauce. Although time-consuming to prepare, feijoãda is a delicious and filling meal. It is popular in Portugal as well as Brazil.

Tripe Soup
CHKEMBE TCHORBA

3 tablespoons butter
1 onion, finely chopped
1 red bell pepper, cut in thin strips
2 tablespoons all-purpose flour
1 (6-oz.) can tomato paste
1-1/2 lbs. tripe, cooked
3-1/2 cups meat stock or broth
1 teaspoon salt
1/2 teaspoon dried leaf marjoram
1 bay leaf
2 tablespoons finely chopped parsley
1 garlic clove, crushed
2/3 cup grated kashkavàl or feta cheese (2 oz.)

Melt butter in a large saucepan. Add onion and red pepper; sauté until soft. Sprinkle flour over onion mixture; stir in. Stir in tomato paste. Cut tripe in thin strips. Add tripe pieces, stock or broth, salt, marjoram and bay leaf to onion mixture. Partially cover pot; simmer 30 minutes. Remove and discard bay leaf. Pour soup into a tureen or serve in individual bowls. In a small bowl, combine parsley, garlic and cheese; sprinkle over hot soup. Serve immediately. Makes 4 servings.

Cheese-Stuffed Chilies
TSCHUSCHKI SIS SIRENE

4 fresh or canned whole green chilies
1-1/4 cups crumbled siréné or feta cheese (5 oz.)
1 egg, slightly beaten
Dairy sour cream, if desired
1/2 teaspoon salt
1/4 cup vegetable oil

Preheat oven to 400F (205C). To peel fresh chilies, cover your hands with rubber or plastic gloves. After handling chilies, do not touch your face or eyes. Place fresh chilies on a baking sheet; place in hot oven until surface becomes dark brown and begins to curl away from flesh. Place browned chilies in a pan with a tight-fitting lid. Let stand 10 minutes; remove skins. Cut chilies open lengthwise; remove seeds and pith. In a small bowl, beat together cheese and egg until creamy. Add a little sour cream, if desired. Stuff peeled chilies with cheese mixture; press cut edges together. Place stuffed chilies, cut-side up, in a shallow baking dish. Sprinkle with salt and oil. Reduce oven heat to 350F (175C). Bake about 40 minutes. Makes 4 servings.

Cook's Tip

In Bulgaria, this simple, tasty dish is served with fresh white bread.

Duck with Sauerkraut

PATKA SIS SELE

1 (3-1/2- to 4-lb.) duck with giblets
1-1/2 cups cooked long-grain white rice
3/4 cup chopped walnuts
1/8 teaspoon black pepper
1/8 teaspoon red (cayenne) pepper
1 teaspoon dried leaf marjoram
Salt
1/4 teaspoon white pepper
1 tablespoon lard
2 onions, coarsely chopped
1 (24-oz.) can or 2-1/4 lbs. fresh sauerkraut
2 tablespoons sweet paprika

Preheat oven to 350F (175C). Finely chop giblets; stir in rice, nuts, black pepper, red pepper, marjoram and 1/2 teaspoon salt. Place duck, neck-side down, in a large bowl. Loosely fill body cavity with giblet mixture. Truss duck or close with skewers. Rub stuffed duck with 1 teaspoon salt and white pepper. Prick duck skin all over to let fat drain during roasting. Place duck, breast-side down, on a rack in a shallow roasting pan. Pour 1 cup water in bottom of pan. Roast duck 2 hours. Turn duck breast-side up. Insert a meat thermometer in center of inner-thigh muscle. Roast 45 minutes longer or until thermometer registers 180F to 185F (80C to 85C) and juices run clear when a knife is inserted between thigh and breast. Stuffing should reach a temperature of 165F (75C). Melt lard in a large skillet. Add onions; sauté until lightly browned. Add sauerkraut; toss with onions. Stir in paprika. Spoon into a large baking dish. Bake 45 to 60 minutes with duck. Remove duck from oven; let stand 15 minutes before carving. Place carved duck on hot sauerkraut. Makes 4 servings.

Stuffed Cabbage with Pork

SARMA

Water
Salt
1 large cabbage, core removed
3/4 cup cooked long-grain white rice
1-1/4 lbs. ground pork
3 large onions, chopped
1/2 teaspoon dried leaf marjoram
1/2 cup butter
1/3 cup tomato paste
1 cup water
1/8 teaspoon red (cayenne) pepper
1 (24-oz.) can or 2-1/4 lbs. fresh sauerkraut
4 smoked pork spareribs

Bring a large saucepan of salted water to a boil. Plunge cabbage into boiling water. Boil gently 4 to 5 minutes. Use a slotted spoon to remove cabbage from water. Carefully remove outer leaves. Repeat 2 to 3 times or until 12 large outer leaves have been removed. In a medium bowl, combine rice, pork, 3 tablespoons chopped onion, marjoram and 1 teaspoon salt. Divide stuffing mixture into 12 portions. Roll or pound each cabbage leaf to soften center rib. Spread stuffing over each leaf, leaving a 1-inch border uncovered around edges. Roll leaves, enclosing stuffing. Preheat oven to 350F (175C). Melt butter in a large skillet. Add remaining onions; sauté until transparent. Add tomato paste, 1 cup water and red pepper. Stir sauerkraut into sauce. Stir occasionally until hot. Spoon 1/2 of the sauerkraut mixture into a large baking dish. Arrange spareribs on top. Spoon remaining sauerkraut mixture over ribs. Arrange stuffed cabbage leaves on top. Bake 1-1/2 hours or until ribs are tender. Makes 4 to 6 servings.

Fried Vegetables
AKYAW

2 tablespoons vegetable oil
1 onion, finely chopped
8 to 10 green onions, chopped
1 garlic clove, crushed
1 tablespoon fish sauce or oyster sauce
1 teaspoon salt
1/8 teaspoon pepper
1 cup chopped peeled eggplant
1 cup French-cut fresh green beans
1/2 cup shredded Chinese cabbage
1/2 cup shredded or julienned carrot
1 medium zucchini, thinly sliced
1/2 cup fresh or frozen green peas
1-1/2 cups fresh or canned bean sprouts
4 water chestnuts, thinly sliced
1/2 to 1 teaspoon soy sauce
Cilantro

Heat oil in a wok or large skillet. Add onion, green onions, garlic, fish sauce or oyster sauce, salt and pepper. Sauté over medium heat 2 minutes. Add eggplant, green beans, cabbage, carrot, zucchini, peas, bean sprouts and water chestnuts. Stir-fry until crisp-tender. Season with soy sauce. Garnish with cilantro. Spoon onto a platter; serve immediately. Makes 6 servings.

Cook's Tip

In Burma, vegetables are not boiled or steamed but stir-fried in a wok. Fried vegetables are served as a main course with rice or to accompany a meat or fish curry. It is important to cut all vegetables into small pieces or thin slices for even cooking. To prevent vegetables from losing their crispness, serve immediately after cooking.

Chicken Curry
KYETHA HIN

1 onion, cut in wedges
2 garlic cloves, crushed
1 (1-inch) cube gingerroot
1 teaspoon salt
1 teaspoon grated lemon peel
1 teaspoon ground turmeric
4 dried red chilies
1/4 cup vegetable oil
About 1 cup water
1 (3-lb.) chicken, cut in 12 to 14 pieces
2 medium tomatoes, peeled, diced
2 potatoes, peeled, diced
1 cup julienned pumpkin or squash
1 teaspoon shrimp paste
1 teaspoon chopped cilantro or parsley
1/4 teaspoon crushed cardamom seeds

In a blender, puree onion, garlic, gingerroot, salt, lemon peel, turmeric, chilies and 2 teaspoons oil. Heat remaining oil in a wok or large skillet. Add pureed mixture; stir over medium heat 3 to 4 minutes. Add 1 cup water and chicken; cook over low heat 20 minutes. Add tomatoes, potatoes, pumpkin or squash and shrimp paste. Cook 3 to 5 minutes, adding more water, if needed. Simmer curry 30 to 35 minutes longer or until chicken is tender. Sprinkle with cilantro or parsley and cardamom seeds. Serve hot. Makes 3 to 4 servings.

Wild Rice & Mushroom Casserole

3/4 cup uncooked wild rice
1/4 teaspoon dried leaf thyme
1/4 teaspoon dried leaf basil
Salt
1-1/2 cups chicken stock or broth
1 lb. mushrooms
1/4 cup butter
1 onion, finely chopped
Pepper
2 tablespoons chopped parsley

In a medium saucepan, combine rice, thyme, basil, 1/2 teaspoon salt and stock or broth. Cover and bring to a boil. Reduce heat; simmer 40 minutes. Preheat oven to 350F (175C). Trim mushrooms; slice large mushrooms. Cut small mushrooms in half. Melt butter in a large stovetop casserole. Add onion; sauté until golden brown. Add prepared mushrooms; sauté until lightly browned. Season to taste with salt and pepper. Stir in rice mixture and any stock or broth not absorbed. Cover and bake 15 to 20 minutes. To serve, sprinkle parsley over top. Makes 4 servings.

Beef Daube

1 cup dried Great Northern beans, navy beans or white kidney beans
Water
2 tablespoons vegetable oil
1 onion, finely chopped
1-3/4 lbs. beef round steak, cut in 3/4-inch cubes
1 teaspoon all-purpose flour
2 tablespoons tomato paste
1/3 cup dry red wine
1 cup beef stock or broth
1 bay leaf
Pinch of dried leaf thyme
Salt
1/8 teaspoon pepper
1/2 lb. fresh carrots, cut in 2-inch pieces

Soak beans in cold water to cover 12 hours. Heat oil in a large stovetop casserole. Add onion; sauté until tender. Add beef; sauté until lightly browned. Sprinkle with flour; sauté 3 to 5 minutes longer. Stir in tomato paste, wine, stock or broth, bay leaf, thyme, 1/2 teaspoon salt and pepper. Bring to a boil. Preheat oven to 400F (205C). Add beans and soaking water to beef mixture. Cover and bake 1 hour or until beef and beans are tender. Meanwhile, cook carrots in salted water until crisp-tender. Remove and discard bay leaf from stew. Stir in cooked carrots. Serve hot. Makes 4 to 6 servings.

Canadian Pastry

3 cups all-purpose flour
Pinch of salt
1/2 cup plus 2 tablespoons
  butter, chilled
5 to 7 tablespoons cold water
1 egg yolk, beaten

Sift flour and salt into a medium bowl. Dot with butter. Use a pastry blender or fork to cut in butter until mixture resembles coarse crumbs. Using a fork, gradually stir in water to form a pastry dough. Wrap dough in plastic wrap to prevent drying; refrigerate 15 to 30 minutes. Divide dough in half. Roll out half of dough to make a thin pastry. Use to line a 10-inch pie pan. Fill with 1 of fillings at right. Roll out remaining dough for top crust. Place over filling; fold top crust under bottom crust. Flute edge as desired. Before baking, brush top pastry with beaten egg yolk. Makes 1 (10-inch) double-crust pastry.

Walnut Pie

2 eggs
1/2 cup plus 2 tablespoons sugar
1 teaspoon vanilla extract
1/2 cup pure or artificial maple
  syrup
2 tablespoons butter, melted
3/4 cup chopped walnuts
Unbaked Canadian Pastry,
  opposite

Preheat oven to 400F (205C). In a small bowl, beat eggs lightly. Stir in sugar, vanilla, syrup, butter and nuts. Spread mixture evenly in bottom pie crust. Cover with top crust. Bake 10 minutes. Reduce heat to 350F (175C); bake 30 minutes longer. Makes 1 (10-inch) pie.

Apricot Pie

1/3 cup ground almonds
2 tablespoons fresh breadcrumbs
2 tablespoons chopped walnuts
Unbaked Canadian Pastry,
  opposite
1 lb. fresh or frozen apricots or 1
  (29-oz.) can apricots in heavy
  syrup, drained
1/2 cup sugar

Preheat oven to 400F (205C). In a small bowl, combine almonds, breadcrumbs and walnuts; sprinkle over bottom pie crust. Peel and halve fresh apricots. Spread fresh, frozen or canned apricot halves over nut mixture. Sprinkle sugar over fresh or frozen apricots. If using canned apricots, omit sugar. Cut top crust into strips; arrange in a lattice pattern over filling. Bake 30 minutes. Makes 1 (10-inch) pie.

Blueberry Pie

1/2 cup sugar
1/4 teaspoon ground cinnamon
Pinch of salt
1 tablespoon all-purpose flour
Unbaked Canadian Pastry,
  opposite
2 cups frozen, fresh or drained
  canned blueberries
1-1/2 teaspoons lemon juice
1 tablespoon butter

Preheat oven to 400F (205C). In a small bowl, combine sugar, cinnamon, salt and flour. Sprinkle half of the sugar mixture over bottom pie crust. Cover with blueberries. Sprinkle remaining sugar mixture over blueberries. Sprinkle with lemon juice; dot with butter. Cover with top crust; bake 30 minutes. Makes 1 (10-inch) pie.

Ginger Mousse

1 (1/4-oz.) envelope unflavored gelatin (1 tablespoon)
2 tablespoons cold water
1 cup half and half
2 eggs, separated
1/4 cup plus 2 tablespoons sugar
2 to 3 tablespoons finely chopped crystallized ginger
2 tablespoons white rum
1/8 teaspoon salt
Crystallized-ginger pieces

In a small glass bowl, soften gelatin in water, 3 to 5 minutes. Place bowl over hot water; stir until gelatin dissolves. Keep warm. Pour half and half into a small saucepan. Stir constantly over low heat until almost boiling. In top of a double boiler, beat egg yolks until blended; beat in 1/4 cup sugar. Gradually stir in hot half and half; place over hot water. Stir constantly until warmed through. Stir in dissolved gelatin and chopped ginger. Let stand 10 to 15 minutes. Stir in rum. In a medium bowl, beat egg whites until stiff but not dry; stir in remaining 2 tablespoons sugar and salt. Carefully fold egg-yolk mixture into egg-white mixture. Spoon mousse into a serving bowl or individual dessert dishes. Cover; refrigerate about 3 hours. To serve, decorate with crystallized-ginger pieces. Makes 4 servings.

Mango Cream

2 large or 3 medium, ripe mangoes
2 tablespoons fresh lemon juice
1/4 cup plus 1 tablespoon sugar
2 egg whites
Pinch of salt
6 tablespoons whipping cream
2 tablespoons grated chocolate or chocolate flakes

Peel mangoes and cut flesh from stones; finely dice half of the fruit. In a blender or food processor, puree remaining fruit, lemon juice and 1/4 cup sugar. Beat egg whites until soft peaks form. Beat in remaining 1 tablespoon sugar and salt until stiff but not dry. Whip cream until stiff. Gently fold beaten egg whites into whipped cream. Fold in mango puree, then fold in diced mango. Spoon into a serving bowl or individual dessert dishes; refrigerate 30 minutes. To serve, decorate with chocolate. Makes 4 servings.

Variation

As an interesting change of flavor, substitute freshly squeezed lime juice for lemon juice. The delicate lime flavor blends well with mangoes.

Stuffed Potato Croquettes
PATATAS RELLENOS

3 medium potatoes, peeled, cut in quarters
Water
1 teaspoon salt
1 tablespoon butter
1 onion, finely chopped
1 teaspoon finely chopped parsley
1/4 teaspoon dried leaf thyme
1 tablespoon chicken stock or broth
1 hard-cooked egg, finely chopped
3 cups finely chopped, cooked chicken
1 teaspoon raisins
1 egg yolk
Vegetable oil for deep-frying
2 to 3 tablespoons cornstarch

In a large saucepan, cover potatoes with water; add salt. Cook 15 to 30 minutes or until tender. Melt butter in a medium saucepan. Add onion; sauté until transparent. Add parsley, thyme and stock or broth. Simmer 3 to 5 minutes, stirring constantly. Stir in hard-cooked egg, chicken and raisins. Remove from heat; cool slightly. Drain and mash potatoes; quickly beat in egg yolk. Set aside to cool. In a medium saucepan, heat oil to 375F (190C) or until a 1-inch cube of bread turns golden brown in 50 seconds. Dust your hands with flour. With floured hands, shape chicken mixture into walnut-size balls. Cover each with potato puree. Roll potato croquettes in cornstarch. Carefully fry 2 or 3 at a time in hot oil until golden brown. Keep hot until ready to serve. Makes 4 servings.

Marinated Chicken
ESCABECHE DE GALLINA

1 cup celery leaves
2 parsley sprigs
2 whole cloves
1/4 teaspoon dried leaf thyme
1/3 cup olive oil
1 (2-1/2-lb.) chicken, cut in pieces
1 cup dry white wine
1/3 cup wine vinegar
1 teaspoon salt
1 cup hot water
2 onions, cut in rings
1 carrot, sliced
1 leek, sliced
1 lemon, cut in 8 wedges

Reserve a few celery leaves for garnish. Chop remaining celery leaves. Tie chopped celery leaves, parsley, cloves and thyme in a small piece of cheesecloth; set aside. Heat oil in a large saucepan. Fry chicken in oil, a few pieces at a time, until golden brown. Discard oil after frying chicken pieces; wipe pan with paper towels. Return browned chicken to saucepan. In a small bowl, combine wine, vinegar, salt and water. Pour over chicken; add onion rings, carrot, leek and bag of herbs. Cover and simmer 30 minutes; discard bag of herbs. Place cooked chicken pieces in a large bowl. Spoon off fat from cooking liquid. Stir cooking liquid, vegetables and lemon wedges into chicken. Cool to room temperature. Cover and refrigerate 6 hours. Serve cold, garnished with reserved celery leaves. Makes 4 servings.

Stewed Jumbo Shrimp
DUEI HSIA

4 fresh or frozen jumbo shrimp
2 tablespoons vegetable oil
2 garlic cloves, slightly crushed
1 (1/2-inch) cube gingerroot, thinly sliced
1/3 cup water
1 teaspoon sugar
1/2 teaspoon salt
1 tablespoon rice wine or dry sherry
1/2 teaspoon vinegar
1 teaspoon cornstarch
2 tablespoons tomato juice
1 green onion, finely chopped

Thaw frozen shrimp; remove shrimp shells and veins. Cut shrimp in halves lengthwise. Heat oil in a medium skillet. Add garlic and gingerroot; sauté until soft. Add shrimp halves; brown lightly. Stir in water, sugar, salt, wine or sherry, vinegar, cornstarch and tomato juice. Stirring gently, simmer 3 to 5 minutes. Add green onion. Boil liquid until slightly reduced. Remove garlic. Arrange cooked shrimp on a plate. Spoon sauce over top. Makes 1 serving.

Jumbo Shrimp in White Wine
HUNG SHAO DUEI HSIA

4 fresh or frozen jumbo shrimp
1/3 cup stock or broth
1/4 teaspoon salt
2 teaspoons sugar
2 tablespoons rice wine or dry sherry
1 to 2 tablespoons water
1 tablespoon cornstarch
4 cooked broccoli spears

Thaw frozen shrimp; remove shrimp shells and veins. Slit each shrimp along the back with a sharp knife. Bring stock or broth to a boil in a medium saucepan. Add shrimp; boil 2 minutes. Use a slotted spoon to remove shrimp from pan. Add salt, sugar and wine or sherry to hot stock or broth. In a small bowl, combine water and cornstarch; stir until smooth. Stir in about 1/4 cup hot stock or broth mixture. Stir cornstarch mixture into remaining stock or broth mixture. Bring to a boil. Reduce heat and simmer 2 minutes. Skim foam from surface until surface is clear. Add cooked shrimp; heat through. To serve, arrange in a small bowl with broccoli. Makes 1 serving.

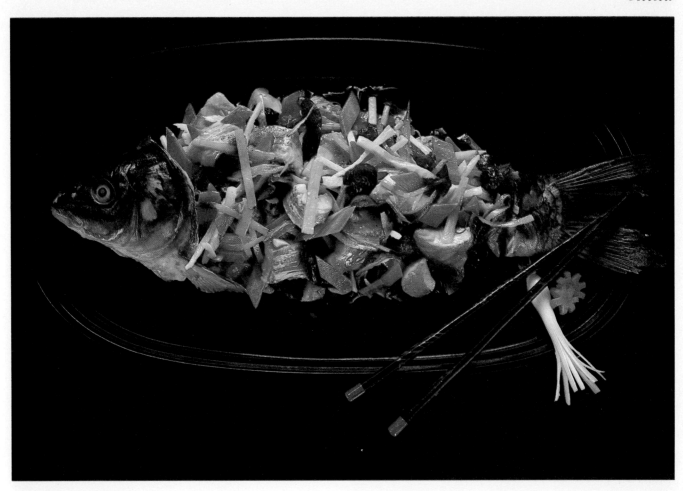

Stuffed Carp

LI YÜ

3 carrots
1 (8-oz.) can bamboo shoots, drained
2 oz. dried Chinese mushrooms
Water
1 (2-lb.) oven-ready carp
1 onion, finely chopped
1 tablespoon chopped parsley
1 bay leaf
2 whole cloves
Salt
2 cups white wine
1/4 cup butter
1 leek, thinly sliced
1 cup fresh or canned bean sprouts, drained
1 tablespoon soy sauce
Juice of 1 lemon
1/4 teaspoon pepper
1/2 teaspoon ground ginger

Peel 2 carrots; slice lengthwise. Cut slices into small diamond-shape pieces; set aside. Chop remaining carrot. Cut bamboo shoots into thin strips. In a small bowl, soak mushrooms in hot water 30 minutes or until softened. Fillet carp, keeping head, tail and backbone intact. To fillet carp, remove skin from body. Cut along bones on each side of back from head to tail. Cut behind gills to free fillet at head. Lift fillet and make short cuts along middle bone, freeing fillet completely. Cut each fillet into 3/4-inch pieces; set aside. Steam head, tail and backbone 5 to 10 minutes. Refrigerate until serving time.

To make filling, in a large saucepan, combine chopped carrot, onion, parsley, bay leaf, cloves, 1 teaspoon salt, wine and 2 cups water. Bring to a boil; boil 5 minutes. Add carp pieces; simmer 3 minutes. Drain and chop soaked mushrooms. Melt butter in a medium skillet. Add chopped mushrooms, carrot diamonds, bamboo-shoot pieces, leek and bean sprouts. Sauté 8 to 10 minutes or until vegetables are crisp-tender. Do not overcook vegetables. In a small bowl, combine soy sauce, lemon juice, pepper and ginger. Stir soy-sauce mixture and sautéed vegetables into fish mixture.

To complete, arrange chilled head, tail and backbone on a platter. Spoon fish-and-vegetable mixture onto backbone, shaping mixture like body of a fish. Makes 3 to 4 servings.

Cook's Tip

In China, this is a way of making fish serve more people, yet giving the impression that a whole fish is being served.

Crispy Fried Duck

TZUOI JIA

1 (3- to 4-lb.) duck
Water
Salt
2 teaspoons finely chopped gingerroot
2 egg whites
1/3 cup cornstarch
White pepper
Vegetable oil for deep-frying
2 green onions, thinly sliced
1 leek, thinly sliced
1 onion, thinly sliced
1 yellow or green bell pepper, cut in narrow strips
1 red bell pepper, cut in narrow strips
1 (4-oz.) can bamboo shoots, drained, chopped
2 oz. dried Chinese mushrooms, soaked in water, chopped
2 tablespoons soy sauce
Pinch of sugar

In a large pot, cover duck with water. Add 1 teaspoon salt and
gingerroot. Bring to a boil. Reduce heat and simmer 50 minutes.
Remove duck; reserve cooking liquid. Cut wings and legs from
cooked duck. Cut remaining meat from carcass in large pieces.
In a medium bowl, beat egg whites until frothy, gradually
beating in cornstarch, a pinch of salt and white pepper. Roll
duck in egg-white mixture. In a wok or large skillet, heat oil to
350F (175C) or until a 1-inch cube of bread turns golden brown
in 50 seconds. Deep-fry coated duck until crisp. Drain; keep
warm. Drain wok or skillet; wipe with paper towels. Heat 3
tablespoons oil in wok or skillet. Add green onions, leek, onion,
bell peppers, bamboo shoots and chopped mushrooms. Sauté
until heated through. Stir in 6 tablespoons reserved cooking
liquid. Cook 8 to 10 minutes. Season with soy sauce and sugar.
Makes 3 to 4 servings.

Szechwan Chicken

SZE CHUEN JAR GAI

1 (2- to 3-lb.) chicken
2 tablespoons soy sauce
1 teaspoon cornstarch
1 fresh red chili
1/4 cup vegetable oil
3 carrots, cut in thin strips
3 green onions, cut in thin strips
1 tablespoon soy sauce, if desired

Using a cleaver or sharp knife, cut chicken in half. Cut chicken
from bones. Chop chicken; discard bones. Place chicken pieces
in a shallow bowl; sprinkle with soy sauce and cornstarch. Stir
well. Cover and marinate 30 minutes. To handle fresh chilies,
cover your hands with rubber or plastic gloves. After handling
chilies, do not touch your face or eyes. Cut chili into rings;
remove seeds. Heat 2 tablespoons oil in a wok or large skillet.
Add marinated chicken; cook 4 to 5 minutes, stirring
constantly. Using a slotted spoon, remove meat from pan. Heat
remaining oil in pan. Add chili rings, carrots and green onions.
Sauté 5 to 6 minutes. Add chicken; heat through, stirring
frequently. Season with soy sauce, if desired. Serve with hot
cooked rice. Makes 3 to 4 servings.

Chicken with Rice Hai Nan

KAI FAN

1 (2-1/2- to 3-lb.) chicken
1 garlic clove, crushed
2 teaspoons salt
1 teaspoon oyster sauce
5-1/2 cups water
1 green onion, sliced
1 cup sliced celery
2 teaspoons finely chopped gingerroot
1 fresh red chili
1/4 cup canned coconut milk or 1/4 cup Coconut Milk, page 7
1 cup uncooked long-grain white rice
1 onion, chopped

Radish Sauce:
1 white radish, finely grated
3 tablespoons wine vinegar
3 tablespoons soy sauce

Rub chicken inside and out with garlic, salt and oyster sauce. Cover and refrigerate 1 hour. In a large saucepan, combine water, green onion, celery, 1 teaspoon gingerroot and whole chili. Bring to a boil. Add chicken. Reduce heat and simmer 1 hour or until tender. Pour 1-1/2 cups cooking liquid into a medium saucepan. Add coconut milk; bring to a boil. Add rice, onion and remaining gingerroot. Cook over low heat 15 to 20 minutes or until rice is tender but still firm. Remove chicken from cooking liquid. Cut cooked chicken into pieces by boning entire chicken or by boning breast only. Cut breast meat into slices; arrange on lettuce as shown. Serve with cooked rice, vegetables, cooking liquid and soy sauce, chili sauce or radish sauce. Makes 3 to 4 servings.

To make radish sauce, in a small bowl, squeeze liquid from radish; discard liquid. Stir in vinegar and soy sauce.

Cook's Tip

This recipe originated on the island of Hai-Nan-Pao in the South China Sea. It has now become popular throughout China. Wherever the Chinese have settled throughout the world, several variations are served.

Pork with Curry Sauce

CHOW YOOK PIN

1-1/4 lbs. boneless pork, cut in thin slices
5 tablespoons vegetable oil
4 green onions, cut in strips
2 cups fresh or canned bean sprouts, drained

Marinade:
1/4 cup soy sauce
1/4 cup rice wine or dry sherry
1/8 teaspoon salt
Pinch of sugar
1/8 teaspoon ground ginger
4 teaspoons cornstarch

Curry Sauce:
2 tablespoons vegetable oil
3 tablespoons curry powder
1 tablespoon rice wine or dry sherry
1/3 cup stock or broth
1 teaspoon cornstarch
Water

Place pork in a shallow bowl. In a small bowl, combine marinade ingredients. Pour over pork; cover and marinate 20 minutes. Drain pork well. Heat oil in a wok or large skillet; add drained pork. Stir-fry 5 minutes. Using a slotted spoon, remove cooked pork pieces. Heat oil again. Add green onions and bean sprouts; stir-fry 2 to 3 minutes. Add cooked pork.
To make sauce, heat oil in a wok or large skillet. Stir in curry powder, wine or sherry and stock or broth. In a small bowl, combine cornstarch and a little water. Stirring constantly, add cornstarch mixture to curry mixture. Cook until thickened. Serve with cooked pork and vegetables, hot rice, mango chutney and canned sweet-and-sour fruit. Makes 4 servings.

Stuffed Shiitake Mushrooms

JING YEUNG BUCK GWOO

24 large fresh shiitake mushrooms
1 green onion, white part only, finely chopped
8 canned water chestnuts, chopped
1/2 lb. ground pork
1 tablespoon cornstarch
2 tablespoons soy sauce
1/2 teaspoon salt
1/8 teaspoon sugar
1/8 teaspoon grated fresh gingerroot
About 1 cup stock or broth
1 egg, slightly beaten

Lightly oil a shallow stovetop casserole; set aside. Cut stems from mushrooms; rub mushroom caps with a damp cloth. In a medium bowl, combine green onion, water chestnuts, pork, cornstarch, soy sauce, salt, sugar and gingerroot. Place 1 heaping tablespoon pork mixture on each of 12 mushroom caps. Top with remaining mushroom caps; press firmly together. Arrange stuffed mushrooms in oiled dish; cover tightly. Cook over medium heat 25 to 30 minutes. Remove stuffed mushrooms from dish; keep warm. In a small saucepan, heat stock or broth. Add enough hot stock or broth to mushroom cooking juices in dish to make 1 cup liquid. Whisk egg into cooking-liquid mixture. Do not boil. Pour sauce over mushrooms. Serve with hot cooked rice. Makes 4 servings.

Beef with Bamboo Shoots
YÜ-HSIANG-NIV-JOU

1/4 cup vegetable oil
2 green onions, finely chopped
1 lb. beef top round, cut in thin strips
2 green or red bell peppers, cut in strips
1 (8-oz.) can bamboo shoots, drained, chopped
1 garlic clove, crushed
1 tablespoon ketchup
1/4 cup soy sauce
1/2 teaspoon salt
1/2 teaspoon red (cayenne) pepper
1/3 cup chicken stock or broth
2 teaspoons chopped fresh cilantro or parsley

Heat oil in a wok or large skillet. Add green onions; sauté until transparent. Add 1/3 of the beef to pan. Stir-fry over high heat until browned, 1 to 2 minutes. Using a slotted spoon, remove browned beef from pan; keep warm. Repeat with remaining beef strips, cooking 1/3 at a time. Heat oil remaining in wok or skillet. Add green or red peppers and bamboo shoots; stir-fry 2 to 3 minutes. Add garlic, ketchup, soy sauce, salt and red pepper; cook 2 minutes. Add cooked beef and stock or broth; heat through. To serve, spoon into a serving bowl; sprinkle with cilantro or parsley. Serve with transparent Chinese noodles and a bean-sprout salad. Makes 4 servings.

Sweet & Sour Pork
KU LAO JOU

1 lb. boneless pork loin, cut in thin slices
2 oz. dried Chinese mushrooms
Water
1/4 cup vegetable oil
1 green bell pepper, cut in strips
1 red bell pepper, cut in strips
1 leek, cut in strips
2 carrots, sliced
1/2 cucumber, thinly sliced
1 cup stock or broth
1 tablespoon cornstarch

Marinade:
3 tablespoons soy sauce
2 tablespoons vinegar
1/2 teaspoon sugar
1 teaspoon salt

Place pork in a shallow bowl. In a small bowl, combine marinade ingredients. Pour over pork; marinate 1 hour, stirring occasionally. In a small bowl, soak mushrooms in hot water 30 minutes or until softened. Drain and chop mushrooms. Drain pork, reserving marinade. Heat oil in a wok or large skillet. Add drained pork; stir-fry 2 to 3 minutes or until browned on all sides. Add green and red peppers, leek, carrots and cucumber. Stir-fry 5 minutes. Add stock or broth; simmer 15 minutes. Stir in chopped mushrooms. In a small bowl, combine cornstarch, 1 teaspoon reserved marinade and a little water. Stir into mixture; continue stirring over low heat until thickened. Spoon pork mixture into a serving bowl. Serve with transparent Chinese noodles and a Chinese cabbage salad. Makes 4 servings.

Hot & Sour Soup

SUAN-LA TANG

1/2 lb. boneless pork
Water
Salt
1/3 cup uncooked long-grain white rice
4 dried Chinese mushrooms
About 3 cups chicken stock or broth
1/4 cup chopped bamboo shoots
1 teaspoon grated fresh gingerroot
1 tablespoon cornstarch
1 egg, slightly beaten
1 tablespoon vinegar
1/8 teaspoon black pepper
1/8 teaspoon red (cayenne) pepper
2 teaspoons sesame oil
2 green onions, finely chopped

Cook pork in boiling, lightly salted water 30 minutes. Cook rice in boiling salted water 15 minutes; drain. In a small bowl, soak mushrooms in hot water 30 minutes or until softened. Drain and chop mushrooms. Drain pork, reserving cooking liquid. Finely chop pork; set aside. Skim fat from surface of cooking liquid. Add stock or broth to make about 5-1/2 cups liquid. Bring liquid to a boil in a large saucepan. Add chopped mushrooms, chopped pork, cooked rice, bamboo shoots and gingerroot. Reduce heat and simmer 1 minute. In a small bowl, combine cornstarch and a little cold water. Stir into soup until slightly thickened. Stirring constantly, cook about 5 minutes longer. Stir egg into soup, then immediately remove soup from heat. Season with vinegar, black pepper and red pepper. Stir in sesame oil and green onions. Pour into a tureen or serve in individual bowls. Makes 4 servings.

Vegetable Soup

TZAI TANG

4 dried Chinese mushrooms
4 medium tomatoes
3 tablespoons vegetable oil
2 green onions, finely chopped
1/2 garlic clove, crushed
1 celery stalk, thinly sliced
1/4 head Chinese cabbage, thinly sliced
1/2 cup fresh or canned bean sprouts, drained
3 tablespoons soy sauce
1/2 teaspoon salt
1/4 teaspoon white pepper
1/8 teaspoon ground ginger
2 teaspoons chopped parsley
3-1/2 cups hot chicken stock or broth

In a small bowl, soak mushrooms in hot water 30 minutes or until softened. Peel tomatoes; remove and discard seeds. Chop tomatoes. Drain and coarsely chop mushrooms. Heat oil in a wok or large skillet. Add onions and garlic; sauté until transparent. Add chopped mushrooms, chopped tomatoes, celery, cabbage and bean sprouts. Stir-fry over high heat 2 to 3 minutes. Stir in soy sauce, salt, white pepper, ginger, parsley and stock or broth. Bring to a boil. Reduce heat and simmer 2 to 3 minutes. Pour into a tureen or serve in individual bowls. Serve hot. Makes 4 servings.

Creole Steak with Beans & Rice
PABELLON CRIOLLA

Beans:
1 cup dried black beans
Water
2 tablespoons olive oil
1/2 green bell pepper, finely chopped
1/2 onion, chopped
1 garlic clove, finely chopped
1/2 teaspoon salt

Beef:
4 (8-oz.) boneless beef top-loin steaks
5 medium tomatoes
3 tablespoons olive oil
2 onions, coarsely chopped
1 teaspoon salt
1/8 teaspoon ground cumin

Rice:
1 whole green chili
3 tablespoons olive oil
1 small onion
1 cup uncooked long-grain white rice
2 cups boiling water
1 teaspoon salt

Garnish:
4 green bananas
3 tablespoons vegetable oil

To prepare beans, soak beans in cold water to cover 12 hours. Bring beans, uncovered, to a boil in soaking water. Boil 1 to 1-1/4 hours, adding water as necessary. Heat olive oil in a large skillet. Add green pepper, onion and 1/2 the garlic. Reserve remaining garlic for beef. Sauté green-pepper mixture until onion is transparent; stir in salt. Add green-pepper mixture to cooked beans. Cover and simmer 15 minutes.

To prepare beef, preheat grill or broiler. Cook beef 4 minutes on each side. Cut cooked beef into thin strips; set aside. Peel tomatoes; remove and discard seeds. Chop tomatoes. Heat olive oil in a large skillet. Add onions and reserved garlic; sauté until transparent. Stir in chopped tomatoes, salt and cumin; simmer 30 minutes. Arrange beef over top of vegetables. Cover and keep warm over low heat.

To prepare rice, preheat oven to 250F (120C). To peel fresh chili, cover your hands with rubber or plastic gloves. After handling, do not touch your face or eyes. Place fresh chili on a baking sheet; place in hot oven until surface becomes dark brown and begins to curl away from flesh. Place browned chili in a pan with a tight-fitting lid. Let stand 10 minutes; remove skin. Cut green chili in half lengthwise; remove seeds and pith. Heat olive oil in a small skillet. Add whole onion and chili halves; sauté 5 minutes. Stir in rice; sauté 5 minutes. Add boiling water and salt. Cover and bake 20 minutes or until rice is tender. Remove and discard onion and chili halves. Cover and keep warm.

To prepare garnish, peel bananas; cut in halves lengthwise. Cut each half crosswise into 3 pieces. Heat vegetable oil in a medium skillet. Fry banana pieces in oil until browned on all sides. To serve, spoon vegetables and beef onto a warm platter. Add alternate portions of rice and black beans, as shown. Arrange cooked banana over beef mixture. Makes 4 servings.

Stewed Rabbit
ZAJÍE NA ČERNE

1 (3- to 4-lb.) rabbit, cut in pieces
Water
Vinegar
6 to 8 bacon slices, diced
1 large onion, chopped
1 bay leaf
1/2 teaspoon dried leaf thyme
6 whole peppercorns
6 whole allspice
1 piece lemon peel
1 teaspoon salt
2 tablespoons butter
2 tablespoons all-purpose flour
2 tablespoons red-wine vinegar
1 tablespoon sugar

Rub rabbit pieces with a cloth moistened in water and vinegar; set rabbit aside. Fry bacon in a medium saucepan until nearly crisp; remove bacon, leaving drippings in saucepan. Add onion to bacon drippings; sauté until transparent. Add bay leaf, thyme, peppercorns, allspice, lemon peel and salt. Add rabbit pieces and enough warm water to cover. Cover and simmer 1-1/2 to 2 hours or until rabbit is tender. Place cooked rabbit on a platter; keep warm. Strain and reserve cooking liquid. Melt butter in another medium saucepan. Stir in flour to make a smooth paste. Gradually stir in 2 cups reserved cooking liquid. Stir over medium heat until thickened. Stir in wine vinegar and sugar; boil 5 minutes, stirring occasionally. Add remaining cooking liquid to sauce. Bring to a boil; pour over rabbit. Makes 4 servings.

Bohemian Ham & Noodle Dish
SCHINKENFLECKERL

1 lb. flat noodles, broken in pieces
Water
Salt
5 tablespoons butter
1 onion, chopped
3/4 lb. boiled ham, diced
3 eggs
1/3 cup dairy sour cream
1/8 teaspoon ground nutmeg
1/8 teaspoon pepper

Cook noodles in 2-1/2 quarts lightly salted water, 10 minutes or until *al dente* or tender but firm to the bite. Drain; rinse with cold water and drain again. Preheat oven to 400F (205C). Butter a baking dish; set aside. Melt 2 tablespoons butter in a large skillet. Add onion; sauté until golden brown. Add ham and sautéed onion to noodles; pour into buttered baking dish. In a small bowl, beat together eggs, sour cream, nutmeg, pepper and 1 teaspoon salt. Pour over noodle mixture. Bake in center of oven 30 minutes. Dot with remaining butter. Cover and bake 10 minutes longer. Serve with a lettuce-and-tomato salad. Makes 4 servings.

Beef with Bread Dumpling

SVÍČKOVÁ/KNEDLIKY

1 (1-1/4-lb.) beef-tenderloin roast
Salt and white pepper
3 onions, chopped
1/2 small celeriac or 4 celery stalks, chopped
1 carrot, chopped
1 parsnip, chopped
4 or 5 bacon slices, diced
4 whole peppercorns
2 whole cloves
1 bay leaf
2 tablespoons butter, melted
1 cup beef stock or broth
2 tablespoons all-purpose flour
1 cup dairy sour cream
1 tablespoon lemon juice

Bread Dumpling:
1/4 cup butter
6 bread rolls, cut in cubes
1 onion, finely chopped
1 cup all-purpose flour
Salt and white pepper
1/8 teaspoon ground nutmeg
1 tablespoon chopped parsley
1/3 cup milk
2 egg yolks
Water
1 tablespoon butter, melted

Preheat oven to 425F (220C). Rub beef with salt and white pepper; place in a shallow roasting pan. Cover beef with onions, celeriac or celery, carrot, parsnip, bacon, peppercorns, cloves and bay leaf. Drizzle butter over top. Roast, uncovered, in center of oven 20 minutes. Turn after first 10 minutes roasting time. In a small saucepan, bring stock or broth to a boil. Reduce heat to 350F (175C). Pour hot stock or broth over vegetables and beef. Bake 15 to 20 minutes longer or until tender. Turn off oven; place beef on a heatproof platter. Place in oven to keep warm. Strain pan drippings; return strained drippings to roasting pan. Bring to a boil on stove. In a small bowl, beat flour into sour cream; stir in 2 tablespoons hot beef drippings. Stir flour mixture into remaining drippings. Cook, stirring constantly, until thickened. Season with lemon juice, salt and white pepper. Slice beef. Serve with gravy and Bread Dumpling.

To make dumpling, melt 3 tablespoons butter in a large skillet. Add bread cubes; sauté until lightly browned. Pour browned bread cubes into a large bowl. Melt remaining butter in same skillet. Add onion; sauté until transparent. Add sautéed onion to browned bread cubes. Stir in flour, salt, white pepper, nutmeg and parsley. In a small saucepan, warm milk slightly; beat in egg yolks. Pour milk mixture over bread mixture; blend thoroughly. Let stand 20 minutes. In a deep pan, bring 2-1/2 quarts salted water to a boil. Brush 1 tablespoon melted butter over a large clean cloth. Spoon bread mixture onto cloth. Use your hands and the cloth to form mixture into a roll. Tie cloth at one end, pushing a long wooden-spoon handle under knot. Hang dumpling from spoon into water; boil 40 minutes. Rinse dumpling under cold water. Slice to serve. Makes 6 servings.

Plum Turnovers
POVIDLOVĚ TAŠKY

Plum Puree:
1 lb. purple plums, stones removed
1/2 cup granulated sugar
1 tablespoon rum
1/2 teaspoon ground cinnamon

Dough & Topping:
3 cups all-purpose flour
2 eggs, slightly beaten
Salt
Water
1 egg yolk, beaten
1 cup dry breadcrumbs, browned in 1/2 cup butter
3 tablespoons powdered sugar

To make puree, in a large saucepan, combine plums and 1/2 cup granulated sugar. Simmer, stirring occasionally, until plums are soft; cool slightly. Puree plum mixture in a blender or food processor. Beat in rum and cinnamon.
To make dough, combine flour, 2 eggs, 1/4 teaspoon salt and 6 tablespoons water. Stir with a fork until mixture pulls away from bowl. Cover; let stand 30 minutes. On a lightly floured surface, roll out dough until 1/8 inch thick. Cut into 3-1/2-inch circles.
To complete, spoon 1-1/2 teaspoonfuls plum puree onto center of each dough circle. Brush edge of dough with egg yolk; fold dough over filling. Use your fingers or tines of a fork to press edges together to seal. In a large pot, bring 2-1/2 quarts water to a gentle boil; add 1/2 teaspoon salt. Add turnovers, a few at a time. Be sure water continues to simmer. Cook turnovers 8 minutes. Drain well over pan. Dip cooked turnovers in browned breadcrumbs. Dust with powdered sugar. Makes 20 to 25 turnovers.

Bohemian Livancy
LĬVANCY

1/4 cup warm water (110F, 45C)
2 teaspoons active dry yeast
3/4 cup warm milk (110F, 45C)
3-1/2 cups all-purpose flour
5 tablespoons butter
2 eggs, slightly beaten
2 tablespoons granulated sugar
1/8 teaspoon salt
Grated peel of 1/2 lemon
Powdered sugar

Plum Filling:
1 tablespoon rum or 1 teaspoon rum extract
1/2 teaspoon ground cinnamon
1 cup Plum Puree, opposite, or plum jam

To make batter, in a large bowl, combine water and yeast; stir until yeast dissolves. Stir in 1/4 cup milk and 1 cup flour; beat until smooth. Cover and let stand 20 minutes. Melt 2 tablespoons butter; set aside. Stir yeast mixture; stir in remaining milk, melted butter, eggs, granulated sugar, salt and lemon peel; beat well. Stir in enough remaining flour to make a medium-thick batter. Cover and let rise in a warm place, free from drafts, until light and bubbly, 30 to 60 minutes.
To make filling, in a small bowl, stir rum and cinnamon into plum jam. Plum Puree is already flavored.
To complete, in a large skillet, melt remaining 3 tablespoons butter until bubbly. Stir raised batter; drop by teaspoonfuls into hot butter. Spread slightly; cook until golden brown on both sides. Cover half of the browned cakes with 1 tablespoon Plum Puree or plum jam; top with a second cake. Sprinkle powdered sugar over top. Makes 8 servings.

Karlsbad Cake

PIŠINGRUV DORT

1 cup butter, room temperature
1 cup granulated sugar
8 oz. semisweet chocolate
4 egg whites
1 cup ground hazelnuts
2 tablespoons vanilla sugar or 2
**   tablespoons sugar and 1/2**
**   teaspoon vanilla extract**
6 large Karlsbad or oblaten
**   circular wafers**
3/4 cup powdered sugar
2 to 3 tablespoons hot water

In a small bowl, cream butter with 1/2 cup granulated sugar; set aside. Break 5 ounces chocolate into small pieces; place in a medium, glass or metal bowl. Place bowl over hot water; stir until chocolate is melted. In a medium bowl, beat egg whites until soft peaks form. Gradually beat in remaining granulated sugar until stiff but not dry. Stir butter-sugar mixture into melted chocolate, 1 tablespoon at a time. Stir in nuts and vanilla sugar or 2 tablespoons granulated sugar and 1/2 teaspoon vanilla extract. Fold in egg-white mixture. Place 1 wafer on a cake plate; cover with some of the chocolate mixture. Top with another wafer. Continue until all wafers and chocolate mixture have been used, ending with chocolate mixture. In bowl used for chocolate mixture, melt remaining chocolate over hot water. Add powdered sugar and 2 tablespoons water. Stir until smooth; add more water, 1/2 teaspoon at a time, if needed to make a spreadable mixture. Cover top and side of cake with powdered-sugar mixture. Refrigerate 3 to 4 hours before serving. To serve, cut in wedges. Makes 8 to 10 servings.

Variations

Substitute any plain, not too sweet, square or rectangular cookies for oblaten. Or, use small wafers to make several small cakes instead of 1 large cake. They make attractive gifts.

Cook's Tip

Oblaten are large round cookies, usually available in import stores.

Smoked Salmon with Spinach
RØGET MED SPINAT

1-1/2 lbs. fresh spinach
1/4 cup butter
2 tablespoons all-purpose flour
1 cup half and half
Salt and white pepper
Pinch of ground nutmeg
4 eggs
4 large smoked-salmon slices

Wash spinach. Place wet spinach in a saucepan with a tight-fitting lid. Add no water. Cook over medium heat 5 minutes; drain well. Melt 3 tablespoons butter in a medium saucepan. Add cooked spinach; sprinkle with flour. Gradually stir in 1/2 cup half and half. Stirring constantly, cook 2 minutes. Season with salt, white pepper and nutmeg. Pour spinach mixture into a warm bowl; keep warm. In a small bowl, beat eggs with remaining 1/2 cup half and half. Season with salt and white pepper. Melt remaining 1 tablespoon butter in a medium skillet. Pour in egg mixture. Cook over low heat. As eggs begin to set, stir gently. Spread hot scrambled eggs over salmon slices; roll up salmon. Serve salmon rolls with creamed spinach, toast and butter. Makes 4 servings.

Greens with Glazed Potatoes
GRØNLANDKAAL MED GLASEREDE KARTOFFLER

Greens:
2 lbs. cabbage, beet greens, collard greens, kale or other greens
Water
Salt and pepper
1/2 cup butter
3 tablespoons all-purpose flour
1/2 cup milk
1 cup half and half

Potatoes:
1-1/2 lbs. small new potatoes
3 tablespoons sugar

To prepare greens, wash cabbage or greens; tear leaves into small pieces. Bring a small amount of water to a gentle boil. Add 1 teaspoon salt and torn cabbage or greens. Cover and simmer 25 to 30 minutes. Drain and squeeze to remove excess water. Melt 1/4 cup butter in a large skillet. Sprinkle flour over melted butter. Stirring constantly, cook until golden brown. Gradually stir in milk and half and half. Beat with a whisk until smooth and creamy. Fold drained cabbage or greens into sauce; season with salt and pepper.

To glaze potatoes, boil potatoes in their skins until tender. Peel cooked potatoes; rinse under cold water. Dry on paper towels. In a small saucepan, cook sugar over medium heat, stirring constantly, until golden. Reduce heat; stir in remaining 1/4 cup butter until melted. Add cooked potatoes; stir gently until golden brown and evenly glazed. Spoon cooked cabbage or greens and glazed potatoes into separate serving bowls. Makes 4 servings.

Roast Pork with Prunes
SVINEMØRBRAD MED SVEDSKER OG AEBLER

8 to 10 pitted prunes
Water
2 cooking apples
1 (3-1/2- to 4-lb.) boneless pork blade roast
Salt and pepper
1/8 teaspoon ground ginger
2 tablespoons butter
1 to 2 cups hot stock or broth
1/3 cup half and half
1 tablespoon black-currant jelly

In a small saucepan, cover prunes with water; bring to a boil. Set aside to cool. Chop cooled prunes. Peel and dice apples. Cut pork roast lengthwise nearly in half; open to lay flat. Rub inside of pork with salt, pepper and ginger. Spread pork with chopped prunes and apples. Roll up pork; tie securely with kitchen string. Preheat oven to 350F (175C). Melt butter in a shallow roasting pan. Sear stuffed roast in butter until browned on all sides. Pour off most of cooking fat. Pour 1 cup hot stock or broth around browned pork. Bake 1-1/2 to 2 hours or until tender, adding stock as needed. Remove pork from roasting pan; keep warm. Add half and half; cook over low heat, stirring to loosen drippings from bottom of pan. Stir in jelly; season with salt and pepper. Remove string from pork. Cut in thick slices. Serve with sauce. Makes 4 servings.

Sailor's Stew
SKIPPERLABSKOVS

2-1/2 cups water
1-1/2 lbs. beef cubes for stew
5 or 6 new potatoes, peeled, diced
2 onions, chopped
1 teaspoon salt
1 or 2 bay leaves
6 whole peppercorns
1 whole clove
2 tablespoons chopped parsley

In a large pot, bring water to a boil. Add beef cubes; boil 4 to 5 minutes. Skim foam from surface until surface is clear. Add potatoes, onions and salt. Tie bay leaves, peppercorns and whole clove in a small piece of cheesecloth; add to pot. Cover and cook 1-1/2 to 2 hours. In this time, potatoes and onions will become very soft and beef tender. Remove spice bag. Spoon stew into a serving bowl; sprinkle with parsley. Serve with pickled cucumbers or mixed pickles, beet salad and black bread with butter. Makes 4 servings.

Fruit Blancmange
RØDGRØD MED FLØDE

**3 cups fresh, frozen or drained canned red currants, blackberries,
    raspberries or strawberries**
About 2-1/4 cups water or juice from fruit
3/4 cup sugar
1/3 cup plus 2 tablespoons cornstarch

If using fresh fruit, wash and stem currants; rinse and hull
berries. Reserve a few currants or berries for decoration. In a
large saucepan, combine fruit and 2 cups water or juice; bring to
a boil. Stirring occasionally, boil 5 minutes; press through a fine
sieve. Add water or juice to make 4 cups fruit puree. In
saucepan, heat fruit puree; stir in sugar. Dissolve cornstarch in
1/4 cup water or juice. Stir into fruit puree. Stirring constantly
over medium-low heat, bring almost to a boil. Do not boil; cook
5 to 10 minutes. After 5 minutes, taste mixture; if a cornstarch
flavor remains, cook longer. Set aside to cool, stirring
occasionally to prevent a skin from forming over top. Rinse a
1-quart bowl or mold with cold water. Pour cooled blancmange
into rinsed bowl or mold. Refrigerate 3 to 4 hours. To serve,
invert onto a platter; remove bowl or mold. Decorate with
reserved fruit. Serve with half and half. Makes 4 to 6 servings.

Variation

If blancmange will not be served as a molded dessert, reduce
cornstarch to 1/3 cup.

Peasant Girl with a Veil
BONDEPIGE MED SLØR

1 tablespoon butter
2 cups dry rye breadcrumbs or dry chocolate-cake crumbs
2 tablespoons sugar
1 (16-oz.) can applesauce
1/2 cup whipping cream
1 tablespoon cranberry jelly

Melt butter in a medium skillet. Add breadcrumbs or cake
crumbs and sugar. Stir constantly over medium heat until
crumbs are crisp. Sprinkle crumbs onto a plate; set aside to cool.
Sprinkle some of cooled crumbs over bottom of a 1-quart
casserole or 4 to 6 individual dessert dishes. Top with a layer of
applesauce. Continue alternating layers, ending with a layer of
crumbs. Whip cream until stiff. Spoon whipped cream over top,
swirling only on center or spreading to cover. Top with a dollop
of cranberry jelly. Makes 4 to 6 servings.

Cook's Tip

**In some parts of Denmark this traditional dessert is known as *brown
bride with a white veil*.**

Rice & Almond Pudding
RIS A L'AMANDE

1/2 cup uncooked short-grain white rice
3-1/2 cups milk
1-1/2 cups whipping cream
1/2 teaspoon vanilla extract
3 tablespoons sugar
3/4 cup chopped blanched almonds
1 tablespoon toasted sliced almonds

Quick Cherry Sauce:
1 (16-oz.) can dark sweet cherries
1 tablespoon cornstarch
Water
Cherry liqueur, if desired

In a medium saucepan, combine rice and milk. Cook over medium heat 45 minutes or until rice is tender; set aside to cool. In a medium bowl, whip cream until stiff; stir in vanilla. Stir whipped cream, sugar and chopped almonds into cooled rice mixture. Spoon into a serving dish. Refrigerate 3 to 4 hours. Sprinkle with toasted almonds.
To make sauce, heat cherries with juice. Dissolve cornstarch in a little water. Stir into cherries; gently stir over medium heat until thickened. Flavor with liqueur, if desired. Serve rice pudding with hot cherry sauce, if desired. Makes 4 servings.

Cook's Tip

It was once traditional in Denmark to include 1 whole almond in the rice pudding. The person who found it would receive the prize—a marzipan pig.

Lemon Cream
CITRONFROMAGE

4 eggs, separated
7 tablespoons sugar
2 teaspoons freshly grated lemon peel
1 (1/4-oz.) envelope unflavored gelatin (1 tablespoon)
6 tablespoons fresh lemon juice
1/2 cup whipping cream, whipped
Shaved chocolate or chocolate flakes

In a medium bowl, beat egg yolks until light. Beat in 5 tablespoons sugar and lemon peel until light and fluffy; set aside. Pour gelatin into a small saucepan; stir in lemon juice until gelatin is softened. Stir over low heat until gelatin dissolves; do not boil. Remove from heat; stir occasionally until cooled. In a large bowl, beat egg whites until frothy. Beat in remaining 2 tablespoon sugar until stiff but not dry. Fold cooled gelatin mixture into egg-yolk mixture. Fold egg-yolk mixture into beaten egg whites. Spoon into 4 to 6 individual serving dishes. Refrigerate 3 hours. To serve, top each serving with a dollop of whipped cream and shaved chocolate or chocolate flakes. Makes 4 to 6 servings.

Tomato Soup with Bananas
SOPA DE TOMATES CON PLÁTANOS

7 or 8 medium tomatoes, peeled, chopped
2 cups chicken stock or broth
1/2 teaspoon salt
2 tablespoons vegetable oil
2 onions, finely chopped
4 bananas
2 tablespoons cornstarch
1/4 cup half and half
1/8 teaspoon white pepper
2 tablespoons grated coconut

In a large saucepan, combine tomatoes, stock or broth and salt. Bring to a boil; cover and simmer over low heat until tomatoes are soft. Heat oil in a second saucepan. Add onions; sauté until transparent. Peel and slice bananas. Add banana slices to sautéed onions. Sauté bananas, crushing slightly. Strain tomato mixture; pour juice over onion mixture. Press tomato pulp through a strainer or puree in a blender or food processor. Stir tomato puree into onion mixture. In a small bowl, combine cornstarch and half and half. Stir in about 1/4 cup hot tomato soup. Stir cornstarch mixture into remaining soup. Stir constantly over medium heat until soup thickens slightly. Season with white pepper. Pour into a tureen or serve in individual bowls. Sprinkle with coconut. Makes 4 servings.

Variation

Substitute 1 (29-ounce) can tomatoes for fresh tomatoes.

Lamb with Green Beans
PIERNA DE CARNERO CON HABAS

3 tablespoons vegetable oil
1 teaspoon prepared mustard
Salt
1/8 teaspoon pepper
1 (2- to 3-lb.) lamb-leg roast, shank portion
1 cup hot stock or broth
1 lb. fresh green beans
2 onions, chopped

Preheat oven to 325F (165C). In a small bowl, combine 2 tablespoons oil, mustard, 1/2 teaspoon salt and pepper. Brush oil mixture over lamb; place in a roasting pan. Place on lowest oven rack. Roast 1-1/2 to 2 hours. After 30 minutes roasting time, spoon a little hot stock or broth around lamb. Throughout remaining roasting time, baste lamb frequently with pan drippings, adding stock or broth as needed. Trim beans; leave small beans whole and cut large beans in half. Cook beans, covered, in a saucepan of boiling salted water 10 minutes. Heat remaining tablespoon oil in a medium skillet. Add onions; sauté until transparent. Drain cooked beans; stir into onions. During last 10 to 20 minutes of roasting time, arrange bean mixture around lamb. To serve, place roast lamb on a platter. Spoon bean mixture around lamb. Serve with boiled potatoes. Makes 3 to 4 servings.

Lentil & Garlic Soup
SHURIT ADS

7 cups chicken stock or broth
2 cups dry lentils
2 tomatoes, peeled, cut in quarters
4 garlic cloves, coarsely chopped
3 onions
2 tablespoons butter
1 teaspoon salt
Pinch of pepper
2 teaspoons ground cumin
Lemon wedges

In a large saucepan, bring stock or broth to a boil. Add lentils, tomatoes and garlic. Quarter 2 onions; add to lentil mixture. Chop remaining onion; set aside. Partially cover pan. Simmer lentil mixture 45 minutes or until lentils are tender. Melt 1 tablespoon butter in a medium skillet. Add chopped onion; sauté until lightly browned. Press lentil mixture through a sieve or puree in a blender or food processor. Reheat in saucepan; season with salt, pepper and cumin. Stir in remaining 1 tablespoon butter. Pour into a tureen or serve in individual bowls. Sprinkle sautéed onion over top. Serve with lemon wedges. Makes 6 servings.

Beef & Okra Casserole
BAMIA

1-1/2 lbs. okra
6 tablespoons vegetable oil
1 onion, finely chopped
6 tomatoes, peeled, chopped
1 lb. ground beef
1 cup stock or broth
2 garlic cloves, crushed
1 teaspoon salt
3 tablespoons plain yogurt
3 tablespoons dairy sour cream
1/2 teaspoon white pepper
1 tomato, thinly sliced
1 lemon, thinly sliced

Cut stalks from okra. Heat 3 tablespoons oil in a large saucepan. Add okra; sauté 6 minutes. Drain sautéed okra on paper towels. Discard oil; wipe pan with paper towels. Heat 2 more tablespoons oil in saucepan. Add onion and tomatoes; sauté until heated through. Add ground beef; cook, stirring occasionally, until browned. Add stock or broth; bring to a boil. Add garlic and salt. Simmer until most of liquid has evaporated. Preheat oven to 350F (175C). Brush a large baking pan with oil. Stir yogurt, sour cream and white pepper into beef mixture. Spoon half of the beef mixture over bottom of oiled pan. Cover with okra, then with remaining beef mixture. Sprinkle with remaining tablespoon oil. Bake 50 to 60 minutes. Garnish with tomato and lemon slices. Makes 4 to 6 servings.

Corn-Stuffed Pigeon

HAMAM MAHSHI

4 pigeons or Cornish hens with giblets
2/3 cup butter
10 green onions, chopped
Salt and pepper
1/2 cup coarsely ground cornmeal
1 tablespoon chopped fresh mint or 2 teaspoons dried leaf mint
1-1/2 cups water
2-1/2 cups chicken stock or broth

Chop giblets. Melt 1/3 cup butter in a medium skillet. Add chopped giblets, green onions, 1 teaspoon salt and a little pepper. Stir occasionally until giblets are browned. Stir in cornmeal and mint. Rub inside each bird with salt and pepper. Stuff each bird with 2 tablespoons cornmeal mixture. Pull loose skin over cavity; secure with wooden or metal picks. Place birds in a stovetop casserole. Set remaining stuffing aside. Preheat oven to 400F (204C). Melt remaining 1/3 cup butter; brush over stuffed birds. Add water to dish; bring to a boil on stove. Cover and place in oven. Bake 50 minutes or until tender, basting birds every 10 minutes with pan drippings. In a medium saucepan, bring stock or broth to a boil; add remaining cornmeal stuffing. Bring to a second boil. Cover and simmer 30 minutes. Serve with baked birds. Makes 4 servings.

Ground-Rice Pudding

MEHALLABIA

1/3 cup raisins
2 tablespoons hot water
1 cup plus 2 tablespoons uncooked long-grain white rice
3/4 cup sugar
3 tablespoons cornstarch
3-1/2 cups hot milk (140F, 60C)
1 teaspoon vanilla extract
2 tablespoons chopped pistachios
2 teaspoons rose water or a sprinkle of ground cinnamon

In a small bowl, soak raisins in hot water. In a blender, process rice 5 minutes on high. In a medium saucepan, combine sugar, 1 cup ground rice and cornstarch. Stirring constantly over medium heat, gradually add milk; continue stirring until slightly thickened. Simmer 15 minutes. Preheat oven to 400F (205C). Butter a 9-inch baking dish; set aside. Drain and dry raisins. Stir soaked raisins, vanilla and pistachios into pudding. Pour into buttered dish. Bake 40 to 45 minutes or until a brown crust forms. Stir crust into pudding; set aside to cool. Sprinkle pudding with rose water or ground cinnamon. Serve warm with half and half or, refrigerate 3 to 4 hours before serving. Makes 4 servings.

Cook's Tip

The hard surface crust is stirred into the pudding giving it a delicate caramel flavor.

Vegetable Soup
KASÄKEITTO

1 small head cauliflower
4 oz. spinach
7 cups water
1 tablespoon sugar
Salt
2 medium carrots, finely chopped
3 medium potatoes, peeled, finely chopped
1/2 lb. fresh green beans, cut in pieces
5 radishes, cut in halves
1 cup fresh or frozen green peas
3 tablespoons butter
3 tablespoons all-purpose flour
1 cup milk
2 egg yolks
1/3 cup half and half
White pepper
7 oz. peeled cooked shrimp
2 tablespoons chopped fresh dill or 1 to 2 teaspoons dill weed

Divide cauliflower into flowerets. Wash and chop spinach. In a large pot, bring water to a boil with sugar and 2 teaspoons salt. Add cauliflower, carrots, potatoes, green beans, radishes and peas. Cover and simmer until vegetables are nearly tender, 5 to 8 minutes. Add spinach; cook 5 minutes longer. Strain and reserve cooking liquid; set vegetables aside. Melt butter in a large saucepan; stir in flour. Stirring constantly, gradually add strained cooking liquid and milk. In a small bowl, beat egg yolks with half and half; stir in 1/4 cup hot cooking liquid. Stir egg-yolk mixture into saucepan; season with salt and white pepper. Return cooked vegetables to soup. Add shrimp; heat through. Pour into a tureen or serve in individual bowls. Sprinkle with dill. Makes 6 servings.

Mushrooms in Sour Cream
PAISTETUT SIENET

3 tablespoons butter
1 onion, finely chopped
1 lb. mushrooms, sliced
1/4 cup fresh breadcrumbs
Salt and pepper
3/4 cup dairy sour cream
1 tablespoon chopped parsley

Melt butter in a large skillet. Add onion; sauté until transparent. Add mushrooms; cook 5 minutes, stirring occasionally. Sprinkle breadcrumbs over mushroom mixture; stir in. Season with salt and pepper. Remove pan from heat. Gently stir in sour cream. Spoon into individual serving dishes. Garnish with parsley. Makes 4 servings.

Cook's Tip

Mushroom Salad is another Finnish speciality. To make Mushroom Salad, thinly slice 1 pound fresh mushrooms. Steep 3 to 5 minutes in a little boiling water and lemon juice. Drain and pat dry. In a small bowl, combine 3/4 cup sour cream, a pinch of sugar, salt, pepper and 1 tablespoon grated onion. Pour over mushrooms; carefully fold in. Serve immediately.

Turnip Casserole
LANTTULAATIKKO

6 medium turnips, peeled, diced
Water
Salt
1/3 cup fresh breadcrumbs
1/3 cup half and half
2 eggs, beaten
Ground nutmeg
2 tablespoons butter

Cook turnips in boiling salted water 15 to 20 minutes or until tender. Drain turnips; press through a fine sieve or puree in a blender or food processor. In a medium bowl, soak breadcrumbs in half and half 3 to 4 minutes. Preheat oven to 350F (175C). Butter a soufflé dish or an 11'' x 7-1/2'' baking dish; set aside. Stir eggs into soaked-breadcrumb mixture. Stir in turnip puree. Season to taste with nutmeg and salt. Spoon turnip mixture into buttered dish. Dot with butter. Bake 1 hour or until surface is browned and mixture is set. Serve with roast pork. Makes 6 servings.

Ground-Meat Pastie
LIHAMUREKE PIIAAS

Pastry:
2-3/4 cups all-purpose flour
Salt
3/4 cup plus 2 tablespoons butter
2 eggs
6 tablespoons dairy sour cream

Filling:
1-1/2 lbs. mixed ground meat (beef, pork, veal, ham)
1/4 cup butter
4 oz. mushrooms, finely chopped
1 onion, finely chopped
1 parsley sprig, finely chopped
1 cup grated Jarlsberg cheese (4 oz.)
Salt
White pepper

In a large bowl, stir together flour and 1 teaspoon salt. Add butter, 1 egg and sour cream. Blend into a smooth dough. Wrap dough to prevent drying; refrigerate 1 hour.
To make filling, in a large skillet, cook meat until no pink remains. Pour off fat; set meat aside. Melt butter in skillet. Add mushrooms and onion; sauté 3 minutes. Stir in cooked meat, parsley and cheese; season with salt and white pepper.
To complete, preheat oven to 375F (190C). Grease a large jelly-roll pan; set aside. Divide dough in half. On a lightly floured surface, roll out each piece of dough to 14'' x 6''. Place 1 piece on greased pan. Spread meat filling in an oval on dough; cover with remaining rolled dough. Trim edges; crimp edges together with a fork. Use trimmings to decorate pastry as shown. Beat remaining egg; brush over top. Bake 45 minutes or until golden brown. Serve hot with cranberry sauce and sour cream. Makes 8 to 10 servings.

French Onion Soup
SOUPE À L'OIGNON

1/4 cup butter
3 large onions, thinly sliced
1 tablespoon all-purpose flour
2-1/2 cups water
Salt and white pepper
4 French-bread slices, 1 inch thick
1 cup dry white wine
1/2 cup grated Gruyère cheese (2 oz.)

Melt 2 tablespoons butter in a large saucepan or skillet. Add onions; sauté over low heat until golden brown. Sprinkle flour over onions; stir until slightly browned. Gradually stir in water, salt and white pepper. Bring to a boil. Cover and simmer 20 minutes, stirring occasionally. Preheat oven to 375F (190C). Melt remaining 2 tablespoons butter in a medium skillet. Fry bread slices in butter until golden brown on both sides. Arrange browned bread in 4 heatproof soup bowls. Stir wine into soup. Immediately pour soup over bread; sprinkle with cheese. Place on top shelf in oven. Bake 10 to 20 minutes or until cheese melts. Brown cheese under broiler, if desired. Makes 4 servings.

Baked Pumpkin Soup
SOUPE DE COURGE À LA CRÈME

1 (2-lb.) pumpkin or squash
1 cup milk
1 teaspoon salt
1/8 teaspoon white pepper
Pinch of ground nutmeg
1-1/2 cups chicken stock or broth
1 tablespoon whipping cream
1 tablespoon dairy sour cream
2 white-bread slices
2 tablespoons butter
2 tablespoons grated Gruyère cheese (1/2 oz.)

Preheat oven to 350F (175C). Lightly butter a large baking dish; set aside. Peel pumpkin or squash; remove seeds. Finely dice pumpkin or squash; spread over bottom of buttered dish. In a medium bowl, combine milk, salt, white pepper, nutmeg, stock or broth, whipping cream and sour cream. Pour over diced pumpkin or squash. Cover and bake 1 hour. Cut bread into small cubes. Melt butter in a medium skillet. Add bread cubes; sauté until golden brown. Puree cooked pumpkin mixture in a blender or food processor. Pour into 4 soup bowls. Sprinkle browned bread cubes and cheese over top. Makes 4 servings.

Niçoise Salad
SALADE NIÇOISE

1/2 small head lettuce
1 (6-1/2-oz.) can tuna, drained
4 anchovy fillets
1/4 cup olive oil
1 tablespoon wine vinegar
1/2 teaspoon salt
1/8 teaspoon white pepper
Pinch of mixed dried leaf basil, oregano and thyme
1/2 small cucumber, thinly sliced
4 tomatoes, cut in wedges
1 onion, cut in rings
24 ripe olives
2 hard-cooked eggs, cut in wedges

Separate lettuce leaves; if large, tear into small pieces. Place lettuce leaves into a large salad bowl. Flake tuna; into small pieces. Cut each anchovy fillet in half lengthwise; set aside. In a small bowl, beat together oil, vinegar, salt, white pepper and dried herbs. Pour over lettuce. Gently fold in cucumber, tomatoes, onion, flaked tuna and olives. Arrange anchovies and eggs on salad. Makes 4 servings.

Artichoke-Heart Salad
COEURS D'ARTICHAUTS EN SALADE

12 fresh or frozen, peeled, cooked shrimp
8 small artichokes
Water
Salt
Juice of 1-1/2 lemons
1/2 small head lettuce
1 garlic clove
1/4 cup vegetable oil
Pinch of sugar
Pinch of white pepper
2 hard-cooked eggs, cut in wedges
1 tablespoon chopped fresh dill

Thaw shrimp if frozen. Remove artichoke stalks and top 2/3 of leaves. In a large saucepan, combine 3 cups water, 1 teaspoon salt and juice of 1 lemon. Add artichokes and enough hot water to cover. Bring to a boil; reduce heat and simmer 30 minutes. Set aside to cool in cooking water. Remove choke and outside leaves from each cooled artichoke. Cut large artichoke hearts into quarters; cut small hearts in halves. If lettuce leaves are large, tear into small pieces; arrange in a serving bowl. Crush garlic with a pinch of salt. In a small bowl, beat together remaining lemon juice, garlic-salt mixture, oil, sugar and white pepper. Arrange artichoke hearts, egg wedges and shrimp on lettuce. Pour dressing over top; sprinkle with dill. Makes 4 servings.

Savory Omelet
OMELETTE SAVOYARDE

6 to 8 bacon slices
3 tablespoons vegetable oil
2 potatoes, peeled, finely chopped
1 leek, sliced
8 eggs
Salt and white pepper
1/2 cup finely chopped Gruyère cheese (2 oz.)
2 tablespoons chopped parsley
1 parsley sprig

In a large skillet, fry bacon until crisp. Crumble cooked bacon; set aside. Add 1 tablespoon oil to bacon drippings. Add potatoes and leek; sauté until tender. Stir in crumbled bacon; set aside. In a large bowl, beat together eggs, salt and white pepper. Stir in sautéed-potato mixture and cheese. Heat remaining 2 tablespoons oil in skillet. Pour in egg mixture. Cook over low heat until underside is browned and top is soft and moist. Sprinkle chopped parsley over top. Fold cooked omelet in half. Use a broad spatula to place omelet on a platter. Garnish with parsley sprig. If desired, cook 4 small omelets instead of 1 large omelet. Makes 4 servings.

Garden Peas with Onions
PETITS POIS

1 small head lettuce
1 cup fresh or frozen green peas
12 shallots or small onions
4 parsley sprigs
1/2 cup butter
6 tablespoons water
1 teaspoon salt
1/2 teaspoon sugar

Remove outer leaves from lettuce. Cut off stem; cut lettuce head into quarters. Loosely tie lettuce quarters together with kitchen string; place in a large saucepan. Add peas and shallots or onions. Tie parsley sprigs together; place on top. Dot with butter. Add water; sprinkle salt and sugar over top. Cover and bring slowly to a boil. Stir carefully; cover and simmer 30 minutes, shaking pan occasionally. Remove parsley; remove string from lettuce. Serve as an accompaniment to roasted meats. Makes 4 servings.

Snails with Garlic Butter
ESCARGOTS À LA BOURGUIGNONNE

2 garlic cloves
Salt
6 tablespoons butter, room temperature
2 shallots or small onions, finely chopped
Pinch of white pepper
1 tablespoon chopped parsley
1/4 cup chopped chervil
1 teaspoon lemon juice
24 to 36 canned snails with shells

Crush garlic with a little salt. In a medium bowl, combine garlic-salt mixture, butter, shallots or onions, white pepper, parsley, chervil and lemon juice. Preheat oven to 400F (205C). Press a little herb-butter mixture into each snail shell. Place a snail in each shell. Pack shells to rim with additional herb butter. Place filled shells on snail plates. Or, fill base of an heatproof dish with 1/2-inch salt. Place snails in dish open-side up. Cook snails until butter begins to bubble, about 10 minutes. Serve with toasted French bread. Makes 4 servings.

Scallops St. Jacques
COQUILLES SAINT-JACQUES AU GRATIN

1 lb. scallops
Water
1/4 cup butter
1 shallot or small onion, finely chopped
4 oz. mushrooms, sliced
1 tablespoon chopped parsley
2 tablespoons all-purpose flour
6 tablespoons white wine
1 egg yolk, well beaten
1/4 cup dry breadcrumbs
2 tablespoons butter

In a medium saucepan, blanch scallops 3 minutes in a little boiling water; drain well, reserving 6 tablespoons cooking liquid. Cut drained scallops into small pieces. Preheat oven to 400F (205C). Melt 1/4 cup butter in a large skillet. Add shallot or onion; sauté until transparent. Add mushrooms and parsley; sauté 2 to 3 minutes. Sprinkle flour over top. Stirring constantly, cook until golden brown. Gradually stir in reserved cooking liquid and white wine. Boil sauce 2 minutes. Remove from heat; fold in egg yolk, then scallop pieces. Spoon evenly into scallop shells or a baking dish. Sprinkle breadcrumbs over top; dot with 2 tablespoons butter. Bake 10 minutes. Makes 4 servings.

Stuffed Vegetables Provençale

LES FARCIS À LA
PROVENÇALE

4 large tomatoes
4 medium zucchini
2 Spanish onions
About 1/4 cup olive oil
1 lb. mixed ground beef and pork
3 garlic cloves, crushed
2 tablespoons chopped mixed
   parsley, basil, sage and
   rosemary
2 eggs, slightly beaten
1/2 cup grated Gruyère cheese
   (2 oz.)
Salt and white pepper
1/4 cup dry breadcrumbs

Cut a slice from top of each tomato. Cut each zucchini in half lengthwise. Peel onions; plunge in boiling water 2 to 3 minutes. Lift from water with a slotted spoon. Cut a slice from top of blanched onions. Remove centers from tomatoes, zucchini and onions. Finely chop centers and slices from tomatoes, onions and zucchini. Preheat oven to 350F (175C). Lightly grease a baking sheet; set aside. In a medium saucepan, heat 1 tablespoon oil; add chopped vegetables. Stirring constantly, cook until tender; spoon into a bowl. In the same pan, heat 2 more tablespoons oil. Add meat; stir over medium heat until no pink remains. Stir in cooked vegetables, garlic, herbs, eggs and cheese. Season to taste with salt and white pepper. Spoon mixture into centers of tomatoes, zucchini and onions. Press down gently with the back of a spoon; sprinkle evenly with breadcrumbs. Sprinkle on a little oil. Arrange vegetables on greased baking sheet. Bake about 45 minutes or until tender; cooking time will depend on size of vegetables. Serve hot or cold. Makes 4 servings.

Tomato Torte
TARTE AUX TOMATES

1 pkg. frozen patty shells (6 shells)
3 medium tomatoes
3 eggs
Salt and white pepper
1 teaspoon chopped fresh basil or 1/2 teaspoon dried leaf basil
1 tablespoon butter, melted
1/3 cup half and half
1/3 cup grated Gruyère cheese (1-1/2 oz.)
1 basil sprig

Thaw patty shells. Arrange patty shells on a lightly floured surface with edges overlapping. Roll out dough to a 12-inch circle. Use to line a 10-inch flan or quiche pan. Preheat oven to 400F (205C). Peel tomatoes; remove and discard seeds. Finely chop tomatoes. In a medium bowl, beat together eggs, salt, white pepper and basil. Gradually stir in butter and half and half. Stir in chopped tomatoes. Pour into dough-lined pan. Sprinkle cheese over top. Bake 8 minutes; reduce heat to 350F (175C). Bake 20 to 25 minutes or until a knife inserted off-center comes out clean. If torte browns too quickly, cover with parchment or brown paper. Let stand 10 minutes before serving. Serve hot. Makes 6 servings.

Cook's Tip

Puff Pastry, page 8, frozen puff pastry or any pie pastry can be used in place of frozen patty shells.

Mushroom Quiche
QUICHE AUX CHAMPIGNONS

2 tablespoons butter
2 onions, finely chopped
1 lb. mushrooms, thinly sliced
3 eggs
1 cup half and half
1/2 cup dairy sour cream
1/2 teaspoon salt
1/8 teaspoon pepper

Pastry:
1-1/2 cups all-purpose flour
1/4 teaspoon salt
1/2 cup butter
4-1/2 teaspoons vegetable oil
Water
1 tablespoon chopped parsley

Melt butter in a large skillet. Add onions; sauté until transparent. Add mushrooms. Sauté over low heat until liquid evaporates; set aside to cool. In a small bowl, beat eggs. Beat in half and half, sour cream, salt, pepper and mushroom mixture.
To make pastry, preheat oven to 400F (205C). Sift flour and salt into a large bowl. Add butter and oil. Use a pastry blender or fork to work all ingredients together. Add a little water if necessary to make a smooth firm dough. Roll out dough to a 14-inch circle. Use to line a 12-inch flan or quiche pan. Cover with parchment or brown paper. Cover bottom of paper with dried beans. Bake 7 to 10 minutes. Remove beans and paper. Reduce heat to 375F (190C).
To complete, pour filling into baked crust. Bake 30 to 40 minutes or until a knife inserted off-center comes out clean. Let stand 10 minutes before serving. Sprinkle with parsley; serve hot. Makes 6 to 8 servings.

Grilled Lobster

HOMARD GRILLÉ

2 live lobsters
Water
3 tablespoons salt
1 cup white wine
Juice of 1 lemon
1 carrot, finely chopped
1 onion, cut in wedges
6 whole peppercorns
1/4 cup olive oil

Seasoned Butter:
1/2 cup butter, room temperature
2 garlic cloves
2 tablespoons finely ground almonds
2 tablespoons finely chopped shallot or onion
2 tablespoons finely chopped parsley
1/2 teaspoon salt
1/8 teaspoon white pepper
Pinch of red (cayenne) pepper

Cream Sauce:
6 tablespoons whipping cream
6 tablespoons dairy sour cream
1 teaspoon tarragon mustard
1 tablespoon chopped mixed chervil, chives and tarragon
1 teaspoon cornstarch
1/8 teaspoon salt
1/8 teaspoon white pepper
Pinch of red (cayenne) pepper
1/4 cup apple brandy

Rinse lobsters under cold running water. In a pot large enough to submerge lobsters, bring 5 quarts water to a boil with salt, wine, lemon juice, carrot, onion and peppercorns. Plunge 1 lobster, head first, into boiling water. Boil a 1-pound lobster 7 to 8 minutes. Add 2 minutes for each additional 1/2 pound. Use tongs to remove lobster from water. Plunge briefly into cold water; set aside to cool. Repeat with remaining lobster. Grease a large baking sheet; set aside. Place lobster on its back. Split lobster down middle, from end to end. Remove and discard small sac near eyes and attached vein. Remove orange coral and creamy contents of head; place in a medium bowl. Crack open claws. Dice meat from claws; add to coral mixture. Break off empty head section; discard. Brush lobster halves with oil. Arrange cut-side up on greased baking sheet. Preheat oven to 425F (220C).

To make butter, place butter in a small bowl. Press garlic cloves through a garlic press into butter. Beat in almonds, shallot or onion, parsley, salt, white pepper and red pepper. Place prepared lobster in oven; immediately reduce heat to 350F (175C). After 5 minutes, spread seasoned butter over lobster. Bake 5 minutes longer. Mix reserved diced-lobster mixture with remaining seasoned butter. Spread over lobster halves. Bake on top oven rack 5 minutes. Keep hot.

To make sauce, in a small saucepan, heat whipping cream and sour cream. Stir in mustard and mixed herbs. In a small bowl, blend together cornstarch, salt, white pepper and red pepper. Stir in brandy. Stir brandy mixture into cream mixture. Stirring gently, bring to a simmer over medium-low heat; immediately pour into a serving bowl or gravy boat. Serve with lobster. Makes 4 servings.

Bouillabaisse

BOUILLABAISSE MARSEILLAISE

1 lb. mussels or clams
Water
Salt
2 lbs. flounder, monkfish, whiting, bass, perch, haddock or red
  snapper
2 tablespoons lemon juice
3 medium tomatoes
5 garlic cloves
1/2 cup olive oil
1 onion, finely chopped
1 carrot, finely chopped
1 leek, white part only, sliced
1/4 celery stalk, sliced
1 bay leaf
1 thyme sprig
1 fennel sprig
2 parsley sprigs
1 (2-inch) piece orange peel
2 potatoes, peeled, sliced
Pinch of powdered saffron
1/8 teaspoon white pepper
12 peeled cooked shrimp
8 French-bread slices

Clean mussels or clams. Soak mussels or clams 2 hours in several changes of salted water. Wash and clean fish; remove heads, tails and fins. Reserve trimmings. Pat fish dry with paper towels; cut fish into 2- to 3-inch pieces. Sprinkle with lemon juice; cover and let stand 20 minutes.

To make stock, pour 5 cups water into a large saucepan. Add fish trimmings and 1 teaspoon salt. Bring to a boil; boil, uncovered, 15 minutes. Strain fish stock; discard trimmings. Pour fish stock back into pan; bring to a boil.

To complete, scrape soaked mussels or clam shells clean; pull out and cut off beards. Rinse mussels or clams in cold water. Add cleaned mussels or clams to fish stock; boil 10 minutes or until shells open. Discard any that do not open. Remove mussels or clams from liquid; set aside to cool. Strain fish stock again; set aside. Peel tomatoes; remove and discard seeds. Coarsely chop tomatoes; set aside. Set 1 garlic clove aside; crush remaining 4 garlic cloves. Heat 1/3 cup oil in a large saucepan. Add crushed garlic, onion, carrot, leek and celery. Sauté over medium heat 5 minutes. Tie bay leaf, thyme, fennel, parsley and orange peel in a small piece of cheesecloth. Add herb mixture and potatoes to onion mixture. Add reserved fish stock. Bring to a boil; add trimmed fish. Boil, uncovered, 15 minutes. Add chopped tomatoes, saffron and white pepper; cook 10 minutes. Add cooked mussels or clams and shrimp; heat through. Finely chop reserved garlic; combine with remaining oil. Use to coat both sides of bread; brown bread in a skillet. Keep browned bread warm in a covered bread basket. Pour soup into a tureen or serve in individual bowls. Serve hot. Makes 6 to 8 servings.

Breton Sole
SOLE BRETONNE

4 large or 8 small sole fillets
1 teaspoon lemon juice
1/4 cup butter
2 small leeks, white part only, sliced
2 celery stalks, sliced
2 shallots or small onions, finely chopped
Salt
About 1/2 cup all-purpose flour
1/3 cup light white wine
1/3 cup half and half
1 tablespoon chopped parsley

Sprinkle sole with lemon juice; cover and let stand 15 minutes. Preheat oven to 400F (205C). Melt butter in a large skillet. Add leeks, celery and shallots or onions; sauté over low heat 10 minutes. Pat sole fillets dry with paper towels; season with a little salt. Coat with flour, shaking off excess. Place sautéed vegetables in a casserole; arrange sole fillets on top, folded in half. Sprinkle lightly with wine. Cover and bake 15 minutes, basting sole with wine every 5 minutes. After 15 minutes, pour half and half over sole and vegetables. Bake, uncovered, 10 minutes longer. Garnish with parsley. Makes 4 servings.

Pike Quenelles
QUENELLES DE BROCHET

1-1/2 to 2 lbs. pike, haddock, shad or other firm fish fillets
4 eggs, separated
1 teaspoon salt
1/8 teaspoon white pepper
Pinch of grated nutmeg
2/3 cup butter
1 cup milk
3/4 cup all-purpose flour
1 qt. fish stock, chicken stock or water

Finely chop or grind fish. In a small bowl, beat egg whites until stiff; fold into ground or chopped fish. Beat with a whisk until light. Beat in salt, white pepper and nutmeg. Cover and refrigerate 30 minutes. In a large saucepan, combine 1/3 cup butter and milk. Bring to a simmer. Stir in flour until mixture forms a ball; set aside to cool. Melt remaining 1/3 cup butter in a small saucepan; cool slightly. Use a fork, spoon or your hands to blend together egg yolks, fish mixture and melted butter. Shape mixture into egg-shape dumplings. In a large pot, bring stock or water to a boil. Reduce heat until liquid simmers. Using a slotted spoon, carefully add dumplings. Simmer gently 15 minutes or until dumplings float. Serve over cooked spinach. Makes 4 servings.

Veal Cutlets with Mushrooms
ESCALOPES DE VEAU AUX CÈPES

3 tablespoons vegetable oil
2 shallots or small onions, chopped
1 lb. mushrooms, coarsely chopped
Salt
Pinch of dried leaf thyme
1 tablespoon cornstarch
2 tablespoons stock, broth or water
1/3 cup half and half
4 veal cutlets
White pepper
1 tablespoon mild prepared mustard
1 tablespoon tomato paste
2 tablespoon all-purpose flour
2 tablespoons butter
2 tablespoons chopped parsley

In a large saucepan, heat 2 tablespoons oil. Add shallots or onions; sauté until transparent. Add mushrooms; sprinkle lightly with salt and thyme. Sauté 7 to 8 minutes. In a small bowl, combine cornstarch and stock, broth or water; stir in half and half. Pour over mushroom mixture. Cover and cook over low heat 5 minutes. Season cutlets with salt and white pepper. In a small bowl, combine mustard and tomato paste; spread over cutlets. Dip each cutlet in flour, covering completely. Heat remaining tablespoon oil in a large skillet. Fry cutlets on one side about 4 minutes. Turn cutlets; add butter to skillet. Fry 3 to 4 minutes longer. Arrange cooked cutlets on warm plates; top with mushroom sauce and parsley. Serve with green peas. Makes 4 servings.

Burgundy Beef
BŒUF BOURGUIGNON

3 to 4 bacon slices, finely chopped
1/4 cup vegetable oil
2 lbs. beef round or top-round steak, cut in 1-inch cubes
2 onions, cut in wedges
Salt and pepper
1 garlic clove, crushed
1 tablespoon all-purpose flour
3/4 cup burgundy or other red wine
1 cup beef stock or broth
1 parsley sprig
1 thyme sprig
4 oz. mushrooms, thinly sliced

In a large saucepan, fry bacon until crisp. Remove cooked bacon; set aside. Add oil to bacon drippings. Fry beef cubes in hot oil and bacon drippings until browned on all sides, about 10 minutes. Add onions; sauté about 10 minutes. Add salt, pepper and garlic. Stir in flour; cook 2 to 3 minutes, stirring constantly. Stir in wine and stock or broth. Add parsley and thyme. Cover and simmer 3 hours. Add mushrooms and cooked bacon. Simmer 20 minutes longer. Spoon into a large bowl. Makes 4 servings.

Auvergne Leg of Lamb
GIGOT BRAYAUDE

1 (3-lb.) boneless lamb-leg roast
3 garlic cloves, cut in slivers
Salt and white pepper
6 to 8 bacon slices
1/2 cup lard
2 carrots, sliced
2 onions, sliced
1 thyme sprig
1 bay leaf
1 qt. stock or broth
4 or 5 medium potatoes

Make several small cuts in lamb; insert garlic slivers. Rub lamb with salt and white pepper. Wrap bacon around lamb; secure with wooden picks. Melt lard in a deep roasting pan with a lid. Add carrots and onions; sauté 10 minutes. Add lamb; brown on all sides. Add thyme, bay leaf and 2 cups stock or broth. Cover and cook over low heat 5 to 6 hours. Add more stock or broth, as needed. Peel and thickly slice potatoes; sprinkle with salt. Add potato slices to roast 30 to 40 minutes before end of cooking time. Cook until lamb and potatoes are tender. Remove and discard bay leaf. Makes 4 to 6 servings.

Roast Lamb Saddle
CÔTE D'AGNEAU BONNE FEMME

1 (6-lb.) lamb loin saddle
6 to 8 bacon slices, diced
Salt and pepper
1/4 cup olive oil
2 large carrots, sliced
1 large onion, sliced
2 garlic cloves, cut in quarters lengthwise
2 teaspoons dried leaf thyme
2 teaspoons rubbed sage
1 bay leaf
1-1/2 cups white wine
8 small tomatoes

Preheat oven to 375F (190C). Score fat covering lamb, as shown. In a large roasting pan, fry bacon until crisp. Season lamb with salt and pepper. Add oil to bacon drippings; when hot, add lamb. Sear in oil and bacon drippings until browned on all sides. Add carrots, onion, garlic, thyme, sage, bay leaf and wine. Cover and roast 1-1/2 hours. Peel tomatoes; remove and discard seeds. Chop tomatoes. Reduce heat to 325F (165C). Add chopped tomatoes to lamb mixture. Roast, uncovered, 30 minutes longer. Remove and discard bay leaf. To serve, slice lamb; arrange on a platter. Serve with cooked vegetables and baked potatoes or crusty French bread. Makes 8 servings.

Veal Fricassee

BLANQUETTE DE VEAU À L'ANCIENNE

1-3/4 lbs. boneless veal, cut in 1-inch pieces
1 carrot, chopped
1 onion, chopped
1 leek, chopped
1/2 celery stalk, chopped
1/8 teaspoon dried leaf thyme
Salt
3-1/2 cups chicken stock or broth
10 small onions
1 lb. mushrooms, cut in quarters
3 tablespoons butter
2 tablespoons all-purpose flour
1 egg yolk, slightly beaten
1/3 cup half and half
White pepper
2 tablespoons chopped parsley

In a large pot, combine veal, carrot, chopped onion, leek, celery, thyme, 1/2 teaspoon salt and 2-1/2 cups stock or broth. Bring to a boil. Reduce heat; simmer, uncovered, 1-1/4 hours. In a medium saucepan, simmer whole onions in remaining stock or broth, 15 minutes. Remove onions; keep warm. Reserve liquid in saucepan. Add mushrooms; simmer 7 minutes. Remove mushrooms; add to onions. Strain veal mixture, reserving liquid in saucepan with other cooking liquid. Add veal and vegetables to mushroom mixture. Bring combined cooking liquids to a boil; boil until reduced by 1/2. Melt butter in a large saucepan. Stir in flour; stirring constantly, cook 1 minute. Slowly stir in reduced cooking liquid. Stirring constantly, bring to a boil. In a small bowl, combine egg yolk and half and half. Season with salt and white pepper; stir into sauce. Add veal mixture; heat through. Pour into a large dish. Sprinkle with parsley. Makes 4 servings.

Veal Chops with Apple Brandy

CÔTES DE VEAU AU CALVADOS

4 veal-rib chops
Salt and white pepper
2 tablespoons all-purpose flour
1/2 cup plus 2 tablespoons butter
2 tablespoons vegetable oil
4-1/2 teaspoons apple brandy
1/3 cup tomato paste
1/3 cup half and half
2 egg yolks
1 teaspoon lemon juice
1/3 cup champagne
Noodles alla Carbonara, page 125

Season veal with salt and white pepper; coat with flour. Reserve leftover flour. In a large skillet, heat 2 tablespoons butter with oil. Add coated chops; fry 5 minutes on each side. Arrange cooked chops on a platter; keep hot. Stir reserved flour into pan drippings. Stir in brandy and tomato paste. Bring to a boil; remove from heat. Immediately stir in half and half; keep warm. Melt remaining 1/2 cup butter in a small saucepan; keep warm. In a heatproof bowl, beat together egg yolks, a pinch of salt and lemon juice. Stand bowl in a pan of hot, not boiling, water. Stirring constantly, add melted butter, a few drops at a time. When all butter has been added, remove bowl from pan of water. Season butter mixture with white pepper; stir in champagne. Stir in tomato-paste mixture. Serve cooked chops on platter or, place chops on individual plates. Serve hot sauce over cooked chops. Serve with Noodles alla Carbonara and a green salad. Makes 4 servings.

Pot-au-Feu

POT-AU-FEU

2 beef shanks
Water
2 bay leaves
1-1/2 teaspoons salt
1 (3-lb.) stewing chicken
1 (1-1/2-lb.) beef rump roast
2 carrots, cut in 8 strips
4 parsnips, each cut in 4 or 8 pieces
2 onions, cut in wedges
4 leeks, cut in 1-inch pieces
1/4 cup chopped parsley
1/8 teaspoon pepper
1-1/2 tablespoons brandy

Place beef shanks in a large pot; add water to cover. Bring to a boil; boil 5 minutes. Discard boiling water. In same large pot, bring 2 quarts water to a boil. Add blanched shanks, bay leaves, salt, chicken and beef roast; bring to a boil. Skim foam from surface until surface is clear. Cover and simmer 2 hours. Add carrots and parsnips. Cook 10 minutes longer. Add onions and leeks; cook 10 to 15 minutes longer. Remove and discard shanks and bay leaf. Remove meat from pot. Slice beef; arrange on a platter. Cut chicken into pieces; arrange on same platter. Arrange cooked vegetables around meat or, serve in a separate bowl. Sprinkle parsley over vegetables. Strain cooking liquid; season with pepper and brandy. Serve cooking liquid separately. Makes 6 servings.

Steak with Wine Sauce

BIFTECK MARCHAND DE VIN

3/4 cup butter
4 shallots or small onions, finely chopped
1 cup red wine
1/4 bay leaf
Pinch of dried leaf thyme
3 parsley sprigs
1 teaspoon lemon juice
1 teaspoon all-purpose flour
1 tablespoon chopped parsley
2 tablespoons vegetable oil
4 (8-oz.) boneless beef-sirloin or top-loin steaks
Salt and pepper

Melt 1 tablespoon butter in a small saucepan. Add shallots or onions; sauté until transparent. Add wine, bay leaf, thyme and 1 parsley sprig. Bring to a boil; boil until wine is reduced by 1/2. Strain wine mixture, squeezing all liquid from shallots or onions and herbs by pressing with the back of a spoon. Discard shallots or onions and herbs. Return liquid to pan. Bring back to a boil; set slightly off heat but keep hot. In a medium bowl, beat 1/2 cup plus 2 tablespoons butter until light and fluffy. Continue to beat while adding lemon juice, flour and chopped parsley; set aside. Heat remaining 1 tablespoon butter and oil in a large skillet. Add beef; cook 3 to 5 minutes on each side. Season with salt and pepper. Place on a warm plate; keep warm. Pour wine sauce into skillet. Stirring constantly, bring to a boil. Remove from heat; stir in parsley butter. Serve beef with sauce. Garnish with parsley sprigs. Serve with thin slices of French bread, fried in butter. Makes 4 servings.

Beef Fillet on a String

BŒUF À LA FICELLE

1 (1-3/4-lb.) beef-tenderloin roast
2 whole cloves
1 onion
1 tarragon sprig
1 thyme sprig
2 parsley sprigs
Water
2 teaspoons salt
5 leeks, white part only, sliced
3 carrots, cut in strips
1/4 celeriac or 2 celery stalks, cut in strips
2 medium tomatoes, peeled, cut in wedges
2 tablespoons cornstarch
3 tablespoons chopped chives

Tie beef with kitchen string. Fasten a 6-inch piece of string to 1 end of beef roast; set aside. Insert cloves into whole onion. Tie tarragon, thyme and parsley into a bundle. In a large deep pot, bring 6 cups water to a boil; add salt, onion with cloves, herb bundle, leeks, carrots, celeriac or celery and tomatoes. Cover and boil 30 minutes. Remove and discard onion and herbs. Using a slotted spoon, lift vegetables from liquid; keep vegetables warm. Using string attached to beef, tie beef to a wooden spoon; suspend over pan so beef hangs in liquid. Cover and simmer 20 minutes. Remove beef from liquid; keep warm in oven. Boil liquid until reduced by about 1/3. In a small bowl, combine cornstarch and 2 tablespoons water. Stir into reduced cooking liquid. Stir over medium heat until slightly thickened. Slice beef; arrange on a platter. Arrange vegetables around beef. Pour thickened sauce into a serving bowl; sprinkle chives over top. Serve beef with vegetables and sauce. Makes 4 servings.

Béarnaise Vegetable Stew

GARBURE À LA
BÉARNAISE

1 qt. water
Salt
1/2 onion
1/2 bay leaf
1 lb. boneless beef chuck or round
2 goose or chicken legs
1/2 small head cabbage
1 large carrot, finely chopped
2 to 4 small turnips, finely chopped
3 potatoes, peeled, finely chopped
1/3 cup drained canned Great Northern beans or navy beans
1/2 lb. fresh green beans, cut in 2-inch pieces
1 celery stalk, coarsely chopped
2 chervil sprigs, coarsely chopped
1 lovage sprig, if desired, coarsely chopped
White pepper
1/4 cup grated Gruyère cheese (1 oz.)
2 tablespoons chopped parsley

Bring water to a boil in a large pot. Add 1 teaspoon salt, onion, bay leaf, beef and goose or chicken legs. Cover and simmer 1-1/2 hours. Remove core from cabbage. Shred cabbage; set aside. Remove beef and goose or chicken legs from pot. Strain cooking liquid; discard onion and bay leaf. Return liquid to pot. Add shredded cabbage, carrot, turnips, potatoes, canned beans, green beans, celery, chervil and lovage, if desired. Bring to a boil. Cut cooked beef into 1-inch cubes. Remove and discard bones from goose or chicken legs; cut meat into small pieces. Return meat to pot; simmer 25 to 30 minutes longer. Pour into a tureen or serve in individual bowls. Season with salt and white pepper; sprinkle with cheese and parsley. Makes 6 servings.

France

Basque Chicken
POULET BASQUAIS

6 medium tomatoes
5 tablespoons vegetable oil
1 (3-lb.) chicken, cut in pieces
2 onions, chopped
2 green bell peppers, cut in thin strips
3 garlic cloves, finely chopped
Salt and white pepper
1 cup uncooked long-grain white rice
Water
1 teaspoon sweet paprika

Peel and quarter tomatoes. Remove and discard seeds; set tomato quarters aside. Heat 3 tablespoons oil in a large saucepan. Add chicken pieces; fry until golden brown on all sides. Add onions; sauté until transparent. Add tomato quarters, green peppers and garlic. Season with salt and white pepper. Cover and cook over low heat 50 minutes. About 20 minutes before end of cooking time, heat remaining oil in a medium saucepan. Add rice; stir constantly over medium heat 2 to 3 minutes. Add 2 cups water; season with salt and white pepper. Cover and simmer 16 to 20 minutes or until tender. Add more water, if necessary, to prevent rice from becoming dry. Stir in paprika; spoon rice into a serving bowl. Arrange chicken pieces and vegetables on a platter. Makes 4 servings.

Béarnaise Chicken
POULET FARCIE BÉARNAISE

1 thyme sprig
2 parsley sprigs
1 bay leaf
2 tablespoons chopped chives
2 cups dry breadcrumbs
2 garlic cloves, crushed
1 cup diced cooked ham
1/2 lb. bulk pork sausage
Salt
1 (2-1/2-lb.) chicken
Water
1/2 head Savoy cabbage, coarsely shredded
2 carrots, sliced
3 leeks, white part only, diced
1 onion, coarsely chopped
1/8 celeriac or 1 celery stalk, chopped
1/2 lb. fresh green beans

Tie thyme, parsley and bay leaf into a bundle; set aside. In a large bowl, combine chives, breadcrumbs, garlic, ham, sausage and salt. Stuff chicken with sausage mixture. Pull loose skin over cavity; secure with wooden or metal picks. Place chicken in a large saucepan. Add salt, if desired, and water to cover. Bring to a boil; cover and simmer 1 hour. In a large saucepan, bring 3 cups water to a boil. Blanch cabbage in boiling water 3 minutes. Drain and discard water. Add blanched cabbage, carrots, leeks, onion, celeriac or celery, beans and herb bundle to chicken mixture. Simmer 30 minutes longer. Place cooked chicken on a warm platter. Strain cooking liquid, reserving liquid and vegetables. Arrange cooked vegetables around chicken. Pour cooking liquid into a serving bowl. Serve with pickled cucumbers and toasted bread cubes. Makes 4 servings.

74

Stuffed Pheasant
(center front)
FAISAN FARCI AUX NOIX

1 (2-1/2-lb.) oven-ready pheasant with heart and liver
1/3 cup golden raisins
3 tablespoons brandy
2 day-old white-bread slices, cut in cubes
1/3 cup milk
1-3/4 cups chopped walnuts
1 egg, slightly beaten
Salt and white pepper
6 to 8 thin bacon slices
1 thyme sprig
2 parsley sprigs
1 bay leaf
1/4 cup butter
1 small onion, chopped
1 small carrot, sliced

Finely chop heart and liver. Soak raisins in brandy until plump; drain, reserving brandy. In a small bowl, soak bread cubes in milk. Squeeze milk from bread; discard milk. In a medium bowl, combine chopped heart and liver, drained raisins, soaked bread, nuts, egg, salt and white pepper. Stuff pheasant with raisin mixture. Secure skin with wooden or metal picks. Sprinkle pheasant with salt and white pepper. Wrap bacon around pheasant; secure with wooden picks. Tie thyme, parsley and bay leaf into a bundle. Preheat oven to 400F (205C). Melt butter in a roasting pan. Add pheasant, onion, carrot and herb bundle. Cook on stove until browned. Cover and bake 1 hour. Remove bacon from pheasant. Place cooked pheasant and bacon on a warm platter; keep warm. Spoon vegetables into a bowl. Remove and discard herbs. Stir reserved brandy into pan drippings; strain and pour over pheasant. Serve with vegetables and mashed potatoes. Makes 2 to 3 servings.

Partridge with Lentils
(top right)
ESTOUFFADE DE PERDRIX AUX LENTILLES

2 oven-ready young partridges
Salt and pepper
3 to 4 bacon slices
2 onions
1 whole clove
1/4 cup lard
2 garlic cloves, cut in halves
1 carrot, sliced
1 cup white wine
Water
1-1/2 cups green lentils
1 thyme sprig
1 parsley sprig
1 bay leaf

Season inside of partridges with salt and pepper. Wrap partridges in bacon; secure with wooden or metal picks. Slice 1 onion into rings. Insert whole clove into remaining whole onion. Melt lard in a large saucepan. Add bacon-wrapped partridges; brown on all sides. Add onion rings, garlic and carrot; sauté 3 to 5 minutes. Add wine and 1 cup water. Cover and simmer 50 minutes. Meanwhile, in another large saucepan, cover lentils with cold water; bring to a boil. Add whole onion with clove, salt, thyme, parsley and bay leaf. Simmer 50 minutes. Remove thyme, parsley, bay leaf and whole onion. Place browned partridges on top of cooked lentils. Cook 20 minutes longer. Strain partridge cooking liquid; pour into a serving bowl. Serve separately. Makes 4 servings.

Braised Rabbit

LAPIN À LA BRESSANE

1 (2- to 2-1/2-lb.) oven-ready rabbit
1 garlic clove
Salt
2 tablespoons butter
6 to 8 bacon slices, diced
1 onion, finely chopped
1 tablespoon all-purpose flour
1 cup hot chicken stock or broth
1 cup dry white wine
Pinch of dried leaf rosemary
White pepper
2 egg yolks, slightly beaten
3/4 cup half and half

Cut rabbit into 6 to 8 pieces. Crush garlic with a little salt. Melt butter in a large saucepan. Add rabbit pieces; cook until browned on all sides. Add bacon and onion; sauté until onion is transparent. Sprinkle flour over sautéed bacon and onion. Stir in garlic-salt mixture, hot stock or broth, wine, rosemary and white pepper. Cover and simmer 1 hour or until tender. Remove rabbit from pan; keep warm. In a small bowl, beat egg yolks with half and half; stir in 4 to 5 tablespoons hot cooking liquid. Remove pan from heat; stir egg mixture into remaining cooking liquid. Return rabbit pieces to pan. Stir gently to coat with sauce. Makes 4 servings.

Simple Cassoulet

CASSOULET TOULOUSAIN

3 onions
1 whole clove
3 garlic cloves
Salt
1 parsley sprig
1 thyme sprig
1 bay leaf
3/4 cup dried Great Northern beans, navy beans or white kidney
　beans, soaked 12 hours in cold water to cover
3/4 lb. slab bacon, diced
Water
3 tablespoons lard or vegetable shortening
1 lb. boneless lamb, cut in cubes
1 tablespoon all-purpose flour
1 tablespoon tomato paste
4 oz. garlic sausage, sliced
1 cup dry breadcrumbs
2 tablespoons butter

Chop 2 onions; insert clove into whole onion. Crush 2 garlic cloves with a little salt. Tie parsley, thyme and bay leaf into a bundle. Drain beans. In a large saucepan, combine drained beans, whole onion, crushed and whole garlic, herb bundle and bacon. Add water to cover. Bring to a boil. Cover and gently boil 1-1/2 hours or until beans are nearly tender. Add more water if necessary. Melt lard or shortening in a large skillet. Add lamb and flour; stir over medium heat until browned. Thin tomato paste with a little water; stir into lamb mixture. Cover and cook 1 hour or until tender. Preheat oven to 425F (220C). Discard herb bundle, whole onion and whole garlic. Pour beans into a deep casserole. Add lamb with cooking juices and sausage. Sprinkle breadcrumbs over top; dot with butter. Bake 20 minutes. Makes 4 servings.

Crème Caramel
CRÈME AU CARAMEL

3/4 cup sugar
5 tablespoons water
2 cups milk
3 eggs
2 egg yolks
1 teaspoon vanilla extract
Whipped cream, if desired

In a small heavy saucepan, bring 1/2 cup sugar and water to a boil. Boil steadily over medium heat 8 to 10 minutes or until mixture becomes a rich, golden caramel syrup. Pour hot syrup evenly into 4 (3/4-cup) heatproof molds. Quickly turn and tip each mold to coat base and side evenly; set aside to cool. Preheat oven to 350F (175C). In a small saucepan, heat milk and remaining 1/4 cup sugar, stirring until sugar dissolves; set aside to cool slightly. In a medium bowl, beat together whole eggs and egg yolks; gradually stir in warm milk mixture. Stir in vanilla. Pour evenly into prepared molds. Pour about 1 quart hot water into a 13" x 9" baking pan. Arrange filled molds in baking pan. Water should come half-way up sides of molds. Bake 25 to 30 minutes or until a knife inserted in center comes out clean. Remove molds from baking pan; cool completely. Refrigerate at least 1-1/2 hours. To serve, invert onto individual plates. Decorate with a dollop of whipped cream, if desired. Makes 4 servings.

Cherry Cobbler
CLAFOUTIS

1 lb. fresh or frozen bing cherries or 2 (16-oz.) cans dark sweet cherries
1/4 cup all-purpose flour
2/3 cup granulated sugar
Pinch of salt
3 eggs
1-1/2 cups milk
3 tablespoons powdered sugar

Pit or drain cherries; set aside. Sift flour, granulated sugar and salt into a large bowl. Separate 1 egg; in a small bowl, beat egg white until stiff but not dry. In another small bowl, beat 1 egg yolk and whole eggs; stir into flour mixture. Gradually beat in milk; cover batter and let stand 8 to 10 minutes. Preheat oven to 400F (205C). Butter a 2-quart casserole. Pour pitted or drained cherries into dish. Fold beaten egg white into batter; pour batter over cherries. Bake 45 minutes. Serve hot or cold. Sprinkle with powdered sugar. Makes 6 to 8 servings.

Variation

When cherries are not available, substitute apricots, peaches, apples, gooseberries or black currants.

France

Champagne Sorbet

SORBET AU CHAMPAGNE

1 pint water
2-1/3 cups sugar
1 cup fresh lemon juice
1 bottle dry champagne

In a medium saucepan, combine water and sugar. Stirring constantly, bring to a boil. Stir until sugar dissolves; boil gently 3 to 5 minutes. Stirring occasionally, cool syrup; stir in lemon juice. Stir champagne into cooled syrup; pour into several 9''x 5'' loaf pans or undivided ice-cube trays. Place in freezer until mixture becomes slushy. Puree in a blender to break up ice crystals. Return to freezer. Repeat process after 1 hour. About 45 minutes before serving, place trays in refrigerator to soften sorbet.
To make in an ice cream maker, pour champagne mixture into an ice-cream canister. Freeze in ice-cream maker according to manufacturer's directions. Serve sorbet in chilled glasses or in hollowed-out fruit shells. Decorate as desired. Makes 6 to 8 servings.

Cook's Tip

Substitute white wine, fruit juice or a combination of wine and juice for champagne. Add extra flavor to a fruit sorbet by adding pureed fresh fruit.

Iced Soufflé
SOUFFLÉ GLACÉ

3 (1/4-oz.) envelopes unflavored gelatin (3 tablespoons)
1/2 cup cold water
8 egg yolks
1-1/4 cups sugar
2-1/2 cups cold, strong-brewed coffee
4 teaspoons Cointreau or other orange-flavored liqueur
4 egg whites
1-1/2 cups whipping cream
1 to 2 tablespoons unsweetened cocoa powder, if desired

Cut a piece of waxed paper long enough to wrap round a 1-1/2-quart soufflé dish and wide enough to extend 4 inches above rim. Place inside dish; fasten with tape. In a small bowl, soften gelatin in water, 3 to 5 minutes. In top of a double boiler, beat egg yolks; stir in 1/2 cup plus 2 tablespoons sugar and gelatin mixture. Place over hot water; stir constantly until mixture cooks and resembles thick cream. Pour into a large bowl; stir in coffee and liqueur. Refrigerate 30 minutes or until mixture has consistency of thick egg whites. In a medium bowl, beat egg whites until soft peaks form. Beat in 1/2 cup sugar until stiff but not dry. Gently fold beaten egg-white mixture into partially set coffee mixture. Refrigerate about 30 minutes longer. Whip cream with remaining 2 tablespoons sugar until stiff; fold into chilled coffee mixture. Spoon mixture into prepared soufflé dish. Freeze at least 4 hours. Do not freeze overnight because mixture will develop ice crystals. To serve, sift cocoa powder over top of soufflé, if desired; remove waxed paper. Makes 8 to 10 servings.

Spiced Soufflé
SOUFFLÉ AUX ÉPICES

1/2 cup butter, room temperature
1/2 cup granulated sugar
6 eggs, separated
1 cup gingersnap-cookie crumbs
1/2 cup vanilla-cookie crumbs
1/8 teaspoon ground cinnamon
1/8 teaspoon ground cloves
2 tablespoons candied lemon peel, diced
2 tablespoons candied orange peel, diced
Grated peel of 1/2 lemon
Powdered sugar

Butter 6 ramekins; sprinkle each with granulated sugar. Pour 2 cups water into a deep baking pan; place in oven. Preheat oven to 350F (175C). In a medium bowl, cream butter and 1/4 cup granulated sugar until light and fluffy. Slowly and gently beat in egg yolks. Stir in 1/2 of the gingersnap- and vanilla-cookie crumbs. Add cinnamon, cloves, candied-fruit peels and lemon peel. In a large bowl, whisk or beat egg whites with remaining 1/4 cup granulated sugar until stiff and glossy. Fold beaten egg whites and remaining cookie crumbs into egg-yolk mixture. Divide mixture evenly among buttered ramekins; smooth surfaces. Place ramekins in hot water in baking pan. Water should come half-way up sides of ramekins. Bake 25 to 30 minutes. To serve, dust with powdered sugar. Makes 6 servings.

Floating Islands

OEUFS À LA NEIGE

Custard:
2 cups milk
Pinch of salt
1 teaspoon vanilla extract
4 egg yolks
1/2 cup sugar

Meringues:
4 egg whites
Water
1/3 cup sugar

To make custard, in a small saucepan, bring milk, salt and vanilla to a simmer. Remove from heat. In a medium saucepan, beat egg yolks with 1/2 cup sugar until frothy. Gradually stir in hot milk. Stir constantly over medium heat until thickened; do not boil. Pour into 4 dessert dishes or into a serving bowl; cool.
To make meringues, in a medium bowl, beat egg whites until stiff and glossy. In a large saucepan, bring 2 quarts water to a gentle boil. Using about 1 tablespoonful at a time, carefully drop mounds of egg-white mixture into simmering water. After a few seconds, turn egg-white mound over. Using a slotted spoon, remove cooked egg-white mounds from water. Place on a cloth to drain. Repeat until all egg-white mixture is cooked.
To complete, place cooked meringues on surface of cooled custard. In a small saucepan, boil 1/3 cup sugar and 2-1/2 tablespoons water 8 minutes or until mixture forms a light caramel syrup. Drizzle caramel over meringues and custard. Makes 4 servings.

Chocolate Mousse

MOUSSE AU CHOCOLAT

6 oz. semisweet chocolate
1/4 cup butter
4 eggs, separated
2 tablespoons powdered sugar
3/4 teaspoon orange peel or 1 teaspoon orange-flavored liqueur, if desired
1 cup whipping cream
Pinch of salt
Whipped cream and maraschino cherries, if desired

Break chocolate into small pieces; place in a glass or metal bowl with butter. Stand bowl in a pan of hot, not boiling, water; stir until melted. Still over hot water, vigorously beat in egg yolks, 1 at a time, until mixture thickens. Sift powdered sugar into chocolate. Add orange peel or liqueur, if desired; blend well. In a medium bowl, beat 1 cup whipping cream until stiff peaks form. Fold into chocolate mixture. In another medium bowl, beat egg whites with salt until stiff but not dry. Beat about 3 tablespoons egg-white mixture into chocolate mixture. Gently fold in remaining egg-white mixture until smooth. Do not beat. Spoon into individual dishes; refrigerate until ready to serve. If desired, decorate with whipped cream and maraschino cherries. Makes 4 servings.

Frankfurt Green Sauce
FRANKFURTER GRÜNE SAUCE

5 hard-cooked eggs, cut in halves
1/2 cup vegetable oil
1/2 cup plain yogurt
4-1/2 teaspoons each chopped fresh parsley, chervil, chives,
   watercress, dill, tarragon, lovage, borage and sorrel
1/2 teaspoon salt
1/8 teaspoon garlic salt
1/8 teaspoon white pepper
Pinch of ground nutmeg
2-1/2 teaspoons mild prepared mustard
1/2 cup dairy sour cream

Separate egg yolks and whites; mash yolks in a small bowl. Stir in oil; blend until smooth; set aside. Finely chop egg whites into a medium bowl. Stir in yogurt, herbs, salt, garlic salt, white pepper, nutmeg, mustard and sour cream. Gradually stir in egg-yolk mixture. Serve sauce cold with beef, fish or poultry. It is especially good with cooked asparagus. Makes 6 servings.

Cook's Tip
Some cooks insist that a genuine Frankfurt sauce should contain only 7 herbs, while others find the sauce improves as you use more fresh herbs.

Munsterland Veal Stew
MÜNSTERLÄNDER TÖTTCHEN

2-1/2 qts. water
2 whole cloves
6 small onions
1 bay leaf
10 white peppercorns
1 teaspoon salt
1 calves' tongue
1 (1-1/2- to 2-lb.) veal blade roast
2 tablespoons butter
2 tablespoons all-purpose flour
2 to 3 tablespoons wine vinegar
1 to 2 teaspoons sugar
Dash of Worcestershire sauce
Lemon wedges

In a large pot, bring water to a vigorous boil. Insert a whole clove into 2 onions; add to boiling water. Add bay leaf, peppercorns, salt, tongue and veal. Skim foam from surface until surface is clear. Partially cover; boil 1-1/2 hours. Finely chop remaining 4 onions. Melt butter in a large stovetop casserole. Add chopped onions; sauté until transparent. Sprinkle flour over sautéed onions; cook, stirring constantly, until golden brown. Strain cooking liquid from veal. Gradually stir 2-1/2 cups strained cooking liquid into onion mixture. Simmer 10 to 15 minutes. Peel and slice tongue; bone and dice veal roast. Season with vinegar, sugar and Worcestershire sauce. Add tongue and veal to sauce in casserole; warm through. Garnish with lemon wedges. Makes 6 servings.

Frankish Roast Pork
FRÄNKISCHES SCHÄUFERL

3 carrots
1 (2-lb.) pork arm or blade roast, rind on
1 teaspoon salt
1/2 teaspoon ground caraway seeds
1/2 teaspoon dried leaf marjoram
1 onion, cut in wedges
2 cups hot stock or broth
3/4 lb. mushrooms
Chopped parsley
Potato Dumplings, page 9

Preheat oven to 400F (205C). Cut each carrot lengthwise into 8 strips; set aside. Score pork rind with a crisscross pattern. Combine salt, caraway seeds and marjoram; rub into pork. Place carrot strips, onion and pork in a roasting pan. Add 1 cup hot stock or broth. Roast 1 hour, basting frequently with juices. Add remaining stock or broth as needed. Cut large mushrooms in halves or quarters; leave small mushrooms whole. After 1 hour, arrange mushrooms around pork; baste with pan drippings. Continue roasting pork 45 to 60 minutes or until cooked through. Let stand 10 minutes before slicing pork. Serve with pan drippings, vegetables, Potato Dumplings and red cabbage. Garnish with parsley. Makes 4 servings.

Rabbit Stew
HESSISCHER DIPPEHAS

1 (5-1/2-lb.) oven-ready rabbit
3 onions, finely chopped
2 garlic cloves, finely chopped
2 cups wine vinegar
4 allspice berries
4 whole cloves
1/2 teaspoon pepper
1 thyme sprig
1 bottle Burgundy or other red wine
1-1/4 lbs. slab bacon, diced
2 tablespoons all-purpose flour
1/4 cup butter
1 to 1-1/2 cups pumpernickel breadcrumbs
1 teaspoon salt

Cut rabbit into 6 to 8 pieces. Place rabbit pieces in a large nonmetal casserole; set aside. In a medium bowl, combine onions, garlic, vinegar, allspice berries, cloves, pepper, thyme and wine. Carefully pour over rabbit. Cover and refrigerate 12 hours. Preheat oven to 350F (175C). Sauté bacon in a medium skillet; set aside. Drain marinated rabbit; strain and reserve marinade. Pat meat pieces dry with paper towels; dip in flour. Reserve leftover flour. Melt butter in a stovetop casserole. Add floured meat pieces; brown on all sides. Sprinkle with leftover flour; gradually stir in strained marinade. Stir in sautéed bacon, pumpernickel breadcrumbs and salt. Cover and bake 1-1/2 hours or until meat is tender. Serve with ribbon noodles garnished with fresh breadcrumbs fried in butter. Makes 8 servings.

Swabian Meat Pasties
SCHWÄBISCHE MAULTASCHEN

3-1/2 cups all-purpose flour
Salt
8 to 10 tablespoons warm water (110F, 45C)
1 tablespoon vinegar
5 tablespoons vegetable oil
1-1/2 day-old bread rolls
About 1 cup water
1 bunch fresh spinach (12 oz.), cooked 3 minutes, drained
2 teaspoons chopped parsley
1 lb. mixed ground veal and pork
3/4 lb. bulk pork sausage
2 onions, 1 chopped, 1 sliced
2 eggs, slightly beaten
1/8 teaspoon ground nutmeg
1/2 teaspoon salt
1/4 teaspoon pepper
6 to 8 cups chicken stock or broth
2 tablespoons butter
1 to 2 cups fine dry breadcrumbs, fried in butter

Stir together flour and 1/2 teaspoon salt. Stir in 8 tablespoons water, vinegar and oil until mixture forms a ball. If necessary, add more water. Cover; let stand 20 minutes. Moisten bread in water; squeeze out moisture. Combine with spinach, parsley, ground meats, sausage, chopped onion, eggs, nutmeg, salt and pepper. Roll out 1/4 of the dough at a time until 1/8 inch thick. Cut into an even number of 3-inch squares. Place 1-1/2 tablespoons filling on centers of half the squares. Top with other squares. Crimp edges together with a fork. Bring stock or broth to a boil. Add pasties; simmer in uncovered pan about 10 minutes. Melt butter in a skillet. Sauté sliced onion in butter until golden. Serve pasties with sautéed onion rings. Garnish with breadcrumbs. Makes 6 servings.

Berlin Liver
BERLINER LEBER

2 large sweet apples
1/2 cup butter
2 large onions, cut in rings
4 calves' liver slices
1/4 cup all-purpose flour
Salt and white pepper

Peel and core apples; cut each into 6 to 8 round slices. Melt 3 tablespoons butter in a large skillet. Add sliced apples; fry until golden brown on both sides. Remove from pan; keep warm. In same skillet, fry onion rings until browned and crisp. Remove from skillet; keep warm. Meanwhile, in another large skillet, melt remaining 5 tablespoons butter. Pat liver slices dry with paper towels. Dip liver in flour; shake off excess flour. Fry liver in butter 3 to 4 minutes on each side. Baste repeatedly with butter. Season with salt and white pepper. Arrange cooked liver on warm plates; top with cooked apple slices and onion rings. Serve with mashed potatoes and a fresh salad. Makes 4 servings.

Variation

Substitute fried pineapple rings for fried apple slices.

Silesian Paradise Fruits

SCHLESISCHES HIMMELREICH

1 lb. mixed dried fruit
Water
1 lb. lean slab bacon
1/2 lemon
1 (1-inch) piece cinnamon stick
1 tablespoon cornstarch
Bread Dumplings or Potato Dumplings, page 9

In a large bowl, soak dried fruit in cold water 12 hours. Place bacon in a large saucepan; add 2 cups water. Bring to a boil; cover and simmer 25 minutes. Drain and rinse; set aside. Peel lemon in 1 continuous strip. Squeeze juice from peeled lemon; reserve juice. Pour soaked fruit with soaking water into a large saucepan. Add lemon peel and cinnamon; bring to a boil. Add boiled bacon. Cover and simmer 30 minutes. Remove and discard lemon peel and cinnamon. Remove rind from bacon; slice bacon, if desired. In a small bowl, dissolve cornstarch in 3 tablespoons water. Stir into fruit mixture. Stirring constantly, bring to a boil; continue stirring until slightly thickened. Stir in lemon juice. Spoon fruit and juice into a serving bowl; top with sliced or unsliced bacon. Serve with Bread Dumplings or Potato Dumplings. Makes 4 servings.

Hamburg-Style Pork

BIRNEN, HOHNEN UND SPECK HAMBURGER ART

1 lb. lean slab bacon
2-1/2 cups water
Salt
1 lb. fresh pears
2 lbs. fresh green beans, cut in 2-inch pieces
1 teaspoon chopped parsley
Pepper

In a large pot, combine bacon, water and 1/2 teaspoon salt. Cover and simmer 30 minutes. Peel, quarter and core pears. Add pears to bacon mixture; cook 10 minutes. Add beans. Cover and simmer 30 minutes longer. Remove bacon from pan; cut into slices. Season cooked beans and pears with parsley, salt and pepper. Arrange bacon slices over top. Serve with boiled potatoes. Makes 4 servings.

Variation

Leave pears whole and unpeeled. Add a peeled potato, cut in wedges.

Germany

Pomeranian Roast Goose
POMMERSCHER GÄNSEBRATEN

Water
6 to 8 day-old white-bread slices
1 lb. whole chestnuts, roasted, skins removed
3 tablespoons butter
1 tablespoon sugar
1 cup stock or broth
8 to 10 bacon slices, diced
2 onions, coarsely chopped
Salt
1 egg, beaten
1 (6-1/2-lb.) goose

Sprinkle water over bread; set aside. Cut chestnuts in halves. In a medium saucepan, melt butter. Add sugar, chestnut halves and stock or broth; simmer 10 minutes. Drain chestnuts. In a medium skillet, sauté bacon; remove bacon. Add onions to skillet; sauté until transparent. Squeeze moisture from bread; crumble bread into a medium bowl. Add drained chestnut halves, 1 teaspoon salt, egg, sautéed bacon and onions. Remove excess fat from goose. Preheat oven to 350F (175C). Rub inside of goose with salt. Loosely fill neck and body cavities with chestnut mixture. Fasten skin over body cavities with skewers. Prick goose skin all over to let fat drain during roasting. Place goose breast-side down on a rack in a shallow roasting pan. Roast 1-1/2 hours. Occasionally thin pan drippings with water; use to baste goose. Turn goose over. Insert a meat thermometer in center of inner-thigh muscle. Continue roasting 1-1/2 hours longer or until thermometer registers 180F to 185F (80C to 85C) or juices run clear when a knife is inserted between thigh and breast. Place roasted goose on a large platter. Let stand 10 to 15 minutes before carving. Serve with red cabbage and dumplings, if desired. Makes 6 servings.

Rhineland Spiced Beef
RHEINISCHER SAUERBRATEN

1 cup wine vinegar
Water
1 (1-3/4- to 2-lb.) beef top-round or rump roast
3 to 4 bacon slices, cut in 1-inch pieces
1 carrot, chopped
1 parsnip, chopped
1/4 celeriac or 2 celery stalks, chopped
1 garlic clove, finely chopped
1 bay leaf
3 allspice berries
3 whole peppercorns
1 thyme sprig
1 cup Burgundy or other red wine
1/4 cup lard
1 tablespoon tomato paste
1 gingerbread slice
1 pumpernickel-bread slice
1 tablespoon all-purpose flour blended with 2 tablespoons water
1/2 cup raisins

Boil vinegar and 1/2 cup water; cool. Cut shallow slashes in beef. Insert bacon pieces in slashes. In a large bowl, combine beef, carrot, parsnip, celeriac or celery, garlic, bay leaf, allspice, peppercorns and thyme. Pour vinegar mixture and wine over top. Cover; refrigerate 24 hours. Preheat oven to 375F (190C). Melt lard in a roasting pan. Drain beef; reserve marinade. Brown beef in hot lard. Stir tomato paste into marinade. Pour marinade into roasting pan; roast 1 hour. Crumble gingerbread and pumpernickel bread into pan; roast 1-1/2 to 2 hours longer or until beef is tender. Place beef on a platter. Strain pan drippings; return to pan. Stir flour mixture into pan drippings. Cook until slightly thickened. Stir in raisins. Slice beef; serve with sauce. Makes 6 servings.

Saxony Curd Cakes
SÄCHSISCHE QUARKKEULCHEN

3 medium potatoes, cooked, peeled, chilled
1/2 cup raisins
Water
1-1/2 cups cottage cheese, drained (12 oz.)
2 eggs, slightly beaten
1/3 cup all-purpose flour
1/8 teaspoon salt
1/3 cup plus 2 tablespoons sugar
Grated peel of 1/2 lemon
1/4 cup vegetable oil
1/4 teaspoon ground cinnamon

Press potatoes through a metal sieve or ricer or, mash thoroughly. Rinse raisins in hot water; drain on paper towels. In a blender or food processor, process cottage cheese until smooth. In a large bowl, combine processed cottage cheese, sieved potatoes, rinsed raisins, eggs, flour, salt, 1/3 cup sugar and lemon peel. Press mixture together to form a dough. Flour your hands. With floured hands, shape mixture into 6 to 8 flat cakes, 2 inches in diameter. Preheat oven to 225F (105C). Heat oil in a large skillet. Cook curd cakes in hot oil, a few at a time, 8 minutes or until golden brown on both sides. Keep cooked cakes warm in oven. In a small bowl, combine remaining 2 tablespoons sugar and cinnamon; sprinkle on both sides of cooked cakes. Serve with applesauce, stewed plums or other stewed fruit. Makes 6 to 8 curd cakes.

Swabian Cherry Pudding
SCHWÄBISCHER KIRSCHENMICHEL

8 day-old bread rolls, thinly sliced
2 cups warm milk
2 (15-oz.) cans pie cherries, lightly drained
3/4 cup plus 2 tablespoons granulated sugar
1/2 cup golden raisins
Water
1/4 cup plus 2 tablespoons butter, room temperature
4 eggs, separated
Grated peel of 1 lemon
1/3 cup chopped hazelnuts
Powdered sugar

In a medium bowl, soak bread in milk 30 minutes. Pit cherries, if necessary; sprinkle 1/3 cup granulated sugar over cherries. In a small bowl, soak raisins in hot water 10 minutes; drain. Preheat oven to 400F (205C). Butter a 2- or 3-quart casserole. In a large bowl, beat 1/4 cup butter with remaining granulated sugar until creamy. Stir in egg yolks and lemon peel. Stir in bread mixture, drained raisins, nuts and cherries with any juice that has formed. In a medium bowl, beat egg whites until stiff; fold into cherry mixture. Spoon mixture into prepared dish. Smooth surface; dot with remaining butter. Bake on lowest rack in oven 45 minutes or until golden brown. Dust with powdered sugar; serve with cream or a vanilla custard. Makes 4 servings.

Bavarian Dumplings

BAYERISCHE
DAMPFNUDELN

Dumpling Dough:
1/4 cup warm water (110F, 45C)
2 teaspoons active dry yeast
2/3 cup sugar
1-1/4 cups warm milk (110F, 45C)
1/2 cup butter, melted
2 eggs, slightly beaten
1/8 teaspoon salt
5 to 5-1/2 cups all-purpose flour
1/2 cup butter
2/3 cup sugar
1 cup milk

To make dough, in a large bowl, combine water, yeast and 2 teaspoons sugar; stir until yeast dissolves. Let stand 5 minutes or until foamy. Stir in remaining sugar, milk, butter, eggs and salt. Beat in 2 cups flour until smooth. Cover and let stand 10 minutes. Stir in enough remaining flour to make a medium-soft dough. Shape dough into 16 balls. Cover and let rise until doubled in bulk, 30 to 45 minutes.

To complete, melt butter in an electric skillet, Dutch oven or a shallow, heavy stovetop casserole with a tight-fitting lid. Add sugar. Stir over medium heat until sugar is lightly browned. Stir in milk. Arrange raised dumplings side by side over sauce in pan. Drape a damp cloth over pan; place lid on pan. Cook dumplings at 225F (105C) in electric skillet or over medium heat 30 minutes; do not lift lid during cooking. Serve dumplings with vanilla custard. Makes 16 dumplings.

Variation

Substitute stewed plums or other stewed fruit for custard.

Herrings with Mustard Sauce

Mustard Sauce:
3 tablespoons butter
2 tablespoons all-purpose flour
1 cup milk
1 tablespoon prepared English or Dijon mustard
1 teaspoon lemon juice
Pinch of sugar
Salt and white pepper

Herring:
4 herring
1 cup milk
1/2 cup quick-cooking or regular rolled oats
Salt and pepper
5 tablespoons butter or lard
Lemon slices

To make sauce, melt butter in a small saucepan. Stir in flour; stirring constantly, cook 2 minutes. Slowly stir in milk; stir while simmering 5 minutes. Stir in mustard, lemon juice and sugar. Season with salt and white pepper. Keep warm while preparing herring.
To prepare herring, bone herring, if desired. Dip each herring into milk, then into rolled oats; season with salt and pepper. Melt butter or lard in a large skillet. Cook herring in hot butter or lard 8 minutes on each side or until browned and crisp. Arrange cooked herring on a warm platter; garnish with lemon slices. Serve sauce separately. Makes 4 servings.

Old-English Baked Cod

2 tablespoons butter
1 onion, finely chopped
1/4 cup sliced mushrooms
1/8 teaspoon dried leaf thyme
4 (7-oz.) cod fillets
Salt and white pepper
1 bay leaf
2 cups milk
2 tablespoons cornstarch
3 tablespoons water
4 thin bacon slices
3 tablespoons dry breadcrumbs
Watercress

Preheat oven to 350F (175C). Melt butter in a medium saucepan. Add onion and mushrooms; sauté 5 minutes. Pour mixture into a 13" x 9" baking dish; sprinkle with thyme. Pat cod fillets dry with paper towels; arrange over onion mixture. Season with salt and white pepper; add bay leaf. In a medium saucepan, bring milk to a simmer. In a small bowl, blend cornstarch with water. Stir into hot milk. Continue stirring over medium heat until thickened; pour sauce over fish. Cover and bake 10 minutes. In a small skillet, cook bacon until crisp. Increase heat to 425F (220C). Sprinkle breadcrumbs over cod; top with cooked bacon. Bake 10 minutes longer or until browned. Garnish with watercress. Serve hot. Makes 4 servings.

Poached Salmon with Cucumber
(left)

4 (7-oz.) salmon steaks
1/4 cup wine vinegar
Salt
2 cups water
Juice of 1 lemon
1 cup dry white wine
2 tablespoons butter
1 cucumber, peeled, coarsely chopped
White pepper
1 tablespoon chopped fresh dill
Blender Hollandaise Sauce, page 8

Pat salmon steaks dry with paper towels. Sprinkle salmon with vinegar and salt. In a large shallow pan, bring water to a boil with 1-1/2 teaspoons salt. Add lemon juice and wine; return to a boil. Add salmon steaks; simmer 15 minutes or until salmon flakes easily when pierced with a fork. Place poached salmon on a platter; keep warm. Melt butter in a small saucepan. Add cucumber; season with salt and white pepper. Cover and cook 15 minutes or until tender, stirring occasionally. Sprinkle with dill. Arrange cucumber around salmon steaks. Serve with Blender Hollandaise Sauce. Makes 4 to 6 servings.

Potted Shrimp
(right)

3/4 cup Clarified Butter, page 9
1 lb. peeled cooked shrimp
1/4 teaspoon salt
1/8 teaspoon ground mace
1/8 teaspoon ground nutmeg
1/8 teaspoon ground allspice

Reserve 5 tablespoons clarified butter; heat remaining clarified butter in a small skillet. Pat shrimp dry with paper towels; add shrimp to skillet. Stir until coated with butter. Add salt, mace, nutmeg and allspice. Sauté shrimp 5 minutes. Spoon shrimp and butter from skillet into 4 ramekins, packing fairly tight. Cool until butter is set. Melt reserved clarified butter in a small saucepan. Pour evenly over shrimp and butter in ramekins, covering completely. Cover ramekins with foil; refrigerate 3 to 4 hours. Serve with toast and butter. Makes 4 servings.

Cook's Tip

The flavor will improve even more if dish is kept in the refrigerator at least 2 days.

Irish Lamb Stew

5 medium potatoes, peeled, sliced
2 lbs. boneless lean lamb, cut in 1-inch cubes
3 large onions, sliced
2 teaspoons salt
1 teaspoon dried leaf thyme
About 1-1/2 cups water
2 tablespoons chopped parsley

Preheat oven to 350F (175C). Grease a 2-quart casserole. Line bottom of dish with 1/3 of the sliced potatoes. Cover with 1/2 of the lamb, then with 1/2 of the onions. Sprinkle onion rings with 1/2 of the salt and thyme. Cover onions with another 1/3 of the potatoes, remaining lamb and onion rings. Sprinkle with remaining salt and thyme; top with remaining 1/3 of the potatoes. Pour 1 cup water into dish. Cover and bake 2 hours, adding water after 1 hour, if needed. Bottom potato layer will become soft and combine with liquid to make a thick sauce. Garnish with parsley. Makes 4 servings.

Lancashire Hot-Pot

3 lambs' kidneys
Water
1-3/4 lbs. boneless lamb
4 medium potatoes, peeled, sliced
2 carrots, sliced
1 small rutabaga or turnip, finely chopped
Salt and pepper
1 large onion, cut in thin rings

Soak kidneys in cold water to cover 30 minutes. Cut lamb into thick slices. Skin, core and coarsely chop kidneys. Preheat oven to 350F (175C). Butter a deep casserole. Arrange 1/2 of the potato slices in buttered casserole. Add layers of carrots, rutabaga or turnip and lamb. Season with salt and pepper. Cover with 1/2 of the onion rings. Top with chopped kidneys. Season with salt and pepper. Top casserole with remaining onion rings and potatoes. Add water until it comes about half-way up side of dish. Cover and bake 2 hours. Uncover and bake 30 minutes longer or until top layer is browned and crisp. Makes 4 servings.

Beef Stew with Onion Dumplings

1/4 cup all-purpose flour
Salt and pepper
1-1/2 lbs. beef round steak, cut in cubes
3 tablespoons vegetable shortening or lard
2-1/2 cups hot beef stock or broth
Pinch of grated lemon peel
2 medium carrots, chopped
2 medium onions, chopped
1 small parsnip, chopped

Onion Dumplings:
3/4 cup all-purpose flour
1 teaspoon baking powder
Pinch of salt
2 oz. beef suet, shredded
1 small onion, finely chopped
3 to 5 tablespoons water
1 tablespoon chopped parsley

Season 3 tablespoons flour with salt and pepper. Roll beef cubes in seasoned flour. Melt shortening or lard in a large saucepan. Add seasoned beef cubes; cook until browned on all sides. Remove from pan; set aside. Stir remaining 1 tablespoon flour into pan drippings. Gradually stir in stock or broth and lemon peel. Continue stirring over medium heat until slightly thickened. Add cooked beef. Cover; simmer 1-1/2 hours. Add carrots, onions and parsnip. Cook 1 hour longer.
To make dumplings, sift flour, baking powder and salt into a large bowl. Stir in suet, onion and enough water to make a soft dough. Flour your hands; shape dough into 8 dumplings.
To complete, add dumplings to stew; simmer 30 minutes longer or until beef and vegetables are tender and dumplings are cooked through center. Pour into a tureen or serve in individual bowls. Garnish with parsley. Makes 4 servings.

Roast Pork with Applesauce

1 (4-lb.) boneless pork-leg roast, rolled, tied
Vegetable oil
Salt

Stuffing:
1 lb. bulk pork sausage
5 tablespoons dry breadcrumbs
1 onion, finely chopped
1 egg, slightly beaten
2 tablespoons chopped sage or 1 tablespoon rubbed sage

Chunky Applesauce:
3 to 4 cooking apples, peeled, coarsely chopped
2 to 3 tablespoons water
2 tablespoons butter
Sugar, if desired

Score outer pork fat. Rub oil and salt into fat. Preheat oven to 350F (175C). In a large bowl, combine all stuffing ingredients. Loosen or remove strings from roast. Press stuffing into center of roast. Use kitchen string to tie roast again. Place in a roasting pan; roast 4 hours or until juices run clear. Occasionally baste with pan drippings. To make outer fat especially crisp, increase heat to 425F (220C) during last 30 minutes of roasting.
To make applesauce, in a medium saucepan, simmer apples with a little water until tender. Stir in butter; sweeten with a little sugar, if desired. Serve applesauce and roast pork with baked potatoes and fresh vegetables. Makes 6 to 8 servings.

Cornish Pasties

Pastry:
3 cups all-purpose flour
Pinch of salt
3/4 cup chilled lard
5 to 6 tablespoons water
1 egg, slightly beaten

Filling:
8 oz. boneless beef sirloin or top round, finely chopped
1/2 small onion, finely chopped
1 small potato, peeled, finely chopped
1/8 rutabaga or turnip, finely chopped
1/2 teaspoon salt
1/4 teaspoon pepper
1 tablespoon stock or broth

To make pastry, in a large bowl, stir together flour and salt. Use a pastry blender or fork to cut in lard until mixture resembles coarse crumbs. Sprinkle 5 tablespoons water over flour mixture. Stir in with a fork, adding remaining 1 tablespoon water, if needed. Gather dough into a ball; refrigerate 30 minutes before rolling out.
To make filling, in a large bowl, combine beef, onion, potato, rutabaga or turnip, salt, pepper and stock or broth.
To complete, preheat oven to 400F (205C). On a lightly floured surface, roll out dough until 1/4 inch thick. Cut out 4 (7-inch) circles. Moisten edges with water. Spoon filling evenly on 1 side of each dough circle. Fold pastry over filling. Crimp edges together with a fork. Brush egg over top of pasties. Arrange pasties on an ungreased baking sheet. Bake 20 minutes. Reduce heat to 350F (175C). Bake 40 minutes longer. Makes 4 servings.

Steak & Kidney Pudding

1/3 cup all-purpose flour
1/2 teaspoon salt
1/2 teaspoon pepper
1/3 to 1/2 beef kidney, trimmed, cored, cut in 1-inch pieces
1-1/2 lbs. lean beef for stew, cut in 1-inch cubes
4 oz. fresh mushrooms, cut in quarters
1 medium onion, coarsely chopped
1 cup hot beef stock or broth

Pastry:
1 cup shredded beef suet (4 oz.)
2-1/4 cups all-purpose flour
1 tablespoon baking powder
1/4 teaspoon salt
6 to 8 tablespoons water

In a large bowl or heavy plastic bag, combine flour, salt and pepper. Add kidney and beef; toss to coat. Add mushrooms and onion; toss to distribute.
To make pastry, butter a deep 1-quart mold; set aside. In a large bowl, combine suet, flour, baking powder and salt. Stir in enough water to make a firm dough; knead about 10 strokes. Roll out 3/4 of the dough to a 14-inch circle. Fit dough circle into mold. Dough will extend 1/4 to 1/2 inch over top of mold.
To complete, roll out remaining dough slightly larger than top of mold; set aside. Spoon filling into lined mold, mounding in center. Pour stock or broth over filling. Place top crust over filling. Dampen edges of overhanging dough; press firmly onto top dough. Grease center of a 12-inch square of foil. Place over top of filled mold, folding a wide pleat across center. Tie tightly with string below rim of mold. Attach a damp kitchen towel as shown on page 7. Hang mold in boiling water; water should come 3/4 up side of mold. Cover tightly; steam 4-1/2 hours, adding boiling water as necessary. Makes 4 to 6 servings.

Farmhouse Chicken Casserole

1/4 cup all-purpose flour
Salt and pepper
1 (3-lb.) chicken, cut in pieces
2 tablespoons butter
1 tablespoon vegetable oil
8 shallots or small onions
8 small new potatoes, peeled
1/3 cup mushrooms, cut in halves
4 bacon slices
1-1/2 cups hot chicken stock or broth
1 tablespoon cornstarch
2 tablespoons water
2 tablespoons chopped parsley

Season flour with salt and pepper; coat chicken with seasoned flour. Melt butter in a large skillet; add oil. Add chicken pieces, a few at a time; brown on all sides. Place browned chicken in a large stovetop casserole. Sauté shallots or onions and potatoes in skillet. Add sautéed vegetables to chicken. Sauté mushrooms in skillet; add to chicken mixture. Preheat oven to 350F (175C). Fry bacon in skillet until crisp. Add cooked bacon and drippings to casserole. Pour hot stock or broth over chicken mixture. Bake 1 hour or until chicken is tender. Arrange cooked chicken, potatoes and onions on a platter; keep warm. In a small bowl, combine cornstarch and water; stir into pan drippings. Stir over medium heat until thickened. Pour into a small bowl. Garnish chicken with parsley. Makes 4 servings.

Roast Duck

1 (4-lb.) oven-ready duck
Salt and white pepper
Hot water
2 tablespoons honey

Stuffing:
2 tablespoons butter
1 onion, finely chopped
Few celery leaves, chopped
2 cooking apples, peeled, chopped
1-3/4 cups fresh breadcrumbs
1/8 teaspoon ground cinnamon
1 teaspoon grated lemon peel
Salt and white pepper
1 cup apple cider

Prepare stuffing. Place oven rack in lowest position. Preheat oven to 350F (175C). Loosely fill duck with stuffing. Fasten skin over body cavity. Rub stuffed duck with salt and white pepper. Prick duck skin all over to let fat drain during roasting. Place duck, breast-side down, on a rack in a shallow roasting pan. Pour about 1/2 cup water in bottom of roasting pan. Roast duck 2 hours. Turn duck breast-side up. Insert a meat thermometer in center of inner-thigh muscle, if desired. Roast 45 minutes longer or until thermometer registers 180F to 185F (80C to 85C) and juices run clear when a knife is inserted between thigh and breast. Combine honey and 1 tablespoon hot water. Brush honey mixture over duck 15 minutes before end of cooking time. Remove as much fat as possible from cooking juices. Place roast duck on a platter. Serve with green peas and cooking juices. Makes 4 servings.
To make stuffing, melt butter in a large skillet. Add onion, celery leaves and apples; sauté 3 minutes. Stir in remaining dressing ingredients; set aside.

Gooseberry Fool

1 (15-oz.) can gooseberries, well drained
3/4 cup plus 2 tablespoons sugar
1 cup whipping cream
1/2 teaspoon vanilla extract
Whipped cream, if desired

Reserve 6 gooseberries for decoration. Puree remaining gooseberries. To remove seeds, strain pureed gooseberries through a fine sieve placed over a small saucepan. Stir 1/2 cup sugar into strained puree. Stir over low heat until sugar dissolves; set aside until cool. In a medium bowl, beat whipping cream until soft peaks form. Fold in remaining sugar and vanilla. Continue whipping until sugar dissolves and stiff peaks form. Fold whipped-cream mixture into gooseberry mixture. Spoon into 6 dessert dishes. Refrigerate 3 to 4 hours. To serve, pipe a little whipped cream on top of each, if desired. Top each with 1 reserved gooseberry. Serve with almond or sugar cookies. Makes 6 servings.

Cook's Tip

This is called *Groset Foul* in Great Britain.

Empire Apple Pie

6 or 7 cooking apples
1/2 cup sugar
Juice and grated peel of 1/2 lemon
1 teaspoon ground cinnamon
1/8 teaspoon ground cloves, if desired
1 tablespoon milk

Pastry:
2 cups all-purpose flour
Pinch of salt
1/4 cup chilled lard
1/4 cup chilled butter
2 to 3 tablespoons water

Prepare pastry. Peel, core and slice apples. Preheat oven to 400F (205C). Roll out 2/3 of the chilled dough. Use to line bottom and side of a deep 8- or 9-inch pie dish. Arrange apple slices in layers over pastry, sprinkling each layer with sugar. Sprinkle top layer of apples with lemon juice, lemon peel, cinnamon and cloves, if desired. Roll out remaining dough for top crust. Arrange over filling. Firmly press edges together. Prick top crust several times with a fork. Cut any pastry trimmings into small shapes; use to decorate top of pie. Brush crust with milk. Bake 10 minutes; reduce heat to 350F (175C). Bake 30 to 40 minutes longer or until golden brown. Serve hot or cold with cream or ice cream. Makes 1 (8- or 9-inch) pie.
To make pastry, sift flour and salt into a medium bowl. Use a pastry blender or fork to cut in lard and butter until mixture resembles coarse crumbs. Sprinkle water over top; stir in with a fork. Gather dough into a ball. On a lightly floured surface, knead lightly 5 to 10 strokes. Wrap in plastic wrap; refrigerate 30 minutes.

Christmas Plum Pudding

1 cup currants
3/4 cup raisins
Water
1/3 cup candied orange peel, chopped
1/3 cup candied lemon peel, chopped
1 cup chopped blanched almonds
2/3 cup candied cherries, cut in quarters
4 oz. beef suet, shredded
1 cup all-purpose flour
4 cups fresh breadcrumbs
2/3 cup packed brown sugar
Grated peel and juice of 1 lemon
1/4 teaspoon ground cinnamon
1/4 teaspoon ground cloves
1/4 teaspoon ground allspice
1/2 teaspoon salt
Juice of 1 orange
3/4 to 1 cup milk
3 eggs
3 tablespoons brandy
1/4 to 1/2 cup rum
Cumberland Rum Butter, opposite

Wash currants and raisins in hot water; drain on paper towels. In a large bowl, combine washed currants and raisins, candied fruit peels, almonds, candied cherries, suet, flour, breadcrumbs, brown sugar, lemon peel, cinnamon, cloves, allspice and salt; blend well. Stir in lemon juice, orange juice and 3/4 cup milk. In a small bowl, beat eggs; stir in brandy. Stir into fruit mixture until ingredients are thoroughly bound together. Add more milk, if necessary.

To steam pudding, bring a large pan of water to a boil. Butter a 7- to 8-cup mold; spoon pudding into mold to within 2 inches of top. Butter a large piece of waxed paper or parchment paper. Pleat paper so it can expand as pudding cooks. Place over mold.

Tie in place with kitchen string. Place mold in boiling water. If necessary, add boiling water until it comes 2/3 up side of mold. Steam pudding 4 to 6 hours, adding more boiling water when necessary. Cool pudding in mold. Remove from mold. Soak 4 layers of cheesecloth in rum; wrap cooked pudding in rum-soaked cloth, then in heavy foil. Store in refrigerator at least 4 weeks. Before serving, return pudding to mold; steam 1-1/2 to 2 hours to heat through. Serve with Cumberland Rum Butter. Makes 8 to 10 servings.

Cumberland Rum Butter

6 tablespoon butter, room temperature
1/2 cup packed light brown sugar or fine granulated sugar
1/4 cup rum
1/8 teaspoon grated nutmeg

In a small bowl, beat all ingredients until fluffy. Refrigerate at least 1 hour.

Cook's Tip

Almost as traditional as Christmas Plum Pudding, is the custom of flaming it. Sprinkle pudding with 2 tablespoons warmed brandy; ignite and carry flaming pudding to the table. Make pudding several weeks before Christmas to let flavors blend fully. In England, it is not unusual to prepare it in the weeks before Christmas for Christmas of the following year.

Treacle Tart

Pastry:
1-1/2 cups all-purpose flour
2 teaspoons sugar
6 tablespoons butter, chilled
2 tablespoons lard or vegetable shortening, chilled
3 to 4 tablespoons cold water

Filling:
4 cups fresh breadcrumbs from homemade-style white bread
1/2 teaspoon ground ginger
1 tablespoon lemon juice
1 egg, beaten
1-2/3 cups dark corn syrup
1 tablespoon molasses

To make pastry, in a medium bowl, combine flour and sugar. Use a pastry blender or fork to cut in butter and lard or shortening until mixture resembles coarse crumbs. Stir in enough water to make a soft dough that forms a ball. Wrap in plastic wrap; refrigerate 30 minutes.
To make filling, in a large bowl, combine breadcrumbs, ginger, lemon juice, egg, corn syrup and molasses.
To complete, preheat oven to 350F (175C). Butter a 9-inch pie pan or quiche dish. On a lightly floured surface, roll out pastry until 1/8 inch thick. Fit into buttered pie pan or dish; trim and flute edge. Pour in filling; smooth surface. Bake in center of oven 20 to 30 minutes or until filling is firm and pastry is golden brown. Cut tart into wedges. Serve with ice cream, whipped cream or custard. Makes 1 (9-inch) tart.

Scones

2-1/4 cups all-purpose flour
1 teaspoon baking powder
1/4 teaspoon baking soda
1/8 teaspoon salt
2-1/2 tablespoons butter, chilled
1/4 cup sugar
About 1 cup buttermilk
2 to 3 tablespoons milk
Butter
Jam
Whipped cream

Grease a large baking sheet; set aside. Preheat oven to 450F (230C). Sift flour, baking powder, baking soda and salt into a large bowl. Use a pastry blender or fork to cut in butter until mixture resembles coarse crumbs. Use a fork to work in sugar and enough buttermilk to make a smooth soft dough. Turn out dough onto a lightly floured surface; knead lightly. Roll out dough until 3/4 inch thick. Cut into 10 to 12 (2-1/2-inch) circles. Arrange dough circles on greased baking sheet; brush tops with a little milk. Bake 15 to 20 minutes or until golden brown; set aside to cool. To serve, separate scones into halves; spread with butter and jam. Top each with whipped cream; sandwich 2 halves together. Makes 10 to 12 scones.

Variation

Cook scones on an ungreased griddle until lightly browned, turning once.

Cook's Tip

To preserve their tender texture, pull scones apart with your fingers. Do not cut with a knife.

Avgolemono Soup
SOUPA AVGOLEMONO

5-1/2 cups chicken stock or broth
1/2 cup uncooked long-grain white rice
4 eggs
Juice of 1 lemon
Salt and white pepper

Bring stock or broth to a boil in a medium saucepan; sprinkle rice into boiling liquid. Cover and simmer 15 to 20 minutes. In a small bowl, beat eggs with a whisk; gradually blend in lemon juice. Slowly stir 1/2 cup hot liquid from rice mixture into egg mixture. Remove remaining rice mixture from heat. Gradually whisk in egg mixture. Reheat soup but do not boil. Season with salt and white pepper. Pour into a tureen or serve in individual bowls. Let stand 5 minutes before serving. Makes 6 servings.

Cook's Tip

Avgolemono can also be served as a sauce. Beat together 2 eggs and juice of 2 lemons. Gradually blend in 2 cups hot chicken stock or broth. Stirring constantly with a whisk, heat sauce over low heat; do not boil. Whisk until light and frothy. Serve with cooked meat, poultry, fish or vegetables.

Aegean Calamari
KALAMARÁKJA KRASATA

1 lb. dressed squid
Salt
1 tablespoon finely chopped parsley
2 garlic cloves
1/3 cup olive oil
1/3 cup dry white wine
2 medium tomatoes, peeled, chopped
White pepper
1 tablespoon lemon juice
1 parsley sprig

Cut squid into rings; slice flaps into broad strips and tentacles in 2-inch pieces. Sprinkle with salt and chopped parsley. Crush garlic with a little salt. Heat oil in a large skillet. Add squid pieces; cook about 1 minute. Add wine, tomatoes and garlic-salt mixture. Cover and cook 40 minutes or until tender. Season with salt, white pepper and lemon juice. Spoon into a serving bowl. Garnish with parsley sprig. Serve with a crisp salad. Makes 4 servings.

Feta Cheese in Pastry

TIROPITA

2 pkg. frozen patty shells (12 shells) or 1 (1-lb.) pkg. frozen filo dough
5 tablespoons butter
1/2 cup all-purpose flour
1/3 cup milk
1/2 teaspoon salt
1/8 teaspoon white pepper
7 eggs
1 lb. feta cheese, crumbled (about 4 cups)
Butter, room temperature

Thaw patty shells or filo dough. Melt 5 tablespoons butter in a large saucepan; stir in flour. Gradually stir in milk. Stirring constantly, simmer 5 minutes. Stir in salt and white pepper; set aside to cool, stirring occasionally. Beat eggs into cooled sauce, 1 at a time; stir in cheese. Grease a 9-1/2-inch cake or quiche pan; set aside. Preheat oven to 375F (190C).
To use patty shells, flatten thawed patty shells. Arrange 2 patty shells on a flat surface, slightly overlapping edges. Roll out shells to a 9-1/2-inch circle. Repeat with remaining patty shells, making 6 circles in all.
To use filo dough, flatten thawed dough, cut in 18 (9-1/2-inch) circles. Spread circles with butter. Use 3 buttered filo circles for each layer. Beginning and ending with a buttered pastry circles, alternate layers of pastry and cheese mixture in greased pan. Bake about 45 minutes. Cut into wedges. Serve warm with a green salad. Makes 6 servings.

Partridge in Wine Sauce

PERDIKES KRASATES

2 oven-ready partridges
Salt and white pepper
5 tablespoons butter
1 cup dry red wine
Juice of 1 lemon
Piece of lemon peel
1 cup stock or broth, if needed

Cut each partridge in half; pat dry with paper towels. Season inside each partridge with salt and white pepper. Melt butter in a large skillet. Add partridge halves; cook until evenly browned. Remove partridges from skillet. Stir a little wine into pan drippings to loosen. Stir in remaining wine, lemon juice and lemon peel. Return cooked partridge halves to skillet. Cover and simmer 40 to 50 minutes or until tender. Add stock or broth as needed during cooking. Using a slotted spoon, remove partridge halves from skillet. Place on a warm platter. Season sauce with salt and white pepper; pour over partridge halves. Makes 4 servings.

Cook's Tip

In Greece, this dish is served with potato puree or rice and a green salad or a salad of cooked broccoli. The salad is dressed with olive oil, salt and fresh lemon juice.

Moussaka
MELITSANES MUSAKÁS

2 large eggplants
Salt
1/4 cup vegetable oil
3 tablespoons vegetable shortening
1-1/2 lbs. ground lamb
2 onions, grated
2 tablespoons dry white vermouth
1/3 cup water
1 teaspoon sugar
Pinch of ground nutmeg
1 teaspoon dried leaf oregano
Pepper
1/3 cup dry breadcrumbs
5 to 6 medium tomatoes
1 cup finely shredded mozzarella cheese (4 oz.)
Greek White Sauce, page 9

Peel eggplants; cut in thick slices. Sprinkle both sides of eggplant slices with salt; let stand 1 hour. Rinse eggplant slices; pat dry with paper towels. Heat oil in a large skillet. Add sliced eggplant; cook in hot oil until nearly tender. Melt shortening in a large saucepan. Add lamb and onions; cook until lamb is done. Add vermouth, water, sugar, nutmeg, oregano, salt and pepper. Simmer 10 minutes, then stir in breadcrumbs. Cut tomatoes in thick slices. Butter a large baking dish. In buttered dish, alternate layers of cooked eggplant, cheese and cooked lamb mixture. Arrange sliced tomatoes over final layer of lamb. Preheat oven to 350F (175C). Prepare Greek White Sauce. Pour over layered mixture in baking pan. Bake 1 hour. Makes 6 servings.

Stuffed Grape Leaves
DOLMATHAKIA YALADZI

1/3 cup vegetable oil
3 onions, grated
1 cup uncooked long-grain white rice
Water
1/2 cup pine nuts
2 tablespoons chopped fresh dill
2 tablespoons chopped parsley
1 tablespoon chopped mint
1/2 teaspoon salt
1/8 teaspoon pepper
1 teaspoon sugar
16 fresh or canned grape leaves
2 tablespoons lemon juice
3 tablespoons butter, melted

Heat oil in a large saucepan. Add onions and rice; sauté until onions are transparent. Add 1 cup hot water, pine nuts, dill, parsley, mint, salt, pepper and sugar. Cover and cook over low heat about 10 minutes; set aside to cool.
To use fresh grape leaves, bring 3 cups water to a boil. Dip fresh leaves in boiling water several times to scald. Immediately rinse under cold water; drain on paper towels.
To use canned leaves, drain off liquid.
To complete, arrange 4 leaves over bottom of a large saucepan. Arrange remaining leaves on a flat surface with inside of leaves up. Place 1 to 2 teaspoons rice mixture on each leaf on flat surface. Fold leaf sides over filling; roll up leaves. Place rolled stuffed leaves in pan. Add lemon juice, butter and 1 cup hot water. Place a heatproof plate on top of stuffed leaves. Cover and cook slowly 30 to 40 minutes. Serve cool with chilled yogurt. Makes 12 stuffed grape leaves.

Baked Vegetables
TURLU FURNO

3 small eggplants, peeled, cut in 1/4-inch slices
Salt
3 medium potatoes, peeled, cut in wedges
5 medium zucchini, cut in 1/4-inch slices
1 tablespoon chopped fresh dill
1 tablespoon chopped parsley
1/4 cup olive oil
1 onion, finely chopped
1 garlic clove, finely chopped
Pepper
1-1/2 cups stock or broth
1 tablespoon fresh breadcrumbs
3 tablespoons grated Parmesan cheese
3 medium tomatoes, peeled, cut in wedges

Butter a large baking dish; set aside. Sprinkle both sides of eggplant slices with salt; let stand 1 hour. Rinse and pat dry with paper towels. In buttered dish, arrange eggplant slices, potatoes, zucchini, dill and parsley. Preheat oven to 350F (175C). Heat oil in a medium skillet. Add onion and garlic; sauté until transparent. Stir into eggplant mixture. Stir in salt, pepper and stock or broth. Cover and bake 45 minutes. In a small bowl, combine breadcrumbs and 1 tablespoon cheese. After baking eggplant mixture 45 minutes, stir tomatoes and crumb mixture into vegetable mixture. Bake 15 minutes longer or until tomatoes are cooked. Sprinkle with remaining cheese. Serve hot. Makes 4 servings.

Beef with Chestnuts
KREAS ME KASTANA

1 lb. whole chestnuts
Boiling water
3 tablespoons butter
2 onions, finely chopped
1-1/2 lbs. beef cubes for stew
3-1/2 cups beef stock or broth
1 teaspoon salt
1/8 teaspoon white pepper

To peel chestnuts, cut a cross in pointed end of each chestnut. Drop into boiling water; boil until shells split open, about 20 minutes. Peel chestnuts. Melt butter in a large saucepan. Add onions; sauté until browned. Add beef cubes; stirring constantly, cook until browned. In a small saucepan, heat stock or broth; pour over beef mixture. Stir in salt and white pepper. Cover and cook over low heat 1 to 1-1/2 hours or until beef is tender. About 20 minutes before end of cooking time, stir in shelled chestnuts. Cook with beef until soft but still whole. Spoon into a serving bowl or crock. Serve with cooked cauliflower. Makes 4 servings.

Variation

Substitute drained canned chestnuts for fresh chestnuts. Add to beef; heat through.

Fried Liver

SIKOTAKJA LADORIGHANI I TAGHANITA

1-1/2 lbs. lambs' or calves' liver
1/3 cup olive oil
1 teaspoon salt
1/8 teaspoon white pepper
Juice of 2 lemons
2 tablespoons chopped fresh basil or 1 tablespoon dried leaf basil
1 teaspoon chopped parsley

Cut liver into 1-3/4-inch pieces. Heat oil in a large skillet. Add liver pieces; cook 3 minutes over high heat, stirring constantly. Reduce heat to low. Season liver with salt and white pepper; sprinkle with lemon juice and basil. Cook 6 minutes longer, stirring occasionally. Spoon into a serving bowl. Sprinkle parsley over cooked liver. Serve with a salad of endive or lettuce, onion rings, green peppers, tomatoes and ripe olives. Makes 4 servings.

Cook's Tip

If you can get fresh wild marjoram, use instead of basil. Because of its strong flavor, use only 1 teaspoon chopped wild marjoram leaves.

Piquant Liver

SIKOTAKJA MARINATA

1/3 cup all-purpose flour
Salt and white pepper
1-1/2 lbs. calves' liver, cut in 1/2-inch slices
1/3 cup olive oil
1/3 cup water
1-1/2 cups tomato juice
1 rosemary sprig or 1/2 teaspoon dried leaf rosemary
1 bay leaf
1 teaspoon sugar
3 to 4 tablespoons red-wine vinegar
2 garlic cloves
2 tablespoons chopped parsley

Season flour with salt and white pepper; use to coat liver slices. Heat oil in a large skillet. Add floured liver; cook 3 to 4 minutes on each side. Place cooked liver on a deep platter or shallow dish; keep warm. Add remaining seasoned flour to skillet; stir in water and tomato juice. Add rosemary, bay leaf, sugar and enough vinegar to give liver a slightly sharp flavor. Crush garlic with a little salt. Add garlic-salt mixture to sauce; simmer 5 to 6 minutes. Remove and discard rosemary sprig, if used, and bay leaf. Pour hot sauce over liver. Sprinkle with parsley. Serve hot or cold. Makes 4 servings.

Spinach Pie
SPANAKOPITA

3/4 (1-1/4-lb.) pkg. frozen puff pastry or 1 (1-lb.) pkg. frozen filo dough
1-1/2 lbs. fresh spinach
1/4 cup butter
5 or 6 green onions or 5 shallots, finely chopped
1 garlic clove, finely chopped
2 teaspoons salt
1/4 teaspoon white pepper
1/8 teaspoon grated nutmeg
4 eggs
6 tablespoons half and half
4 to 5 tablespoons fresh breadcrumbs
1/4 cup crumbled feta cheese (1 oz.)
1/2 cup butter, melted for filo dough
1 egg yolk, beaten

Thaw puff pastry or filo dough. Clean spinach; tear into pieces. Set spinach aside. Melt 1/4 cup butter in a large skillet. Add green onions or shallots and garlic; sauté until onions or shallots are transparent. Add spinach; simmer 8 to 10 minutes. Drain well; return drained spinach mixture to skillet. Stir in salt, white pepper and nutmeg. In a medium bowl, beat whole eggs; stir in half and half. Stir into spinach mixture. Stir in breadcrumbs and cheese. Preheat oven to 400F (205C).

To use puff pastry, on a lightly floured surface, roll out thawed puff pastry 1/8 inch thick. Cut into 6 rectangles, 12" x 10" each.

To use filo dough, brush each sheet with melted butter.

To complete, rinse a baking sheet with cold water. Place 2/3 of either dough on wet baking sheet, with edges of dough extending beyond sides of sheet. Spread with spinach mixture; fold sides of dough over filling. Arrange remaining sheets of pastry or filo over top, tucking edges under. Prick top in several places; decorate top as shown, if desired. Brush top with beaten egg yolk. Bake in center of oven, 40 to 50 minutes or until golden brown. Cut pie into squares; serve hot. Makes 4 to 6 servings.

Leg of Lamb with Herbs
ARNI BOUTI STO CHARTI

1 lemon
1/4 cup chopped fresh thyme, oregano and rosemary or 2 tablespoons
    dried mixed herbs
1 tablespoon prepared mustard
1 teaspoon green peppercorns
1/2 teaspoon ground allspice
1 (1-1/2- to 2-lb.) boneless lamb leg roast
3 garlic cloves, cut in thin slivers
1 tablespoon cornstarch dissolved in a little water
1 teaspoon dried leaf mint

Preheat oven to 375F (190C). Grate peel of lemon; remove white pith. Slice lemon; set aside. In a small bowl, make a paste by combining grated lemon peel, herbs, mustard, peppercorns and allspice. With a pointed knife, make small slits in lamb. Fill slits with paste; insert garlic slivers to hold in paste. Oil a large piece of parchment paper or brown paper; place lamb on oiled paper. Arrange lemon slices over lamb. Fold paper over lamb and lemon slices. Overwrap in an ungreased piece of parchment paper or brown paper. Tie with kitchen string; place in a roasting pan. Roast 1 to 1-1/2 hours or until tender. Remove wrappings from lamb; pour cooking juices from wrappings into roasting pan. Place lamb on a platter; keep hot. Stirring constantly, add cornstarch mixture to hot lamb juices. Stirring constantly, cook until slightly thickened. Stir in mint; pour into a serving dish. Serve lamb and sauce separately. Makes 4 servings.

Cook's Tip
Green peppercorns are available in gourmet shops.

Grilled Meat Kabobs
SUWLAKJA

1-1/2-lbs. boneless pork or lamb, cut in 1-1/2-inch cubes
Vegetable oil

Marinade:
1/2 cup olive oil
1/4 cup dry white wine
3 tablespoons lemon juice
1/2 teaspoon pepper
1 teaspoon salt
1 teaspoon chopped fresh oregano
1 teaspoon chopped fresh thyme

Place meat cubes in a deep bowl. In a small bowl, combine marinade ingredients; pour over meat cubes. Cover and refrigerate 12 hours, turning meat occasionally while marinating. Preheat a barbecue grill or broiler. Drain meat, reserving marinade. Slide marinated meat cubes onto 4 long metal or wooden skewers. Place on grill or under broiler 3-1/4 inches from heat. Cook about 20 minutes, turning frequently and basting with oil and reserved marinade, if desired. Serve with cooked carrots and rice that have been sprinkled with a little fresh or dried thyme or oregano. Makes 4 servings.

Cook's Tip
Soak wooden skewers 30 minutes in water before using on a grill.

Greece

Baklava
BAKLAWA

1 (1-lb.) pkg. frozen filo dough (20 sheets)
1 lb. chopped walnuts (3-1/2 cups)
1/4 cup fresh breadcrumbs
1/3 cup sugar
1 teaspoon ground cinnamon
1/2 teaspoon ground cloves
1 cup plus 2 tablespoons butter, melted

Syrup:
1 cup sugar
1 cup water
5 tablespoons honey
Juice and grated peel of 1 lemon

Thaw filo dough. To prevent drying, keep filo covered with a slightly damp cloth or plastic wrap until used. Lightly butter a 13'' x 9'' baking pan; set aside. In a large bowl, combine nuts, breadcrumbs, sugar, cinnamon and cloves. Preheat oven to 350F (175C). Place 1 filo sheet in buttered pan, folding to fit in pan. Lightly brush with melted butter. Repeat with 5 more filo sheets. Spread with about 1 cup nut mixture; cover with 3 filo sheets, brushing each with butter. Top with about 1 cup nut mixture, then 3 more filo sheets, brushing each with melted butter; repeat layers. After layering final cup of nut mixture, layer final 5 sheets of filo, buttering each as before. Brush any remaining butter over top filo sheet. Use a sharp knife to cut or score top layers of filo in diamond shapes. Bake 40 to 50 minutes or until golden brown.
To make syrup, in a small saucepan, combine sugar, water, honey, lemon juice and lemon peel. Bring to a boil; boil 10 minutes. Pour hot syrup evenly over top of baked baklava as it comes from oven. Cool to room temperature; cut through remaining layers, following scoring. Makes about 24 pieces.

Semolina Cake
RAVANI

1-1/3 cups all-purpose flour
1 tablespoon baking powder
1/4 teaspoon salt
6 eggs, separated
3/4 cup sugar
3/4 cup plus 2 tablespoons butter, room temperature
Grated peel of 1 orange
1 cup semolina, farina or regular Cream of Wheat
6 tablespoons orange juice
3/4 cup flaked almonds

Syrup:
1-1/4 cups sugar
1/2 cup water
1 tablespoon brandy or lemon juice

Butter a 13'' x 9'' baking pan; set aside. Preheat oven to 350F (175C). Sift together flour, baking powder and salt; set aside. In a medium bowl, beat egg whites until stiff, gradually adding 1/2 of the sugar; set aside. In another medium bowl, cream butter with remaining sugar, egg yolks and grated orange peel. Stir in flour mixture; semolina, farina or Cream of Wheat; orange juice and almonds. Fold in beaten egg whites. Pour batter into buttered pan. Bake in center of oven 30 to 35 minutes or until golden brown. Cool in pan.
To make syrup, combine sugar and water in a small saucepan. Bring to a boil; boil 5 minutes. Stir in brandy or lemon juice. Immediately pour syrup over cake. To serve, cut cake into 2-inch squares. Makes about 24 (2-inch) squares.

Chicken Soup with Kohlrabi
KALARÁBÉLEVES

2 qts. water
2 teaspoons salt
2 onions
1 (3-lb.) stewing chicken
4 kohlrabi, peeled, cut in 1/2-inch cubes
2 tablespoons butter, room temperature
2 tablespoons all-purpose flour
3 tablespoons chopped parsley

In a large pot, bring water to a boil. Add salt, onions and chicken. Simmer 2 hours or until chicken is tender. Skim foam from surface until surface is clear. Remove cooked chicken from pot. Strain cooking liquid; skim off fat. Discard onions. Pour 5-1/2 cups strained cooking liquid back into pot. Add kohlrabi cubes. Cover and cook over low heat 30 minutes. Remove and discard skin and bones from chicken. Cut meat into 1/2-inch cubes. Return chicken cubes to pot; continue cooking until kohlrabi is tender. Use your fingers to work butter and flour into a ball. Add to soup; beat gently with a whisk until soup thickens slightly. Simmer soup 10 minutes longer. Pour into a tureen or serve in individual bowls; sprinkle with parsley. Serve hot. Makes 6 servings.

Paprika Stew
SERTÉSPÖRKÖLT

1/4 cup lard or vegetable shortening
3 onions, coarsely chopped
1 tablespoon sweet paprika
Water
1-1/4 lbs. boneless pork, cut in 1-1/4-inch cubes
1 to 2 teaspoons salt
1 garlic clove
3 green bell peppers, chopped
2 tomatoes, peeled, quartered

Melt lard or shortening in a large saucepan. Add onions; sauté until transparent. Add paprika and 1 tablespoon water; stir in quickly. Add pork cubes; season with salt. Cover and simmer 50 minutes or until pork is nearly tender, adding more water as needed. Crush garlic with a little salt. Add garlic-salt mixture, green peppers and tomatoes to pork mixture. Cover and cook 20 minutes longer or until pork and vegetables are tender. Pour into a tureen or serve in individual bowls. Makes 4 servings.

Variation

For a hotter stew, cook 1 or 2 whole green chilies with pork. Remove before serving.

Hungarian Goulash
(center front)
MAGYAR GULYÁS

1/4 cup vegetable shortening
5 large onions, cut in rings
1-1/2 lbs. beef-round steak, cut in 3/4-inch
  cubes
1 teaspoon salt
1 tablespoon sweet paprika
2 tablespoons tomato paste
1 teaspoon caraway seeds
5-1/2 cups hot beef stock or broth
1 teaspoon red (cayenne) pepper
Potato Dumplings or Bread Dumplings,
  page 9

Melt shortening in a large saucepan. Add onions; sauté until browned. Add beef; cook until browned on all sides. Add salt, sweet paprika, tomato paste, caraway seeds and enough hot stock or broth to cover. Cover and cook 2 hours. Season with red pepper. Serve with Potato Dumplings or Bread Dumplings. Serve in a large bowl or platter. Makes 4 servings.

Szeged Goulash
(top left)
SZÉKELY GULYÁS

3 tablespoons lard
2 onions, finely chopped
1 tablespoon sweet paprika
1/4 cup water
1-1/2 lbs. boneless pork, cut in 1-1/4-inch
  cubes
1 teaspoon salt
3 green bell peppers, chopped
2 garlic cloves, chopped
1 teaspoon caraway seeds
3 tablespoons tomato paste
2 cups drained sauerkraut
2 tablespoons all-purpose flour
1/3 cup dairy sour cream

Melt lard in a large saucepan. Add onions; sauté until transparent. Stir in paprika and 3 tablespoons water. When water has evaporated, add pork and salt. Cover and simmer 10 minutes. Add green peppers, garlic and caraway seeds. Blend tomato paste and remaining 1 tablespoon water; add to pork mixture. Cook 20 minutes. Stir in sauerkraut; cook 30 minutes longer. In a small bowl, combine flour and sour cream to make a paste. Stir in about 1/4 cup hot cooking liquid from pork mixture. Stir into pork mixture; stir until thickened. Cook 10 minutes longer. Serve on a large platter. Makes 4 to 6 servings.

Veal Paprika
(top right)
BORJUPAPRIKÁS

1/4 cup vegetable shortening
2 onions, finely chopped
1 tablespoon sweet paprika
Water
1-1/2 lbs. boneless veal, cut in 1-1/4-inch
  cubes
1 teaspoon salt
2 green bell peppers, chopped
2 tomatoes, peeled, chopped
2 teaspoons all-purpose flour
3/4 cup dairy sour cream

Melt shortening in a large saucepan. Add onions; sauté until transparent. Sprinkle with paprika. Add 2 tablespoons water, veal and salt. Cover and cook 10 minutes, stirring occasionally. Add green peppers and tomatoes. Cover and cook 30 minutes; add water, if needed. Stir flour into sour cream. Stir in 1/4 cup hot cooking liquid from veal mixture. Stir flour mixture into veal mixture; cook until slightly thickened. Serve in a large bowl or platter. Makes 4 to 6 servings.

Debrecin Steak
DEBRECENI ROSTÉLYOS

4 beef-round eye steaks
Salt
2 tablespoons all-purpose flour
1/4 cup lard
3 onions, coarsely chopped
3 tablespoons sweet paprika
1/8 teaspoon dried leaf marjoram
1/2 teaspoon caraway seeds
1 garlic clove, crushed
Water
4 medium potatoes, peeled, cut in quarters
4 green bell peppers, cut in strips
4 tomatoes, peeled, cut in quarters
4 frankfurters, cut in 1-1/2-inch slices

Season beef with a little salt; coat with flour. Melt lard in a large skillet. Add beef; lightly brown on both sides. Place browned beef in a large saucepan. Brown onions in pan drippings. Sprinkle with 1 to 1-1/2 teaspoons salt, paprika, marjoram, caraway seeds and garlic. Add 6 tablespoons water. Stirring occasionally, bring to a boil; pour over beef. Cover and simmer beef mixture 40 to 50 minutes, adding a little hot water, if needed. Arrange potatoes, green peppers, tomatoes and frankfurters over top of beef. Add enough hot water to half cover. Cover and cook 20 minutes longer. Serve in a large bowl. Makes 4 servings.

Paprika Chicken
PAPRIKÁS CSIRKE

2 (2- to 3-lb.) roasting chickens
2 tablespoons lard
2 onions, finely chopped
1 garlic clove, finely chopped
2 tablespoons sweet paprika
1 cup chicken stock or broth
1/3 cup dairy sour cream
Salt and white pepper

Cut each chicken into quarters. Melt lard in a large skillet. Add chicken quarters; brown on all sides. Remove chicken from pan; pour off all but 1 tablespoon pan drippings. Add onions and garlic to skillet; sauté until browned. Stir in paprika and stock or broth; bring to a boil. Return browned chicken to pan. Cover and simmer 30 minutes or until chicken is tender. Stir in sour cream; season with salt and white pepper. Serve on a platter. Serve with cooked rice and a green salad. Makes 4 servings.

Paprika & Tomato Casserole

PAPRIKÁS-PARADICSOMOS
LECSÓ

4 green or yellow bell peppers
3 to 4 bacon slices, diced
1 large onion, coarsely chopped
3 or 4 small tomatoes, peeled, cut
  in quarters
2 teaspoons sweet paprika
1/2 teaspoon salt
1/8 teaspoon black pepper

Cut bell peppers in half.
Remove seeds; cut into
crosswise strips. Fry bacon in a
stovetop casserole. Add onion;
sauté until browned. Add
bell-pepper strips; sauté with
onion and bacon 5 minutes.
Add tomatoes, paprika, salt and
black pepper. Cover and
simmer 30 to 40 minutes,
stirring occasionally, until
vegetables are tender. Serve
with rice and scrambled eggs,
an omelet or sausages. Makes 4
servings.

Variations

Make with combinations of
tomatoes and eggplant,
tomatoes and zucchini or
tomatoes and fennel. Or, make
with a combination of
tomatoes, eggplant, zucchini
and fennel.

Lamb Korma
KORMA

6 dried red chilies
8 cashews
2 onions, chopped
1 garlic clove, finely chopped
2 teaspoons finely chopped fresh gingerroot
Water
1/2 teaspoon ground cumin
2 teaspoons ground coriander
1/4 teaspoon ground cardamom
1/4 teaspoon ground cinnamon
1/4 teaspoon ground cloves
1/2 teaspoon saffron threads
1 tablespoon Clarified Butter, page 9
2-1/4 lbs. lean lamb, cut in 1-1/4-inch cubes
2 teaspoons salt
2/3 cup plain yogurt
1 tablespoon chopped cilantro or parsley
2 tablespoons grated coconut, if desired

Break open chilies; remove seeds. In a blender, puree seedless chilies, cashews, 1/2 of the onions, garlic, gingerroot and 1/3 cup water. Add cumin, coriander, cardamom, cinnamon and cloves. Continue to puree in blender until thick and smooth. In a small bowl, pour 1 to 2 teaspoons boiling water over saffron; set aside to soak. Heat clarified butter in a large saucepan. Add remaining onions; sauté until transparent. Stir in seasoning puree; cook until butter comes to surface. Add 1/3 cup water; cook until slightly reduced. Stir in lamb, saffron mixture, salt and yogurt. Cover and cook 1 hour. Spoon into a serving dish. To serve, sprinkle with cilantro or parsley and coconut, if desired. Makes 6 servings.

Kofta Curry
KOFTA KARI

1 dried red chili
1-1/2 lbs. boneless lamb, finely ground twice
1-1/2 cups dry white breadcrumbs
1 egg, beaten
1 teaspoon chopped fresh gingerroot
1/8 teaspoon ground cinnamon
1/4 teaspoon ground cardamom
Salt
1 fresh green chili
2 tablespoons vegetable oil
2 onions, coarsely chopped
1/2 teaspoon ground turmeric
1/2 teaspoon ground cumin
1 teaspoon crushed coriander seeds
3 whole cloves
1/2 teaspoon sugar
3-1/2 cups stock or broth
2 tablespoons grated coconut

Break dried red chili in half; remove seeds. Crush red chili in a large bowl. Stir in lamb, breadcrumbs, egg, gingerroot, cinnamon, cardamom and 1 teaspoon salt. Cover and refrigerate 1 hour. To handle fresh chili, cover your hands with rubber or plastic gloves; after handling, do not touch your face or eyes. Cut green chili in half; remove and discard seeds and pith. Chop green chili; set aside. Heat oil in a large skillet. Add onions; sauté until transparent. Add chopped fresh chili, turmeric, cumin, coriander seeds, cloves, sugar and 1/2 teaspoon salt. Stirring occasionally, cook 3 to 5 minutes. Add stock or broth; bring to a boil. Boil 3 minutes. Shape chilled lamb mixture into small balls. Add lamb balls, being sure all are immersed in boiling stock or broth; simmer 15 minutes. Spoon into a serving bowl; sprinkle with coconut. Makes 4 servings.

Chicken Dhansak & Chapatis
DHANSAK/CHAPATIS

1 cup dried red lentils
Water
1/4 cup vegetable oil
1 large onion, finely chopped
2 garlic cloves, finely chopped
1 (3-lb.) chicken, cut in pieces
3-1/2 cups chicken stock or broth
2 or 3 fresh green chilies
4 green onions, white part only, chopped
6 tomatoes, peeled, chopped
3 medium potatoes, peeled, coarsely chopped
2 teaspoons salt
1/2 teaspoon ground cardamom
1/2 teaspoon ground cumin
1/4 teaspoon pepper
1/4 teaspoon ground ginger
1/4 teaspoon ground turmeric
1/8 teaspoon ground cloves
1 teaspoon chopped cilantro or parsley
1/2 teaspoon chopped fresh mint

Chapatis:
3-3/4 cups all-purpose flour
1 teaspoon salt
2 tablespoons vegetable oil
About 1 cup warm water (110F, 45C)

Prepare chapatis dough. In a large saucepan, combine lentils and water to cover. Bring to a boil; remove from heat. Cover and let stand 1 hour. Heat oil in a wok or large skillet. Add onion and garlic; sauté until transparent. Add chicken; cook over high heat until golden brown. Remove browned chicken; set aside. Drain lentils; add to wok or skillet. Stir in stock or broth. Simmer lentil mixture until lentils are tender. To handle fresh chilies, cover your hands with rubber or plastic gloves. After handling, do not touch your face or eyes. Cut chilies in halves; remove and discard seeds and pith. Chop chilies. Add chopped chilies, green onions, tomatoes, potatoes, salt, cardamom, cumin, pepper, ginger, turmeric and cloves to lentil mixture. Cook 30 minutes; return browned chicken to pan. Cook 1 hour longer or until chicken falls from bones. Complete chapatis. Spoon chicken mixture onto a deep platter. Sprinkle with cilantro or parsley and mint.

To make chapatis, in a large bowl, stir together flour and salt. Stir in oil and enough warm water to make a smooth firm dough. Knead 10 to 12 minutes; shape into a ball. Wrap in foil; let stand 1 to 3 hours. Shape dough into balls about the size of walnuts. On a lightly floured board, roll out each ball of dough to a very thin circle. Heat a large cast-iron skillet or flat griddle until very hot. Cook chapatis on ungreased skillet or griddle 1 minute on each side, beginning with first chapatis rolled out. During cooking, gently press down edge of chapatis with a spatula or folded cloth. This causes small air bubbles to form that make chapatis lighter. Wrap cooked chapatis in a cloth until all are cooked. Makes 8 servings.

Cook's Tip
Chapatis is unleavened bread and is similar to flour tortillas.

Eggs on Shrimp & Beef

NASI GORENG

2 eggs
Salt and pepper
6 tablespoons vegetable oil
2 onions, chopped
2 garlic cloves, chopped
1/2 teaspoon shrimp paste
8 oz. fresh shrimp, peeled, deveined
1 lb. boneless beef top loin or sirloin, cut in 2" x 1/8" strips
6 green onions, cut in strips
1-1/2 cups cooked long-grain white rice
2 tablespoons soy sauce
3 tablespoons canned French-fried onion rings
6 fried eggs, if desired

In a small bowl, beat 2 eggs with a little salt and pepper. Heat 1-1/2 teaspoons oil in a large skillet. Pour egg mixture into skillet; cook eggs as for an omelet. Roll up; set aside to cool. In a blender or food processor, puree 2 onions, garlic and shrimp paste. Heat 3 tablespoons oil in a wok or large skillet. Add onion puree; stir constantly until heated through. Add shrimp and beef; cook 5 minutes, stirring constantly. Stir in remaining oil, green onions and rice; cook 3 minutes. Cut rolled omelet into thin slices. Stir omelet slices and soy sauce into shrimp mixture. Spoon onto 6 plates; garnish with canned onion rings. Top each portion with a fried egg, if desired. Makes 6 servings.

Vegetables with Peanut Sauce

GADO-GADO

Peanut Sauce, page 112
4 medium potatoes, peeled, sliced
1 lb. fresh green beans, trimmed, cut in pieces
4 carrots, cut in julienne strips
1/2 head Chinese cabbage, shredded
Water
Salt
1/2 cucumber, sliced
2 bunches watercress, trimmed
4 hard-cooked eggs, cut in quarters
2 cups fresh or canned bean sprouts
1/2 teaspooon white pepper

Prepare Peanut Sauce; set aside. Cook potatoes, beans, carrots and cabbage separately in lightly salted water until crisp-tender. Drain vegetables. Arrange cooked vegetables, cucumber, watercress, eggs and bean sprouts on 4 plates, as shown. Sprinkle white pepper on potatoes. Serve with Peanut Sauce. Makes 4 servings.

Beef Satay with Peanut Sauce
SATAY DAGING/SAUS KACANG PEDIS

Peanut Sauce:
1/3 cup peanut oil
1 tablespoon dried onion flakes
1 garlic clove, crushed
1/4 teaspoon shrimp paste
1 to 2 teaspoons hot chili sauce
1/4 cup smooth peanut butter
1/3 cup water
1/2 teaspoon salt
1 tablespoon soy sauce
2 teaspoons sugar
1 tablespoon lemon juice

Beef Satay:
4 small red onions, grated
2 garlic cloves, grated
1 teaspoon grated lemon peel
1 teaspoon ground coriander
1 teaspoon ground caraway seeds
1 teaspoon ground ginger
1/2 teaspoon salt
1/8 teaspoon sugar
1 lb. beef top round, 1-inch thick,
  cut in long thin slices
5 tablespoons vegetable oil

To make sauce, heat peanut oil in a medium skillet. Add onion flakes; sauté until golden. Drain onions on paper towels. Remove all but 2 tablespoons oil from pan. To remaining oil, add garlic, shrimp paste and chili sauce. Stirring often, cook about 3 minutes. Stir in peanut butter and water; bring to a boil. Stirring occasionally, boil until sauce is thick and smooth. Stir in salt, soy sauce, sugar and lemon juice. Set aside until cool; stir in sautéed onion flakes.

To prepare beef, in a medium bowl, combine red onions, garlic, lemon peel, coriander, caraway seeds, ginger, salt and sugar. Rub onion mixture into beef. Cover and marinate 1 hour. Preheat barbecue grill or broiler. Drain beef strips. Thread beef strips onto metal or wooden skewers. Cook 4 to 6 minutes, frequently turning and brushing with oil. Serve hot with peanut sauce. Serve cucumber chunks and onion slices as accompaniments. Makes 4 servings.

Cook's Tip

Soak wooden skewers in water about 30 minutes before skewering and grilling or broiling meat.

Spinach Soup with Meatballs
ASH SAK

2-1/4 lbs. lamb bones, cut in pieces
Water
3 onions, 2 chopped, 1 cut in rings
3 cups chopped spinach
3 tablespoons chopped parsley
6 tablespoons uncooked long-grain white rice
2/3 cup fresh or frozen peas
Salt
4 teaspoons ground turmeric
1/2 lb. ground lamb
1 shallot or small onion, finely chopped
1 egg, beaten
1/3 teaspoon ground cinnamon
2 tablespoons vegetable oil
1/4 cup butter
1/4 cup chopped fresh mint
1-1/3 cups plain yogurt

In a large pot, cover bones with water. Boil 10 minutes; drain and rinse under cold water. Return bones to pot; add 5-1/2 cups water. Bring to a boil. Skim foam from surface until surface is clear. Simmer 1 hour; strain and discard bones. Pour cooking liquid back into same pot. Add chopped onions, spinach, parsley, 1/4 cup rice, peas, 1 tablespoon salt and 1-1/2 teaspoons turmeric. Cover and simmer 20 minutes. In a large bowl, combine lamb, remaining rice, shallot or onion, egg, cinnamon and 1/8 teaspoon salt. Shape into small balls. Add to hot soup; simmer 15 minutes. Heat oil in a medium skillet; add onion rings. Sauté onion rings until browned; set aside. Melt butter in a small skillet. Stir in mint and remaining turmeric. Stir into soup. Spoon yogurt evenly into 4 individual bowls or mugs. Ladle soup and meatballs over yogurt; top with sautéed onion rings. Makes 4 servings.

Sweet & Sour Meatballs
HODU KABAB

1/2 lb. boneless lean lamb, diced
2 cups water
1/2 cup dried lentils
Salt
1/8 teaspoon ground cloves
1/2 teaspoon ground cardamom
1/2 teaspoon ground cinnamon
1/8 teaspoon saffron threads
4 hard-cooked eggs, chopped
6 prunes, chopped
1 tablespoon raisins, chopped
1 egg, slightly beaten
1 tablespoon sliced almonds
3 tablespoons vegetable oil
4-1/2 teaspoons butter
2 onions, finely chopped
1 cup stock or broth
1/3 cup wine vinegar
Juice of 3 lemons
2/3 cup sugar

In a large saucepan, combine lamb, water, lentils, 1/2 teaspoon salt, cloves, cardamom, cinnamon and saffron. Simmer 1 hour or until lamb and lentils are tender. Drain, reserving cooking liquid. In a blender, process cooked lamb mixture until minced. In a large bowl, combined minced lamb mixture, hard-cooked eggs, prunes, raisins, whole egg and almonds. Shape mixture into balls. Heat oil in a large skillet. Add meatballs; cook until browned. Melt butter in a medium saucepan. Add onions; sauté until transparent. Stir in stock or broth, vinegar, lemon juice, sugar and 1 cup cooking liquid. Boil until slightly reduced. Season with salt. Add cooked meatballs; simmer in sauce 5 minutes. Spoon into a shallow serving bowl. Makes 4 servings.

Date & Nut Cake
GILACGI

1-1/2 cups chopped dates
6 tablespoons water
2 tablespoons honey
1 tablespoon lemon juice
1/2 teaspoon ground cinnamon
3/4 cup chopped walnuts
1 tablespoon dry breadcrumbs
1-1/4 cups semolina, farina or
    regular Cream of Wheat cereal
1-1/4 cups all-purpose flour
1 teaspoon baking powder
1/4 cup sugar
1/2 teaspoon vanilla extract
1/2 cup plus 1 tablespoon butter,
    melted

Combine dates and water in a small saucepan. Bring water to a boil; simmer 5 minutes, stirring constantly. Stir in honey, lemon juice, cinnamon and nuts. Remove from heat. Preheat oven to 400F (205C). Butter a round 8-1/2-inch cake pan; sprinkle with breadcrumbs. In a large bowl, combine semolina, farina or Cream of Wheat; flour; baking powder and sugar. Sprinkle vanilla over mixture. Stir in butter. Spoon half of the mixture into buttered cake pan; press over bottom and up side of pan. Spoon date mixture evenly over top. Sprinkle remaining flour mixture over date mixture. Bake in center of oven 35 to 40 minutes or until golden brown. Cool, then slice. Makes 6 to 8 servings.

Gefilte Fish
GEFILTE FISCH

1 oven-ready carp or pike
2 medium onions, chopped
Water
1 egg white
1/2 lb. sea-trout fillet, chopped
2 tablespoons chopped almonds
1 hard-cooked egg, chopped
5 tablespoons dry breadcrumbs
1 tablespoon sugar
1 teaspoon salt
2 large carrots, thinly sliced
1 scant cup white wine or fish stock

Preheat oven to 350F (175C). Slice carp or pike into 8 thick slices. Place onions in a sieve. Lower sieve into boiling water so onions are covered. Blanch 15 seconds; immediately rinse with cold water. In a medium bowl, beat egg white until stiff. Stir in blanched onions, trout, almonds, hard-cooked egg, breadcrumbs, sugar and salt. Use to stuff cavity of fish slices. In a shallow dish, re-assemble fish slices, as shown. Scatter carrots around fish; pour wine or stock over fish. Cover and bake 20 minutes. Increase heat to 375F (190C). Bake 10 minutes longer. Makes 8 servings.

Variation

Substitute matzo meal for breadcrumbs.

Kreplach
KREPLACH

2 eggs
Salt
1 tablespoon vegetable oil
1 to 1-1/2 cups all-purpose flour
1 cup diced cooked beef or poultry
2 teaspoons chopped parsley
2 teaspoons finely chopped onion
1 tablespoon goose fat or vegetable oil
1/8 teaspoon pepper
1/8 teaspoon ground ginger
Water

In a medium bowl, beat eggs with 1/2 teaspoon salt and 1 tablespoon oil. Gradually add enough flour to make a firm dough. Roll out dough as thin as possible; cut into 2-inch squares. Process beef or poultry in a blender or food processor until finely ground. In a small bowl, combine ground meat, parsley, onion, goose fat or oil, 1/2 teaspoon salt, pepper and ginger. Spoon about 1/2 teaspoon meat filling onto center of each square of dough. Fold dough over filling making triangles. Dip tines of a fork into flour; crimp edges firmly together with fork. Let filled triangles stand on a floured surface 1 hour. Bring 2 quarts water to a gentle boil. Add filled triangles, a few at a time. Cook 15 minutes. Makes 10 kreplach.

Cook's Tip

Kreplach are traditionally served in chicken soup on special occasions, such as the Jewish festival of Succoth.

Savory Blintzes
BLINTZES

Batter:
1 cup all-purpose flour
Pinch of salt
2 eggs
About 1 cup water

Savory Blintze Filling:
2 cups finely chopped cooked beef
    or poultry
Vegetable oil
2 small onions, finely chopped
1/2 teaspoon salt
1/8 teaspoon black pepper
1/8 teaspoon red (cayenne) pepper
1 egg, slightly beaten

To make batter, in a medium bowl, stir together flour and salt. Beat in eggs; gradually beat in enough water to make a smooth, thin batter. Let stand 30 minutes.

To make filling, process meat in a blender or food processor until finely ground. Heat 1 tablespoon oil in a small skillet. Add onions; sauté until browned. In a medium bowl, combine ground meat, sautéed onions, salt, black pepper, red pepper and egg.

To complete, heat 1 teaspoon oil in a 7-inch skillet. Pour in 1 tablespoon batter; swirl in pan to make a thin coating. Cook on one side only until underside is golden and top is firm. Repeat with remaining batter. With browned side down, spread each blintze with a little meat mixture. Fold in half, then in quarters. Heat about 1 cup oil in a large skillet to 375F (190C) or until a 1-inch cube of bread turns golden brown in 50 seconds. Cook filled blintzes in hot oil until golden brown on both sides. Makes 16 blintzes.

Variation

For dessert blintzes, stuff with a mixture of ricotta cheese, honey and chopped almonds. Serve immediately.

Beef, Bean & Potato Casserole
CHOLENT

1 cup dried Great Northern beans, navy beans or white kidney beans
Water
1-1/4 lbs. beef brisket
1 large onion, finely chopped
4 medium potatoes, peeled, sliced
1 or 2 beef shanks
1 teaspoon salt
1 teaspoon sweet paprika
1 teaspoon sugar
1/8 teaspoon pepper

Soak beans in cold water to cover 12 hours. Cut brisket in 3/4-inch-thick slices. Drain beans; discard soaking water. Preheat oven to 350F (175C). In a large casserole with a tight-fitting lid, layer soaked beans, onion and 1/2 of the potatoes. Add sliced beef and shanks; top with remaining potatoes. Sprinkle with salt, paprika, sugar and pepper. Add enough boiling water to cover. Cover dish with foil, sealing well over edge; top with casserole lid. Bake 1-1/2 hours. Makes 4 to 6 servings.

Cook's Tip

Cholent is traditionally served on the Sabbath. It is prepared the day before because no cooking is done on the Sabbath in Orthodox homes.

Liver Casserole

1 lb. calves' or lambs' liver, cut in thin slices
Water
Salt
1/2 cup all-purpose flour
5 tablespoons vegetable oil
2 onions, cut in rings
5-1/2 cups stock or broth
1/8 teaspoon pepper
2 medium potatoes, peeled, sliced
2 medium apples, peeled, sliced

Soak liver in cold water 20 minutes; drain well. Generously coat liver on both sides with salt; let stand 10 minutes. Preheat oven to 350F (175C). Rinse liver; pat dry with paper towels. Coat liver with flour. Reserve leftover flour. Heat oil in a large skillet. Add liver and onions; cook until browned, stirring constantly. Remove browned liver and onions from pan. Arrange in layers in a casserole. Set aside; keep warm. Stir reserved flour into drippings in skillet. Cook until browned; gradually stir in stock or broth. Stirring constantly, simmer until slightly thickened. Season with salt and pepper. Arrange layers of potatoes and apples over liver. Pour sauce over top. Cover and bake 1-1/2 hours or until liver and vegetables are tender. Makes 4 to 6 servings.

Rice Kugel
REIS-KUGEL

1/3 cup raisins
Water
2 apples
1 large egg
Pinch of salt
1/2 cup sugar
1 cup cooked short-grain white rice
6 tablespoons butter, room temperature
1 tablespoon apricot jam
2 tablespoons ground almonds
1 tablespoon sugar

Preheat oven to 350F (175C). Butter a deep baking dish; set aside. Wash raisins in hot water; pat dry with paper towels. Peel and shred apples. In a medium bowl, beat together egg, salt and 1/2 cup sugar. Stir in washed raisins, shredded apple, rice, 1/4 cup butter, jam and almonds. Pour into buttered dish; dot with remaining 2 tablespoons butter. Sprinkle with 1 tablespoon sugar. Bake 40 minutes; serve hot. Makes 6 servings.

Gourmet Turnip Cake
KIHEN FIN VEISSERIBEN

Cake:
1/2 cup plus 1 tablespoon butter
3/4 cup sugar
3 eggs
1 cup pureed cooked turnips (2 medium)
1-1/4 cups all-purpose flour
1/2 teaspoon baking soda
1/2 teaspoon ground cinnamon
1/2 teaspoon ground nutmeg
1/8 teaspoon ground cloves
1/4 teaspoon salt
1/3 cup chopped walnuts

Frosting:
3/4 cup plus 2 tablespoons butter
2 egg yolks
4 cups powdered sugar
3/4 cup grated walnuts

To make cake, preheat oven to 350F (175C). Butter an 8-inch springform pan; sprinkle with flour. In a medium bowl, cream together butter and sugar. Beat in eggs, turnip puree, flour, baking soda, cinnamon, nutmeg, cloves, salt and chopped nuts. Pour cake batter into buttered pan. Bake 50 minutes or until a wooden pick inserted in center comes out clean. Cool on a rack 5 minutes before removing side of pan.
To complete, cream together butter, egg yolks and powdered sugar. Cut horizontally through center of cooled cake, making 2 layers. Spread 1/3 of the frosting over lower half of cake; place other half of cake on top. Spread remaining frosting over top and side of cake; sprinkle evenly with grated nuts. Refrigerate until served; refrigerate unused portion. Makes 8 to 10 servings.

Vegetable Soup
MINESTRONE

1 garlic clove, chopped
Salt
2 tablespoons vegetable oil
3 to 4 bacon slices, diced
1/4 celeriac, finely chopped
1/2 bunch celery, thinly sliced
2 tomatoes, peeled, finely chopped
1/2 red bell pepper, diced
1 carrot, diced
1 onion, finely chopped
1 potato, peeled, diced
1 zucchini, sliced
5 cups meat or vegetable stock or broth
3 tablespoons uncooked long-grain white rice
3/4 cup fresh or frozen green peas
1/4 cup grated Parmesan cheese (1 oz.)

Crush garlic with a little salt. Heat oil in a large saucepan. Add bacon; sauté until crisp. Add garlic-salt mixture, celeriac, celery, tomatoes, red pepper, carrot, onion, potato and zucchini. Cook 3 to 4 minutes, stirring constantly. Add stock or broth; bring to a boil. Cover and simmer 10 minutes. Stir in rice; simmer 15 minutes. Add peas; cook 6 minutes longer. Pour into a tureen or serve in individual bowls; sprinkle cheese over top. Makes 4 servings.

Abruzzi Celery Soup
MINESTRA DI SEDANI

2 tablespoons olive oil
1 onion, finely chopped
3 to 4 bacon slices, diced
2 tablespoons tomato paste
2 bunches celery, cut in 1/2-inch slices
1 qt. hot stock or broth
Salt and pepper
1/2 cup uncooked long-grain white rice
1/4 cup grated Parmesan cheese (1 oz.)

Heat oil in a large saucepan. Add onion and bacon; sauté until onion begins to brown. Stir in tomato paste and celery. Cook 5 minutes, stirring occasionally. Gradually stir in stock or broth. Cover and simmer 20 minutes. Season with salt and pepper. Stir rice into soup. Simmer 15 minutes or until rice is tender. Pour into a tureen or serve in individual bowls; sprinkle cheese over top. Makes 4 servings.

Tuscan Vegetable Soup
ACQUACOTTA

6 to 8 small tomatoes
1/4 cup olive oil
2 onions, finely chopped
2 red bell peppers, cut in strips
1 bunch celery, sliced
1 qt. boiling water
Salt and black pepper
4 eggs, slightly beaten
1/4 cup grated Parmesan cheese (1 oz.)
8 small white-bread slices

Peel tomatoes; remove and discard seeds. Finely chop tomatoes. Heat oil in a large saucepan. Add onions; sauté until transparent. Add red peppers and celery; continue stirring until hot. Stir in chopped tomatoes; cook 2 to 3 minutes. Cover and cook over low heat 10 minutes. Stir in boiling water; season with salt and black pepper. Cover and simmer 10 to 15 minutes. Beat eggs with cheese. Toast bread until golden brown. Remove soup from heat; adjust seasoning, if necessary. Quickly stir in egg mixture. Place 2 pieces of toast in each of 4 soup bowls. Ladle soup over toast. Makes 4 servings.

Piedmont Cabbage Soup
ZUPPA ALLA VALDOSTANA

2 cups water
1 (2-lb.) head cabbage, shredded
Salt
1 lb. day-old white bread, thinly sliced
4 cups hot stock or broth
1/4 cup butter
8 oz. fontina cheese, thinly sliced

Bring water to a boil. Add shredded cabbage and a little salt. Cover and cook 40 minutes or until tender. Drain cabbage; keep hot. Lightly butter a casserole or ovenproof tureen. Preheat oven to 425F (220C). Reserve 5 slices bread; arrange remaining bread on bottom of prepared dish. Sprinkle a little stock or broth over bread in dish. Spoon 1/4 of the drained cabbage over bread; dot with butter. Add a layer of cheese. Continue layering cabbage, butter and cheese, sprinkling each layer with a little stock or broth until all cabbage and cheese are used. Arrange reserved bread over top, as shown. Dot with remaining butter. Pour remaining stock or broth into dish. Bake 20 minutes or until butter and cheese are melted and top pieces of bread are crisp. Makes 4 servings.

Genoese Fish Stew
(left)
BURRIDA

2 lbs. mixed mackerel, squid and red snapper
3 medium tomatoes
6 tablespoons olive oil
1 garlic clove, slightly crushed
1 onion, finely chopped
2 anchovy fillets, chopped
1-1/2 cups water
3 tablespoons chopped parsley
1 bay leaf
1 teaspoon salt
1/3 cup chopped walnuts
1-1/2 cups dry white wine
4 white-bread slices, toasted

Clean, rinse and dry fish; cut into small pieces. Cut squid into rings. Peel tomatoes; remove and discard seeds. Coarsely chop tomatoes. Heat oil in a large heavy skillet or saucepan. Add garlic and onion; sauté 3 to 4 minutes. Remove and discard garlic. Add chopped tomatoes, anchovies, water, parsley, bay leaf and salt. Cover and simmer 10 minutes. Add fish and squid pieces, nuts and wine. Simmer 20 minutes or until fish flakes easily. Remove and discard bay leaf. Pour into a tureen or serve in individual bowls. Serve with toast. Makes 4 servings.

Shrimp in Garlic Oil
(right)
SCAMPI ALL' AGLIO

1 lb. fresh or frozen jumbo shrimp, peeled
1 cup olive oil
2 garlic cloves, finely chopped
1/2 teaspoon salt
Lemon wedges
Parsley or cilantro sprigs

Thaw frozen shrimp; arrange in a casserole. Preheat oven to 475F (245C). Heat oil in a large skillet. Add garlic and salt; sauté 2 minutes. Pour oil mixture over shrimp. Bake 5 minutes. Arrange on a platter. Garnish with lemon and parsley or cilantro. Makes 4 servings.

Cook's Tip

True Italian scampi are caught only in the Adriatic Sea and are characterized by their large size and delicious flavor.

Summer Risotto
RISOTTO DI ESTATE

8 oz. mushrooms
4 tomatoes
3 tablespoons olive oil
1 onion, finely chopped
2 garlic cloves, finely chopped
1-1/4 cups uncooked long-grain white rice
6 oz. prosciutto ham, diced
3-1/2 cups hot stock or broth
1-1/2 cups fresh or frozen green peas
1 cup finely grated pecorino or Romano cheese (4 oz.)
1 tablespoon chopped parsley

Trim and cut mushrooms in halves; cut large mushrooms into quarters. Peel tomatoes; remove and discard seeds. Coarsely chop tomatoes; set aside. Heat oil in a large saucepan. Add onion and garlic; sauté until transparent. Add rice; brown lightly, stirring constantly. Add ham; cook 30 seconds. Add cut mushrooms and chopped tomatoes. Pour in stock or broth. Cover and cook 20 minutes, stirring occasionally. Add more stock or broth, if needed to prevent rice from becoming too dry. Stir in peas; cook 6 minutes longer. Serve in a large bowl; sprinkle cheese and parsley over top. Serve with a radish and endive salad. Makes 4 servings.

Venetian Fennel Risotto
RISOTTO CON I FINOCCHI

1 lb. fennel
6 tablespoons butter
1 onion, finely chopped
1-1/3 cups uncooked long-grain white rice
3-1/2 cups stock or broth
1/4 cup grated Parmesan cheese (1 oz.)

Peel and trim fennel bulbs; chop and reserve fennel leaves. Cut bulb in thin slices. Melt 5 tablespoons butter in a large saucepan. Add onion and sliced fennel; sauté over low heat until fennel begins to soften. Add rice; sauté until golden brown. In a small saucepan, bring stock or broth to a gentle boil. Add about 1/2 cup boiling stock or broth to rice mixture; stir constantly until rice absorbs liquid. Gradually stir in 1-1/2 cups boiling stock or broth. Cook over low heat 20 minutes, adding more stock or broth, as needed to prevent rice from becoming dry. Stir cheese and remaining butter into cooked rice mixture. Let stand 2 to 3 minutes; spoon into a large bowl. Garnish with chopped fennel leaves. Makes 4 servings.

Variation

Substitute fresh asparagus, cut in 1-inch pieces, for fennel.

Potato Gnocchi with Meat Sauce
GNOCCHI DI PATATE

5 medium potatoes, peeled, cooked, mashed
3/4 cup all-purpose flour
2 egg yolks
Pinch of white pepper
1/8 teaspoon dried leaf marjoram
Water
1/4 cup grated Parmesan cheese (1 oz.)
2 tablespoons butter

Meat Sauce:
1/4 cup olive oil
1 onion, finely chopped
1 celery stalk, finely chopped
1 carrot, finely chopped
1/2 garlic clove, crushed
1/2 lb. ground beef
4 medium tomatoes, peeled, seeds removed, chopped
1/2 cup beef stock or broth
1/2 teaspoon salt
1/8 teaspoon white pepper
Pinch of dried leaf oregano

Prepare sauce. Combine potatoes, flour, egg yolks, white pepper and marjoram. Shape into small balls; add more flour, if needed. Bring 2 quarts water to a gentle boil. Cook potato balls in boiling water 5 minutes or until balls float to surface. Drain on paper towels. Preheat oven to 400F (205C). Arrange cooked gnocchi in a greased casserole. Sprinkle with cheese; dot with butter. Bake 10 minutes or until browned. Makes 4 servings.
To make sauce, heat oil in a saucepan. Add onion, celery, carrot and garlic; sauté until browned. Add beef; cook until browned. Add tomatoes and stock or broth; simmer 40 minutes. Stir in salt, white pepper and oregano. Simmer 1 minute. Pour into a bowl.

Cheese Gnocchi with Tomato Sauce
GNOCCHI MALLOREDDUS

2 cups milk
Salt
Pinch of ground nutmeg
1/2 cup butter
Pinch of saffron threads, if desired
1-1/2 cups all-purpose flour
6 eggs
1 cup grated Parmesan cheese (4 oz.)
Water
1/3 cup grated pecorino or Parmesan cheese (1-1/2 oz.)
4 basil sprigs

Tomato Sauce:
1/3 cup olive oil
3 garlic cloves, cut in quarters
1 tablespoon chopped basil
1 tablespoon chopped parsley
6 to 8 small tomatoes, peeled, chopped
1/2 teaspoon salt
1/8 teaspoon white pepper
1 teaspoon chopped fresh oregano

Prepare sauce. Bring milk, a pinch of salt, nutmeg, butter and saffron, if desired, to a simmer. Add flour all at once; quickly beat over high heat until mixture forms a ball. Remove from heat. Beat in eggs, 1 at a time. Stir in 1 cup Parmesan cheese. Shape into small balls or rolls, as shown. Bring 2 quarts salted water to a boil. Add gnocchi, a few at a time. Cook 5 minutes or until gnocchi float to surface; drain. Arrange on a platter. Garnish with pecorino or Parmesan cheese and basil sprigs. Serve gnocchi and sauce separately. Makes 4 servings.
To make sauce, heat oil. Add garlic; sauté until browned. Remove and discard garlic. Add basil, parsley, tomatoes, salt and white pepper. Simmer 30 minutes; stir in oregano.

Spaghetti
SPAGHETTI SVARIATI

2-1/2 qts. water
2 teaspoons salt
1 lb. green or white spaghetti

In a large pot, bring water to a rapid boil; add salt. Gradually add spaghetti, being sure water continues to boil. Stirring occasionally, cook over low heat 8 to 10 minutes or until spaghetti is tender but firm. Drain, but do not rinse. Pour into a warm bowl. Toss spaghetti with sauce before serving or serve sauce separately. Makes 4 servings.

Pesto Sauce
(center front)
PESTO ALLA GENOVESE

5 garlic cloves, finely chopped
1/3 cup pine nuts, coarsely chopped
1 teaspoon salt
1/2 cup crumbled or grated pecorino or Romano cheese (2 oz.)
1 cup grated Parmesan cheese (4 oz.)
2 cups packed chopped fresh basil leaves
1/8 teaspoon white pepper
1 cup olive oil

In a large mortar, blender or food processor, crush garlic and pine nuts with salt. Add cheeses, basil and white pepper. Crush all ingredients thoroughly. Gradually beat in oil. Serve in a separate bowl. Makes 4 servings.

Tuna Sauce
(center)
SPAGHETTI DEL FATTORE

3 medium tomatoes
3 tablespoons olive oil
1 garlic clove
8 oz. mushrooms, sliced
1 (6-1/2-oz.) can tuna, drained
1 teaspoon salt
1/8 teaspoon white pepper
1 tablespoon chopped mixed herbs

Peel tomatoes; remove and discard seeds. Chop tomatoes. Heat oil in a medium saucepan. Add garlic; sauté until browned. Remove and discard garlic. Add mushrooms and chopped tomatoes. Cover and cook over low heat 10 minutes. Flake tuna; add tuna, salt and white pepper to tomato mixture. Before serving, stir in herbs; pour into a serving bowl. Makes 4 servings.

Anchovy Sauce
(left)
SPAGHETTI ALLA GHIOTTA

1/4 cup olive oil
2 garlic cloves
6 to 8 small tomatoes, peeled, finely chopped
6 to 8 pitted green olives, coarsely chopped
6 anchovy fillets, chopped
2 tablespoons capers
1/4 teaspoon salt
1/8 teaspoon ground ginger
1 tablespoon chopped parsley

Heat oil in a medium saucepan. Add garlic; sauté until browned. Remove and discard garlic. Add tomatoes; cook 15 minutes. Add olives, anchovies and capers. Cook 10 minutes. Season with salt and ginger. Pour into a serving bowl; sprinkle with parsley. Makes 4 servings.

Noodles alla Carbonara
FETTUCCINE ALLA CARBONARA

2-1/2 qts. water
Salt
1 lb. egg noodles or fettucini
12 bacon slices, diced
1/2 cup whipping cream
2 tablespoons chopped mixed parsley, borage, sage and marjoram
1/4 cup grated Parmesan cheese (1 oz.)
Pepper
4 egg yolks, in shell halves
1 cup grated pecorino or Romano cheese (4 oz.)

In a large pot, bring water to a rapid boil; add salt. Gradually add noodles or fettucini, being sure water continues to boil. Stirring occasionally, cook over low heat 8 to 10 minutes or until tender but firm. Meanwhile, in a large skillet, cook bacon until crisp. In a small saucepan, warm cream over low heat; do not boil. Stir in herbs and Parmesan cheese. Season with salt and pepper; keep warm. Drain noodles; divide onto 4 warm plates. Pour bacon with drippings and seasoned cream over cooked noodles. Top each portion with a raw egg yolk in its shell, as shown. To serve, garnish with pecorino or Romano cheese. Makes 4 servings.

Variations

Substitute spaghetti for noodles.
Stir egg yolks into seasoned cream.

Manicotti Naples-Style
CANNELLONI ALLA NAPOLETANA

1 tablespoon olive oil
1 lb. ground beef
Salt
Water
5 oz. prosciutto or bacon, finely chopped
5 oz. mushrooms, finely chopped
5 tablespoons butter
3 tablespoons all-purpose flour
1 cup milk
White pepper
Pinch of dried leaf oregano
1 egg yolk
Tomato Sauce, page 123
10 to 12 manicotti tubes, cooked
8 mozzarella-cheese slices

Heat oil in a large saucepan. Add beef; cook until browned. Season with salt; moisten with a little hot water. Cover and simmer 15 minutes. Stir in prosciutto or bacon and mushrooms. Melt 2 tablespoons butter in a medium skillet. Stir in flour to make a paste. Slowly stir in milk. Season with white pepper and oregano. In a small bowl, beat egg yolk; stir in about 1/4 cup hot milk mixture. Stir egg-yolk mixture into remaining milk mixture, then stir sauce into beef mixture. Preheat oven to 400F (205C). Pour 1/2 of the Tomato Sauce into a large casserole. Spoon some beef filling into each cooked manicotti tube. Arrange filled tubes over tomato sauce. Pour remaining Tomato Sauce and beef mixture over filled manicotti. Dot with remaining butter. Arrange cheese slices over top. Bake 15 minutes. Serve with tomato, onion and olive salad. Makes 4 servings.

Baked Polenta with Pork

POLENTA STUFATA

Water
Salt
2 cups coarsely ground yellow cornmeal
3 large tomatoes
2 tablespoons olive oil
1/2 lb. ground pork
Pinch of red (cayenne) pepper
1/3 cup grated pecorino or Romano cheese (1-1/2 oz.)
1/3 cup grated Parmesan cheese (1-1/2 oz.)
1/4 cup butter, chilled

Bring 3 cups water to a boil; add 1/2 teaspoon salt. Meanwhile, stir cornmeal into 2 cups cold water. Stirring constantly with a wooden spoon or whisk, gradually add cornmeal mixture to boiling water. Stir constantly over medium heat until mixture returns to a boil. Stirring occasionally, cook 15 minutes longer or until mixture is smooth and firm. Rinse several large flat pans with cold water; spread cornmeal mixture 1/2 inch thick in pans. Set aside to cool. Peel tomatoes; remove and discard seeds. Chop tomatoes; set aside. Heat oil in a large skillet. Add pork; cook until browned. Add chopped tomatoes, red pepper and a pinch of salt. Cover and simmer 10 minutes. In a small bowl, combine cheeses. Cut butter into shavings; refrigerate cheeses and shaved butter. Butter a 13'' x 9'' baking dish. Preheat oven to 350F (175C). Cut cold cornmeal mixture into 3'' x 1'' strips. Arrange 1/4 of the strips over bottom of buttered dish. Over strips, layer 1/3 of the meat sauce and 1/4 each of the cheeses and butter. Continue layering until all ingredients are used. Top layer will be cornmeal strips, cheeses and butter. Bake 40 to 45 minutes. Makes 4 to 6 servings.

Lombardy Polenta Slices

POLENTA ALLA LODIGIANA

2 cups milk
1/2 teaspoon salt
1 cup finely ground yellow cornmeal
8 oz. Gruyère cheese, cut in 1/4-inch slices
1/2 cup all-purpose flour
1 egg, beaten with 1 teaspoon water
1 cup dry breadcrumbs
1/4 cup butter

In a medium saucepan, bring milk to a simmer; add salt. Stirring constantly, pour cornmeal into hot milk in a fine stream. Stirring frequently, cook over low heat 20 minutes or until mixture begins to thicken. Remove pan from heat; continue stirring 3 to 4 minutes longer. Rinse a 15 1/2''x10 1/2'' jelly-roll pan with cold water. Spread cornmeal mixture about 1/2 inch thick in pan; set aside to cool. Cut cold cornmeal and cheese slices into the same size squares, making twice as many cornmeal square. Sandwich each piece of cheese between 2 cornmeal slices. Gently press together. Dip all sides of cornmeal sandwiches in flour, then in egg mixture, then in breadcrumbs. Melt butter in a large skillet; cook cornmeal sandwiches on both sides until golden brown. Makes 4 servings.

Broccoli Cooked in Wine
BROCCOLI A CRUDO

2 lbs. broccoli
5 tablespoons olive oil
1 garlic clove, finely chopped
Salt and white pepper
1-1/2 cups dry white wine

Rinse broccoli under running cold water. Cut broccoli flowerets from stems; remove any thick stems. Cut a cross into base of remaining stems for even cooking. Heat oil in a large saucepan. Add garlic; sauté about 3 minutes. Add broccoli flowerets; season with salt and white pepper. Sauté 3 to 4 minutes in hot oil. Stir in wine, a little at a time. Cover and simmer 20 minutes or until broccoli is crisp-tender. Drain; serve with roasted meat. Makes 4 servings.

Variation

Substitute boiling salted water for wine. While broccoli cooks, sauté garlic in 2 tablespoons butter or lard. Add 1/2 pound diced prosciutto or bacon. Cook 3 to 4 minutes. Pour garlic mixture over cooked broccoli.

Zucchini with Peppers
ZUCCHINE CON PEPERONI

4 zucchini, cut in halves lengthwise
Water
Salt
5 tablespoons olive oil
4 tomatoes
1 garlic clove, crushed
3 fresh basil sprigs, chopped
2 yellow bell peppers, cut in strips
6 oz. fontina or Gruyère cheese, sliced
4 anchovy fillets, cut in halves lengthwise

Blanch zucchini 2 minutes in boiling salted water; drain thoroughly. Grease a stovetop greased casserole with 1/2 teaspoon oil. Arrange blanched zucchini halves, cut-side up, in greased casserole. Sprinkle with 1/2 teaspoon salt. Cook zucchini halves over medium-low heat until peelings brown and split; remove peelings. Arrange peeled zucchini halves in same casserole; set aside. Peel tomatoes; remove and discard seeds. Chop tomatoes. Heat 2 tablespoons oil in a medium saucepan. Add chopped tomatoes, garlic, 1/2 teaspoon salt and 3/4 of the basil. Cook over low heat 20 minutes. Preheat oven to 425F (220C). Spread tomato mixture and pepper strips over peeled zucchini. Cover with cheese slices as shown. Top with anchovy fillets. Sprinkle remaining oil and basil over top. Bake 15 minutes or until lightly browned. Makes 4 servings.

Osso Buco
OSSOBUCO

1 tablespoon all-purpose flour
Salt and white pepper
Pinch of dried leaf marjoram
2 veal shanks, cut in 2-inch pieces
1/2 cup butter
1 onion, cut in rings
1 garlic clove, finely chopped
1 cup white wine
Small piece of orange peel
Small piece of lemon peel
1/3 cup veal or beef stock or broth
Pinch of grated nutmeg
Cheese Gnocchi with Tomato Sauce, page 123

Combine flour, salt, white pepper and marjoram. Coat veal in seasoned flour; shake off excess. Melt 1/4 cup butter in a large saucepan. Add onion rings and garlic; sauté until transparent. Add floured veal; cook until golden brown on all sides. With cut-side of bones up, add wine and citrus peels. Cover and simmer 1-1/2 to 2 hours or until veal is tender. During cooking, occasionally add 1 tablespoon stock or broth. When cooked, remove veal from pan; keep warm. Strain juices; stir in nutmeg, remaining butter and salt, if needed. Serve with braised mushrooms and Cheese Gnocchi with Tomato Sauce. Makes 4 servings.

Saltimbocca
SALTIMBOCCA

8 (2-oz.) veal scallops
8 sage leaves
8 thin prosciutto or other ham slices
1/4 cup vegetable oil
Salt and white pepper
1/4 cup white wine
3 tablespoons butter

Pound veal pieces to an even thickness. Place a sage leaf and ham slice on each veal piece. Use wooden picks to skewer ham and sage to veal. Heat oil in a large skillet. Add veal packets; cook over medium heat 2 to 3 minutes on each side. Season with salt and white pepper. Sprinkle a little wine over each veal packet. Arrange cooked veal packets on a platter; keep warm. Stir remaining wine into drippings in skillet. Add butter; stir until melted. Pour wine sauce over cooked meats. Serve with hot rice or potatoes and a salad of red and green lettuce, green pepper and onion. Makes 4 servings.

Cook's Tip

Saltimbocca, a Roman speciality, means *jump into the mouth*. In Italy, the scallops are beaten until very thin, rolled with ham and a sage leaf, and then fried. They may be served without the sauce.

Venetian Calves' Liver
FEGATO DE VITELLO ALLA VENEZIANA

3 tablespoons olive oil
4 onions, cut in thin rings
3 tablespoons chopped parlsey
3/4 cup dry white wine
1-1/2 lbs. calves' liver, thinly sliced
Salt and white pepper
2 tablespoons butter
Lombardy Polenta Slices, page 126, if desired

Heat oil in a large skillet. Add onions; sauté over low heat 20 minutes or until softened. Onions should not brown. Add parsley. Gradually stir in wine; increase heat to medium. When wine begins to boil, add liver. Cook about 4 minutes, turning once. Season with salt and white pepper. Add butter; heat until melted. Serve immediately with mashed potatoes or with Lombardy Polenta Slices, if desired. Makes 4 servings.

Roman Oxtail Stew
CODA ALLA VACCINARA

3 lbs. oxtail
1/4 cup olive oil
8 to 10 bacon slices, diced
2 onions, coarsely chopped
1 garlic clove, finely chopped
1 carrot, coarsely chopped
1 red bell pepper, cut in strips
Water
2 tablespoons tomato paste
1/2 teaspoon salt
1-1/2 cups dry white wine
About 1-1/2 cups stock or broth
2 celery stalks, sliced

Cut oxtail into pieces at joints; trim off as much fat as possible. Heat oil in a large saucepan. Add bacon; sauté until partially cooked. Add onions and garlic; sauté until transparent. Add oxtail pieces; cook until browned on all sides. Add carrot and red pepper. In a small bowl, stir 1 or 2 teaspoons hot water into tomato paste. Stir tomato-paste mixture and salt into oxtail mixture. Stir in wine, a little at a time. Stirring constantly, simmer until wine has nearly evaporated. Add 1 cup stock or broth; cook 2 to 2-1/2 hours over low heat, adding stock or broth as needed. Add celery; cook 1 hour longer or until meat and celery are tender. Serve with parsleyed new potatoes. Makes 4 servings.

Pizza Naples-Style
(right)
PIZZA NAPOLETANA

Pizza Crust:
1 (1/4-oz.) pkg. active dry yeast (1 tablespoon)
1 cup warm water (110F, 45C)
3 to 4 cups all-purpose flour
1/2 teaspoon salt

Anchovy Topping:
24 anchovy fillets
Water
6 tablespoons olive oil
1 onion, cut in rings
1 garlic clove, finely chopped
4 medium tomatoes, peeled, sliced
10 oz. mozzarella cheese, sliced
18 ripe olives
12 basil leaves, cut in strips
1/2 teaspoon salt
1/8 teaspoon pepper

To make crust, in a large bowl, dissolve yeast in water. Add 1 cup flour; beat well. Sift together 2 cups flour and 1/2 teaspoon salt. Add to dough. Beat until smooth, adding enough of remaining flour to make a stiff dough. Turn out onto a lightly floured surface; let stand 3 to 5 minutes. Clean and grease bowl; set aside. Knead dough 2 to 3 minutes. Place dough in greased bowl, turning to grease all sides. Let stand in a warm place, free from drafts, until softened and slightly risen, 15 to 20 minutes. Divide dough in half; knead each piece slightly. Wrap each piece in plastic wrap; refrigerate until ready to use, up to 2 hours. Brush 2 large baking sheets with oil. Roll out each piece of dough into a flat base with edge slightly thicker than center. Place 1 on each oiled baking sheet.

To complete, soak anchovy fillets in water to cover 20 minutes; drain. Preheat oven to 425F (220C). Heat 2 tablespoons oil in a large skillet. Add onion rings and garlic; sauté until transparent. Arrange tomatoes, sautéed onion and garlic, cheese slices, soaked anchovies and olives on pizza bases. Sprinkle with basil, salt, pepper and remaining oil. Bake 20 to 25 minutes or until dough is golden brown and cheese is melted; serve hot. Makes 2 pizzas.

Pizza Margarita
(top left)
PIZZA MARGHERITA

Pizza Crust, opposite
3 medium tomatoes, peeled, sliced
12 oz. mozzarella cheese, sliced
Salt and pepper
1 cup grated Parmesan cheese (4 oz.)
1 teaspoon dried leaf oregano
6 tablespoons vegetable oil

Prepare and roll out Pizza Crust dough. Place dough on baking sheets. Preheat oven to 425F (220C). Arrange tomatoes and mozzarella cheese on dough. Season with salt and pepper; sprinkle with Parmesan cheese, oregano and oil. Bake 20 to 25 minutes or until dough is golden brown and cheese is melted; serve hot. Makes 2 pizzas.

Garlic-Sausage Pizza
PIZZA CON SALAME D'AGLIO

Pizza Crust, page 130
3 large tomatoes, peeled, sliced
1/2 lb. garlic sausage, sliced
12 anchovies
12 capers
1 red bell pepper, cut in strips
1 green bell pepper, cut in strips
6 oz. pimiento-stuffed green olives, cut in halves
1-1/2 cups diced mozzarella cheese (12 oz.)
1/2 teaspoon dried leaf oregano
1/2 teaspoon dried leaf basil
2 tablespoons olive oil

Prepare and roll out Pizza Crust dough. Place dough on baking sheets. Preheat oven to 425F (220C). Arrange tomatoes and sausage over dough. Roll each anchovy around a caper. Arrange anchovy rolls, bell-pepper strips and olives over pizza bases. Sprinkle cheese evenly over pizzas. Sprinkle each pizza with 1/2 of the oregano, basil and oil. Bake 20 to 25 minutes or until dough is golden brown and cheese is melted; serve hot. Makes 2 pizzas.

Country-Style Pizza
PIZZA RUSTICA

Pizza Crust, page 130
1 (7-oz.) can artichoke hearts
3 large tomatoes, peeled, sliced
4 oz. salami slices
8 oz. mushrooms, sliced
1 (4-oz.) can shrimp
8 pimiento-stuffed green olives, cut in halves
8 ripe olives, pitted
1/4 cup olive oil
8 oz. mozzarella cheese, cubed
Salt and white pepper
Pinch of dried leaf oregano

Prepare and roll out Pizza-Crust dough. Place dough on baking sheets. Preheat oven to 425F (220C). Drain artichoke hearts; cut in wedges. Arrange artichoke-heart wedges, tomatoes, salami and mushrooms on pizza bases. Rinse shrimp in cold water; drain well on paper towels. Sprinkle drained shrimp, green olives and ripe olives over pizzas. Sprinkle evenly with oil, then with cheese. Season with salt, white pepper and oregano. Bake 20 to 25 minutes or until crust is golden brown and cheese is melted. Makes 2 pizzas.

Zabaglione
ZABAGLIONE

4 egg yolks
1 egg
1/3 cup extra-fine sugar
5 tablespoons Marsala or white wine

In a large heatproof bowl, combine egg yolks, whole egg and sugar. In a saucepan larger than bowl, bring 2 inches water to a gentle boil. Place bowl in pan. Beat egg mixture until light and fluffy. Beat in wine until mixture is fluffy and forms soft mounds. Spoon into 4 glasses; serve immediately. Makes 4 servings.

Variation

Flavor Zabaglione with grated orange or lemon peel or a little Vanilla Sugar, page 7.

Zuppa Inglese
ZUPPA INGLESE

1 (1-lb.) pound cake
1/4 cup kirsch or other cherry-flavored liqueur
1/4 cup rum
3 eggs, separated
1 cup sugar
Grated peel of 1 lemon
1/4 cup all-purpose flour
1-1/2 cups milk
1 cup candied fruit, finely chopped
1 candied cherry

Cut cake into 1/4-inch slices. Sprinkle half of the cake slices with liqueur and half with rum. In a medium bowl, combine egg yolks, 2/3 cup sugar and lemon peel. Beat until light and fluffy. Stir in flour, then stir in milk. Pour into a medium saucepan. Bring to a boil over low heat, stirring constantly. Remove from heat; stir until cool. Cutting slices as needed, line bottom of a round 8- or 9-inch cake or quiche dish with cake slices sprinkled with liqueur. Sprinkle with half of the chopped candied fruit, then half of the egg-yolk mixture. Add another layer of cake slices, using remaining cake sprinkled with liqueur and some of cake soaked with rum. With each successive layer, arrange cake slices as shown above. Sprinkle second cake layer with remaining chopped fruit, then with remaining egg-yolk mixture. Add a final layer, using remaining cake sprinkled with rum, layering cake to a peak. In a medium bowl, beat egg whites until soft peaks form. Beat in remaining sugar until stiff but not dry. Preheat oven to 250F (120C). Cover pudding with meringue or use a piping bag fitted with a medium star nozzle to pipe meringue in a decorative pattern. Bake until golden brown. Refrigerate until chilled; decorate with cherry. Makes 6 to 8 servings.

Almond Cream
CREMA DI MANDORLE

1 tablespoon butter
1/4 cup sugar
1 cup chopped blanched almonds
1 cup whipping cream
2 tablespoons brandy or orange-flavored liqueur

Decoration:
Meringue flowers
Candied-cherry halves

Lightly oil a baking sheet; set aside. Melt butter in a small skillet over low heat. Add sugar; cook until golden brown, stirring constantly. Stir in almonds. Spread almond mixture on oiled baking sheet; cool completely. Crush into crumbs. In a medium bowl, whip cream until stiff. Fold in brandy or liqueur. Reserve some of crumbled almond mixture to sprinkle over top of dessert. Fold remaining crumbs into whipped cream. Spoon into 4 to 6 dessert dishes. Sprinkle with reserved almond mixture. Refrigerate until set. To serve, decorate with meringue flowers and candied-cherry halves. Makes 4 to 6 servings.

Sicilian Cassata
CASSATA ALLA SICILIANA

2 cups cottage cheese, drained (1 lb.)
3/4 cup powdered sugar
1 to 1-1/4 cups whipping cream
1 tablespoon Vanilla Sugar, page 7
2/3 cup golden raisins
Water
2/3 cup candied cherries
1/4 cup chopped pistachios
1 sponge cake or pound cake, loaf shape
3 tablespoons maraschino liqueur or other cherry-flavored liqueur
2/3 cup candied fruit, finely chopped
1/4 cup pine nuts, finely chopped
2/3 cup semisweet chocolate pieces, finely chopped

In a blender or food processor, process cottage cheese until smooth; spoon into a large bowl. Stir in powdered sugar and 5 tablespoons whipping cream. Stir in vanilla sugar. Cover and refrigerate 12 hours or overnight. Wash raisins in hot water; drain on paper towels. Reserve a few cherries and pistachios for decoration; chop remaining cherries. Cut cake into 1/2-inch-thick pieces to fit bottom, top, sides and ends of a 9'' x 5'' loaf pan. Line pan with cake pieces, reserving pieces for top. Sprinkle 2 tablespoons liqueur over cake pieces in pan. Stir chopped fruits, pistachios, washed raisins, pine nuts and chocolate into chilled cheese mixture. Pour into cake-lined pan. Top with remaining cake pieces; sprinkle top with remaining liqueur. Cover and freeze 2 to 3 hours. Or, refrigerate 8 to 10 hours. Invert cassata onto a platter or plate; remove pan. In a medium bowl, whip remaining cream until stiff; spoon or pipe over cassata. If piping whipped cream, use larger amount of cream. Decorate with reserved cherries and pistachios. Refrigerate or freeze unused portion. Makes 6 to 8 servings.

Soup Pot
DOBIN MUSHI

1 fresh or frozen jumbo shrimp
2 dried Japanese mushrooms
Hot water
1 teaspoon soy sauce
2 ginkgo nuts or water chestnuts, sliced
1 parsley sprig
1 lime or lemon wedge

Fish Stock:
4 oz. dried or 8 oz. fresh tuna
7 cups water
1/2 oz. dried seaweed

Prepare stock. Thaw frozen shrimp; peel and remove vein. In a small bowl, soak mushrooms in hot water to cover 30 minutes; drain. In a large saucepan, combine 2 cups fish stock, shrimp, drained mushrooms, soy sauce, ginkgo nuts or water chestnuts, parsley and lime or lemon. Bring to a boil. Remove from heat; keep hot 5 minutes. Makes 1 serving.
To make stock, in a large saucepan, combine tuna and water. Bring to a boil. Add seaweed; return to a boil. Simmer 15 minutes. Strain stock; discard seaweed. Fish may be used in a salad or another dish.

Cook's Tip

In Japan, this soup would be poured into a small jug or teapot and warmed 5 minutes over a spirit burner. The soup is served in the pot, then poured into a small bowl, seasoned to taste with a little lemon juice and sipped slowly. As the soup stands, it becomes quite strong. The shrimp, mushrooms and nuts are eaten.

Raw Fish
SASHIMI

5 oz. fresh tuna
5 oz. fresh pike or perch
1 small carrot, cooked
4 thin lime wedges
Few fine strips leek and radish
3 tablespoons soy sauce
3 tablespoons rice wine or dry sherry
3 tablespoons grated white radish
1 teaspoon grated horseradish

Fillet fish, carefully removing skin and all bones. With a sharp knife, cut fillets into very thin slices; arrange on a plate. Use an hors d'oeuvres cutter to cut each carrot slice to resemble a flower. Garnish fish with lime wedges, leek and radish strips and carrot flowers, as shown. In a small bowl, combine soy sauce and wine or sherry. Serve sauce, radish and horseradish in small bowls for dipping. Makes 1 serving.

Cook's Tip

Raw fish is considered a great delicacy in Japan. When freshly caught, fish has no *fishy* flavor.

Tempura
TEMPURA

6 fresh or frozen jumbo shrimp
2 dried Japanese mushrooms
Water
1 small eggplant
Vegetable oil for deep-frying
1/4 green bell pepper, cut in half
1 (1/2-inch-thick) lotus-root
 slice, if desired
1/3 cup all-purpose flour
2 egg yolks, beaten
Several thin Japanese rice noodles

Thaw frozen shrimp. Leave tails intact; peel and devein. Cut each shrimp in half lengthwise. Cut thick shrimp into 3 slices. In a small bowl, soak mushrooms in hot water to cover 30 minutes; drain well. Cut eggplant in half crosswise. Cut almost through each half several times to make thin fan-like slices. Heat oil in a wok or deep skillet to 350F (175C) or until a 1-inch cube of bread turns golden brown in 65 to 70 seconds. Place shrimp in a large plastic bag. Add eggplant fans, drained mushrooms, green pepper and lotus root, if desired. Add a little flour; shake to coat. Sift remaining flour into a bowl; stir in egg yolks and 2 tablespoons water or enough to make a thin batter. Dip flour-coated shrimp and vegetables in batter; fry in hot oil until golden. Tie noodles together at 1 end. Dip into batter; fry in hot oil 2 to 3 minutes. Use as a garnish. Makes 2 servings.

Cook's Tip

Serve Tempura with a sauce made with 6 tablespoons rice wine or dry sherry, 6 tablespoons soy sauce, 2 cups water in which 4 seaweed leaves have been soaked and 1 teaspoon salt. Bring to a boil; set aside to cool. When cold, pour equally into 2 small bowls. Into 1 bowl, stir grated white radish and gingerroot; into other bowl, stir 1 teaspoon monosodium glutamate, if desired, and a little salt. Lemon or lime wedges may also be served.

Dervish's Rosebed

MASBAHET EL DARWEESH

2 tablespoons all-purpose flour
1 lb. ground beef
3 tablespoons vegetable shortening
3 small onions, cut in halves
1/8 teaspoon ground nutmeg
1/8 teaspoon ground cloves
1 teaspoon salt
1 medium eggplant, cut in 1/4-inch slices
2 medium zucchini, cut in 1/4-inch slices
3 medium tomatoes, peeled, finely chopped
2 small potatoes, peeled, finely chopped
1-1/2 cups stock or broth

Preheat oven to 350F (175C). Butter a large casserole; set aside. In a medium bowl, stir flour into ground beef. Melt shortening in a large skillet. Add onions; sauté until transparent. Add ground-beef mixture; cook until lightly browned. Stir in nutmeg, cloves and salt. Arrange eggplant, zucchini, tomatoes and potatoes in buttered casserole. Spread cooked-beef mixture over top; pour in stock or broth. Bake 40 minutes or until vegetables are tender and beef is cooked. Makes 4 servings.

Variation

Crumble 1 cup (4 oz.) feta cheese over top of casserole. Bake until melted.

Braised Quail

HAMAAN BI NABIED

8 oven-ready quail or Cornish hens
Salt
8 thin bacon slices
1/3 cup vegetable oil
3 tablespoons golden raisins
Water
3 small onions, finely chopped
4 to 5 tablespoons sauterne or other sweet wine
1/8 teaspoon ground allspice

Saffron Rice:
Water
Salt
3 cups uncooked long-grain white rice
1/8 teaspoon saffron threads

Rub inside each quail or hen with salt. Wrap 1 bacon slice around each; secure with a wooden pick or skewer. Heat oil in a large skillet. Cook birds on all sides in hot oil 10 minutes. Set aside; keep warm. Meanwhile, soak raisins in warm water 15 minutes; drain. In oil left from cooking birds, sauté onions until golden brown. Add wine, 4 to 5 tablespoons water and soaked raisins. Stir in allspice and a little salt; simmer 20 minutes. Strain sauce; return to pan. Add birds; simmer in sauce 30 minutes. Serve over Saffron Rice. Makes 8 servings.
To make rice, bring 7 cups water to a boil in a large saucepan. Add salt and rice. Cook over medium heat until fluffy, adding water, if necessary, to prevent sticking. Dissolve saffron in a little hot water. Stir into cooked rice.

Pork in Coconut Milk
BABI LEMAK

2 onions, chopped
8 dried red chilies, crushed
1 teaspoon shrimp paste
3 tablespoons vegetable oil
1 lb. lean pork, cut in 1-1/2-inch cubes
1/4 teaspoon ground ginger
1 teaspoon salt
2 teaspoons sugar
6 tablespoons water
1 cup canned coconut milk or Coconut Milk, page 7
2 tablespoons lime or lemon juice
Grated fresh coconut

In a blender, puree onions, chilies and shrimp paste. Heat oil in a large saucepan. Add puree mixture; cook 1 to 2 minutes. Add pork; cook 2 to 3 minutes or until evenly browned. Stir in ginger, salt, sugar and water. Cover and simmer 30 to 40 minutes or until pork is tender. Stir in coconut milk and lime or lemon juice. Spoon into a tureen or serve in individual bowls. Garnish with coconut. Makes 3 to 4 servings.

Variation

Add extra coconut milk or grated coconut to make this dish less peppery.

Spicy Pineapple
PACHADI BUAH NANAS

1 medium, fresh pineapple
2 tablespoons sugar
1 teaspoon ground turmeric
Water
3 tablespoons vegetable oil
2 onions, finely chopped
2 garlic cloves, finely chopped
2 star anise
1 (3-inch) cinnamon stick
6 whole cloves
2 teaspoons grated fresh gingerroot
1 teaspoon salt
2 jalapeño chilies

Peel pineapple; remove *eyes*. Quarter pineapple lengthwise; remove core. Cut each quarter crosswise into 4 slices. Place in a medium saucepan; sprinkle with 1 tablespoon sugar, turmeric and water to cover. Bring to a boil; boil, uncovered, 10 minutes. Drain pineapple; set aside. Heat oil in a wok or large skillet. Add onions, garlic, star anise, cinnamon stick and cloves; sauté 2 minutes. Stir in gingerroot, 1 cup water, salt and remaining 1 tablespoon sugar. Boil 3 to 4 minutes. To handle fresh chilies, cover your hands with rubber or plastic gloves; after handling, do not touch your face or eyes. Cut chilies open lengthwise; remove seeds and pith. Add chilies and drained pineapple to onion mixture. Cook 3 to 4 minutes longer. To serve, remove star anise, cinnamon stick and cloves. Makes 4 to 6 servings.

Cook's Tips

Star anise is available in Chinese specialty stores and stores specializing in exotic spices.

Chicken Livers in Chili Sauce

SAMBAL GORENG HATI

2 cups grated fresh or packaged unsweetened coconut
1/2 cup milk
1 onion, chopped
2 garlic cloves, finely chopped
8 dried red chilies
4 macadamia nuts or cashews
1 teaspoon shrimp paste
3 tablespoons vegetable oil
1 lb. chicken livers
1 teaspoon salt
1 teaspoon sugar
1/2 teaspoon grated lemon peel
6 tablespoons water

In a medium saucepan, combine coconut and milk; bring to a boil. Let stand 30 minutes; strain through muslin, squeezing out all milk from coconut. Set milk aside; discard coconut. In a blender, puree onion, garlic, chilies, nuts and shrimp paste. Heat oil in a large saucepan. Add puree; cook 1 to 2 minutes, stirring constantly. Add livers; cook 2 minutes over high heat, stirring constantly. Add salt, sugar and lemon peel. Stir in water; simmer 3 to 4 minutes. Add reserved coconut milk; cook over low until liquid is slightly reduced. Serve with cooked rice. Makes 4 servings.

Variation

Substitute canned coconut milk for coconut and milk.

Mussels in Chili Sauce

KEPAH MASAK KUAH PEDAS

1-1/2 lbs. mussels
Water
Salt
1/4 cup vegetable oil
1 bunch green onions, chopped
4 to 6 celery stalks, chopped
8 dried red chilies, crushed
2 garlic cloves, finely chopped
1/4 teaspoon ground ginger

Soak mussels 2 hours in several changes of salted water. Scrape shells clean; pull out and cut off beards. Rinse mussels in cold water; place in a large saucepan. Cover with water; bring to a boil. Boil rapidly 10 minutes or until shells open. Discard any shells that do not open. Heat oil in a wok or large skillet. Add green onions and celery; sauté over high heat 2 minutes. Add chilies, garlic, 1 teaspoon salt, ginger and 1 cup water. Bring to boil. Add opened mussels; simmer 2 to 3 minutes. Serve hot mussels in shells. Makes 2 servings.

Avocado Soup
SOPA DE AGUACATE

3 ripe avocados
6 tablespoons half and half
2-1/2 cups chicken stock or broth
2 tablespoons dry sherry
Salt
Pinch of white pepper
1/4 cup instant masa
Water

In a blender or food processor, puree avocado and half and half. In a medium saucepan, bring stock or broth to a boil. Remove from heat; stir in avocado puree. Season with sherry, 1/2 teaspoon salt and a pinch of white pepper; keep warm. In a small bowl, combine masa, a pinch of salt and enough water to make a firm dough. Shape into a ball. If mixture is crumbly, add a little more water. Place dough between 2 sheets of waxed paper. Roll into a 1/8-inch-thick tortilla. Warm a large, heavy skillet over low heat; do not grease skillet. Cook tortilla until golden brown on both sides. Roll up tortilla; cut into thin strips. Use to garnish soup. Makes 4 servings.

Variation

For a creamier soup, puree another avocado; stir into soup. The riper the avocados, the creamier the soup will be.

Stuffed Bell Peppers
CHILIES RELLENOS CON PICADILLO

4 green bell peppers
1 garlic clove, chopped
Salt and black pepper
1 cup vegetable oil
1 medium onion, chopped
1 lb. ground pork
1/3 cup chopped blanched almonds
2 tablespoons raisins
2 tablespoons chopped green olives
1 tablespoon vinegar
8 small tomatoes, peeled, chopped
2 tablespoons all-purpose flour
1 egg, beaten
1 cup fine dry breadcrumbs
2 tablespoons chopped parsley
Pinch of chili powder
1 banana, sliced

Preheat oven to 350F (175C). Roast peppers until skins split; peel peppers. Cut peppers open on 1 side; remove seeds and pith. Crush garlic with 1/2 teaspoon salt. Heat 2 tablespoons oil in a large skillet. Add onion; sauté until soft. Add pork; cook until browned. Stir in garlic-salt mixture, pinch of black pepper, almonds, raisins, olives, vinegar and 1/4 of the tomatoes. Bring to a simmer; cook 5 minutes. Spoon pork mixture into peeled peppers. Roll peppers in flour; dip in beaten egg, then roll in breadcrumbs. In a large heavy saucepan, heat remaining oil to 365F (185C). Fry peppers in hot oil until golden brown on all sides; drain. Place on a platter; keep warm. Strain oil into a medium skillet. Add remaining tomatoes, parsley and chili powder; stir-fry 2 minutes. Stir in banana. Spoon tomato mixture around peppers; serve immediately. Makes 4 servings.

Cheese Enchiladas
ENCHILADAS DE QUESO

1/4 cup vegetable oil
12 (6-inch) corn tortillas
3 cups shredded Cheddar cheese or combination of Cheddar and
    Monterey Jack cheese (12 oz.)
1 medium onion, chopped
Green onions

Salsa:
2 tablespoons vegetable oil
1 tablespoon all-purpose flour
1/4 cup mild chili powder
4 cups tomato juice
1 (6-oz.) can tomato paste
2 tablespoons canned diced green chilies
1/2 teaspoon dried leaf oregano, crushed
1/4 teaspoon ground cumin
1/2 garlic clove crushed with 1/4 teaspoon salt

Prepare salsa. Preheat oven to 350F (175C). Heat oil in a
medium skillet. With tongs, carefully place 1 tortilla at a time in
hot oil. Quickly turn and dip other side in hot oil. Drain on paper
towels, then dip in salsa. Reserve 1 cup cheese for topping.
Arrange some of the remaining cheese in a strip on tortilla.
Sprinkle with chopped onion. Roll up tightly and place
seam-side down in a medium baking dish. Repeat with
remaining tortillas. Pour remaining sauce over top. Sprinkle
reserved cheese over sauce. Bake 15 to 20 minutes or until
heated through. Garnish with green onions; serve immediately
with shredded lettuce. Makes 4 to 6 servings.
To make salsa, heat oil in a large saucepan. Stir in flour; cook 1
minute. Stir in chili powder until blended. Stir in tomato juice,
tomato puree, oregano, cumin and garlic-salt mixture. Simmer
about 15 minutes; keep warm.

Tortilla Casserole
QUESO E TORTILLAS

8 (6-inch) corn tortillas
1 cup vegetable oil
1 onion, finely chopped
3 medium tomatoes
Salt
1/2 teaspoon dried leaf oregano
1/4 to 1 teaspoon hot-pepper sauce
1-1/2 cups shredded Monterey Jack cheese (6 oz.)
6 hard-cooked eggs, sliced

Tightly roll up each tortilla; cover with a clean dry cloth 15 to 20
minutes. Cut rolled tortillas into 1/4-inch slices. Heat oil in a
medium skillet. Keeping tortilla slices rolled, cook a few at a
time until browned and crisp. Drain on paper towels. Add onion
to oil in skillet; sauté until transparent. Peel tomatoes; remove
and discard seeds. Chop tomatoes. Add to onion in skillet. Stir
in 1/2 teaspoon salt, oregano and hot-pepper sauce. Stirring
frequently, cook over medium-low heat until tomatoes are soft.
Preheat oven to 375F (190C). Grease a large casserole; cover
bottom with a layer of fried tortilla slices. Cover with some of
tomato mixture; sprinkle with cheese. Arrange egg slices over
cheese. Repeat layers until all ingredients are used, ending with
a layer of tomato mixture. Cover and bake 30 minutes. Makes 4
servings.

Pork Casserole

MANCHA MANTELES DE CERDO

3-1/2 cups chicken stock or broth
2-1/4-lbs. boneless pork loin, cut in 1-inch cubes
1 bay leaf
1/8 teaspoon dried leaf thyme
1/8 teaspoon dried leaf oregano
1/8 teaspoon ground cloves
12 small red chilies
3/4 lb. tomatillos or 3 medium, green tomatoes
1 garlic clove
1 teaspoon salt
3/4 cup chopped walnuts
2 onions, chopped
2 tablespoons chopped parsley
1 tablespoon olive oil
3 apples
3 pears
3 bananas
2 medium zucchini, cut in 1/4-inch slices
1 small fresh pineapple, peeled, chopped
2 cups fresh or frozen green peas

Bring 2-1/2 cups stock or broth to a boil in a deep paella pan or wok. Add pork cubes, bay leaf, thyme, oregano and cloves. Cover and simmer 30 minutes. To handle fresh chilies, cover your hands with rubber or plastic gloves. After handling fresh chilies, do not touch your face or eyes. Cut chilies open lengthwise; remove seeds and pith. Chop chilies; set aside. Peel and chop tomatillos or green tomatoes. Crush garlic with salt. Puree nuts in a blender or food processor. Add chopped chilies, chopped tomatillos or tomatoes, garlic-salt mixture, onions, parsley and remaining stock or broth; process until pureed. Heat oil in a large saucepan. Add puree; simmer 5 minutes. Set aside; keep warm. Pour cooking liquid from pork mixture into a large bowl. Cool slightly; skim off fat. Stir cooled cooking liquid into nut sauce. Peel apples and pears. Cut into wedges; remove cores. Peel bananas; cut into 1/4-inch slices. Remove bay leaf from pork mixture. Arrange apple and pear wedges, banana slices, zucchini and pineapple over pork. Spoon sauce over top. Cover and simmer 30 minutes. Sprinkle peas into pan; cook 15 minutes longer. Serve from pan or spoon into a serving dish. Makes 8 servings.

Lamb Soup

HARIRA

4 medium tomatoes
2 tablespoons olive oil
1/2 lb. lean lamb, cut in 1-1/4-inch strips
1/2 teaspoon ground ginger
1/8 teaspoon ground turmeric
2 onions, finely chopped
1 tablespoon finely chopped parsley
1 teaspoon salt
1/2 teaspoon pepper
3-1/2 cups hot meat stock or broth
1 cup broken home-style egg noodles
2 eggs
2 teaspoons lemon juice
Pinch of ground cinnamon

Peel tomatoes; remove and discard seeds. Chop tomatoes. Heat oil in a saucepan. Add lamb; cook, stirring constantly, until browned on all sides. Stir in ginger and turmeric. Add chopped tomatoes, onions, parsley, salt and pepper. Stir well; add stock or broth. Cover and simmer 45 minutes. Add noodles; return to a boil. Simmer, uncovered, 10 minutes longer. Remove from heat. In a small bowl, beat eggs with lemon juice and cinnamon; stir into hot soup. Reheat soup; do not boil. Pour into a tureen or serve in individual bowls. Makes 4 servings.

Chicken with Olives

TAJIEN NTA DJIADJIA

3 tablespoons olive oil
1 (3-lb.) chicken, cut in pieces
2 onions, finely chopped
2 garlic cloves, finely chopped
Salt and pepper
1/8 teaspoon ground turmeric
1/2 teaspoon ground ginger
1 cup hot chicken stock or broth
1/8 teaspoon saffron threads
2 lemons, cut in quarters
1 (6-oz.-drained-wt.) can ripe olives

Heat oil in a large saucepan. Add chicken; cook until golden brown on all sides. Add onions, garlic, salt, pepper, turmeric and ginger. Cook 10 minutes, stirring frequently; add stock or broth, saffron and lemons. Cover and simmer 30 to 40 minutes or until chicken is tender. Arrange cooked chicken pieces on a warm serving dish; keep warm. Heat olives in pan drippings. Garnish chicken with warm olives and lemon quarters. Cook sauce over high heat until thickened; pour over chicken. Serve hot. Makes 4 to 6 servings.

Savory Pie
BASTILA

Crepes:
3-1/2 cups all-purpose flour
1 teaspoon salt
1-3/4 to 2 cups water

Filling:
4 (1-lb.) oven-ready young pigeons or 1 (3-lb.) chicken with giblets
Salt and black pepper
1 cup butter
3 onions, finely chopped
3 tablespoons chopped parsley
2 teaspoons grated fresh gingerroot
1/2 teaspoon ground cumin
1/2 teaspoon red (cayenne) pepper
1/8 teaspoon ground turmeric
1 cup water
1/8 teaspoon saffron threads, if desired
6 eggs
2 egg yolks
3/4 cup blanched whole almonds
1 teaspoon ground cinnamon
2 tablespoons granulated sugar
3 tablespoons vegetable oil
Powdered sugar
Ground cinnamon

To make crepes, the day before using, sift flour and salt into a large bowl. Gradually stir in enough water to make a thin batter. Let stand at least 6 hours. Fry batter in an ungreased skillet making 18 to 20 crepes. Fry on 1 side only; do not brown.

To make filling, chop giblets. Season each bird with salt and black pepper. Melt 1/2 cup butter in a saucepan. Add birds; brown evenly. Remove from pan; set aside. Fry onions and chopped giblets in pan drippings. Add parsley, gingerroot, cumin, red pepper, turmeric, water and saffron, if desired. Bring to a boil. Return birds to pan. Cover; simmer 50 minutes or until tender. Remove meat from bones; chop meat. Discard bones and skin; set meat aside. Pour half of the pan drippings into a medium saucepan; set aside. Cook remaining pan drippings over high heat until reduced to 1/4 cup. Skim off fat; set aside. Bring reserved pan drippings to a simmer. Beat together eggs and egg yolks; stir 1/2 cup hot pan drippings into beaten eggs. Stir egg mixture into remaining hot pan drippings; continue to stir until thickened. Do not boil. Stir in 1/4 cup reduced pan drippings. Melt 1/4 cup remaining butter; add almonds. Stir over medium heat until browned; drain on paper towels. Chop almonds. In a small bowl, combine chopped almonds, 1 teaspoon cinnamon and granulated sugar.

To complete, arrange 6 crepes in a circle on a piece of foil. Cover with 6 more crepes. Then stack 4 crepes, 1 on top of the other, in center of circle. Cover center crepes with almond mixture. Stir meat into sauce; pour over almond mixture. Fold edges of top layer of crepes over filling. Cover with remaining crepes. Fold up edges of bottom layer of crepes. Heat remaining 1/4 cup butter and oil in a large skillet. Slide pie from foil into hot fat. Fry 5 minutes or until golden brown. Use a saucepan lid to help turn pie; fry other side until golden brown. Slide pie from skillet onto a plate. Sift together a little powdered sugar and cinnamon; sprinkle over pie. To serve, cut in wedges; serve hot. Makes 6 servings.

143

Split-Pea Soup
HOLLANDSE ERWTENSOEP

1-1/2 cups dried green split peas
2 pork hocks
1 teaspoon salt
Water
1/4 celeriac or 2 celery stalks, chopped
3 leeks, sliced
3 or 4 celery-leaf sprigs
4 potatoes, peeled, finely chopped
1/2 lb. garlic sausage, sliced

In a large saucepan, combine split peas, pork hocks, salt and water to cover. Bring to a boil; cover and simmer about 25 minutes. Stir in celeriac or celery, leeks, celery leaves and potatoes. Simmer 20 minutes longer or until potatoes are soft. Add sausage; cook 10 minutes longer. Remove pork hocks; remove meat from bones. Dice meat; discard bones. Serve diced meat and sausage separately from soup. Or, stir meat and sausage into soup. Pour into a tureen or serve in individual bowls. Makes 4 servings.

Bean & Pork Soup
SNIJBONENSOEP

1-1/2 cups dried Great Northern beans, navy beans or white kidney beans
Water
1-1/2 lbs. pork spareribs
Salt
3 or 4 celery-leaf sprigs, tied together
1-1/2 lbs. fresh green beans, cut in 2-inch pieces
2 small potatoes, peeled, diced
Pepper

Soak dried beans in cold water to cover 12 hours. Add spareribs, 1 teaspoon salt and water to cover. Bring to a boil. Cover and simmer 1 hour. During last 10 to 15 minutes of cooking, stir constantly with a wooden spoon to break up beans and thicken mixture. Stir in celery leaves, green beans and potatoes. Cook 30 minutes or until potatoes are soft. Remove spareribs and celery leaves from saucepan. Remove and discard bones; chop meat. Serve meat separately or, return meat to soup. Season with salt and pepper. Spoon into a tureen or serve in individual bowls; serve hot. Makes 4 servings.

Braised Pork with Rice
SUB GUM

1/4 cup vegetable oil
12 oz. boneless pork tenderloin, cut in 1/2-inch cubes
1/4 celeriac or 2 celery stalks, chopped
2 leeks, white part only, chopped
1 cup shredded cabbage
1 cup stock or broth
1 tablespoon cornstarch
1-1/2 teaspoons sugar
1/2 teaspoon ground ginger
Salt
Dash of vinegar
Water
2 medium tomatoes
1 cup uncooked long-grain white rice
1/3 cup chopped almonds

Heat oil in a large saucepan. Add pork; cook until browned on all sides. Add celeriac or celery, leeks, cabbage and stock or broth. Bring to a boil. Cover and simmer 30 minutes. In a small bowl, combine cornstarch, sugar, ginger, 1 teaspoon salt, vinegar and a little water. Stir into pork mixture; stir constantly until mixture simmers and begins to thicken. Peel tomatoes; remove and discard seeds. Chop tomatoes. Add chopped tomatoes to pork sauce; simmer 10 minutes longer or until pork is cooked. In a large saucepan, bring 2-1/2 cups water to a boil. Add 1/2 teaspoon salt and rice; simmer 15 minutes or until tender. Drain rice; spoon into a shallow bowl or platter. Spoon pork sauce over rice. Garnish with almonds. Makes 4 servings.

Beef & Onion Ragout
HACHEE

1/4 cup butter or lard
1 large onion, finely chopped
3 tablespoons all-purpose flour
About 1-1/2 cups hot beef stock or broth
3 tablespoons wine vinegar
1 bay leaf
3 white peppercorns
1 whole clove
1/2 teaspoon sugar
2 tablespoons tomato paste
1 lb. cooked roast beef, diced

Melt butter or lard in a large saucepan. Add onion; sauté until transparent. Sprinkle flour over sautéed onion. Stirring constantly, continue cooking 1 to 2 minutes. Gradually stir in 1-1/2 cups stock or broth. Stir in vinegar, bay leaf, white peppercorns, clove, sugar and tomato paste. Bring to a boil. Cover and simmer 15 minutes. Stir beef into sauce. Add more stock or broth if sauce is too thick. Stir occasionally over low heat until beef is heated through. Remove bay leaf; spoon ragout into a serving bowl. Serve with boiled potatoes or cooked rice and red cabbage or green beans. Makes 4 servings.

Boiled Beef & Vegetables
HUTSPOT

1 (1-lb.) beef brisket
Salt
Water
4 carrots, chopped
2 medium parsnips, chopped
4 onions, cut in rings
4 medium potatoes, peeled, chopped
Pepper

In a large saucepan, combine beef, 1 teaspoon salt and water to cover. Bring to a boil. Skim foam from surface until surface is clear. Cover and simmer 2 hours. Add carrots and parsnips; simmer 30 minutes longer. Add onions and potatoes; simmer 30 minutes longer. Remove brisket from pan; cut into small cubes. Stir beef cubes into stew. Season with plenty of pepper. Spoon into a serving bowl; serve hot. Makes 4 servings.

Variations

Substitute slab bacon or beef top round for brisket.

Add cooked Great Northern beans, navy beans or white kidney beans.

Traditional Winter Stew
STAMPPOT

2 tablespoons lard
1-1/4 lbs. boneless pork shoulder
1 qt. beef stock or broth
1 small head green cabbage, shredded
1 small head red cabbage, shredded
5 medium potatoes, peeled, cut in quarters
Salt
1/4 cup butter
White pepper

Melt lard in a large heavy saucepan. Add pork; brown on all sides. Bring stock or broth to a boil; pour over browned pork. Cover and simmer 15 minutes. Add cabbage. Cover and simmer 20 minutes longer. Add potatoes; season with 1 teaspoon salt. Cover and simmer 30 minutes longer. Remove pork; cut into cubes. Use a wooden spoon to gently stir butter and pork cubes into vegetables until butter melts. Season with salt and white pepper. Serve hot. Makes 4 servings.

Braised Rabbit

HAZEPEPER

1 oven-ready rabbit, cut in pieces
2-1/2 cups red wine
1/3 cup red-wine vinegar
3 crushed juniper berries
4 white peppercorns
1/2 bay leaf
Salt and white pepper
1/2 cup butter
6 to 8 bacon slices, cut in thin strips
1 onion, finely chopped
2 cups sliced mushrooms
Water
1/4 cup all-purpose flour
Pinch of sugar
2 white-bread slices, cut in cubes
1 tablespoon chopped parsley

Place rabbit in a deep bowl. Combine wine, vinegar, juniper berries, white peppercorns and bay leaf; pour over rabbit. Cover and refrigerate 2 days. Drain rabbit; reserve marinade. Pat rabbit dry; season with salt and white pepper. Reserve 1 tablespoon butter. Melt remaining butter in a large saucepan. Add marinated rabbit; cook until browned on all sides. Set aside. In saucepan, cook bacon, onion and mushrooms until onion is transparent; remove from pan. Strain reserved marinade; add water to make 2-1/2 cups. Pour into saucepan; stir to loosen pan drippings. Bring to a boil. Add browned rabbit; cover and simmer 1-1/2 hours. Add cooked bacon, onion and mushrooms. Combine flour, sugar and a little water; stir into sauce until thickened. Melt reserved butter in a small skillet. Add bread cubes; sauté until golden brown. Place rabbit on a platter; top with sauce. Sprinkle browned bread cubes over rabbit mixture; garnish with parsley. Makes 4 servings.

Venison Hot-Pot

JACHTSCHOTEL

5 medium potatoes, peeled, cut in quarters
Salt
Water
1/2 cup butter
2 onions, cut in rings
1-1/4 lbs. venison or beef sirloin or tenderloin, cut in cubes
1 cup beef stock or broth
1 bay leaf
2 whole cloves
White pepper
About 1/2 cup milk
1 cooking apple, peeled, sliced

In a large saucepan, combine potatoes, 1 teaspoon salt and 2 to 3 cups water. Bring to a boil; cook about 30 minutes. Melt 1/4 cup butter in a large saucepan. Add onions; sauté until transparent. Add venison or beef cubes; brown on all sides. Stir in stock or broth, bay leaf and cloves; season with salt and white pepper. Bring to a boil. Cover and simmer 20 minutes. Preheat oven to 425F (220C). Grease a large casserole; set aside. Drain and mash potatoes; stir in enough milk to make a smooth, medium-thick mixture. Season with salt; stir in 2 tablespoons butter. Spoon 1/2 of the meat mixture into greased casserole. Top with 1/2 of the potato mixture. Add remaining meat mixture, 1/2 of the remaining potato mixture and apple slices. Spread remaining potato mixture over top. Melt remaining 2 tablespoons butter; sprinkle over potatoes. Bake 15 minutes or until lightly browned. Makes 4 servings.

New Year's Doughnuts
OLIEBOL

1/4 cup warm water (110F, 45C)
1 (1/4-oz.) pkg. active dry yeast
    (1 tablespoon)
1/4 cup granulated sugar
1/2 cup warm milk (110F, 45C)
1/2 teaspoon salt
3 eggs, slightly beaten
3-1/4 to 3-1/2 cups all-purpose
    flour
Vegetable oil for deep-frying
1/2 cup currants
1/3 cup raisins
1/3 cup chopped candied orange
    peel
1 tablespoon grated lemon peel
Powdered sugar

To make dough, in a large bowl, combine water, yeast and 2 teaspoons granulated sugar; stir until yeast dissolves. Let stand 5 minutes or until foamy. Stir in remaining granulated sugar, milk, salt and eggs. Beat in 2 cups flour until smooth. Cover and let stand 10 minutes. Stir in enough remaining flour to make a medium-soft dough. Turn out dough onto a lightly floured surface. Clean and grease bowl; set aside. Knead dough lightly; place kneaded dough in greased bowl, turning to coat all sides. Let rise in a warm place, free from drafts, until doubled in bulk.

To complete, pour oil 3 inches deep into a large saucepan or deep fryer. Heat oil to 350F (175C) or until a 1-inch cube of bread turns golden brown in 50 seconds. Punch down dough; quickly knead in currants, raisins, orange peel and lemon peel. Shape dough into 12 small balls. Fry 4 or 5 balls at a time in hot oil, about 5 minutes on each side. Drain cooked doughnuts on paper towels. Let temperature of oil return to 350F (175C) before frying more doughnuts. Generously dust drained doughnuts with powdered sugar. Serve hot. Makes 12 doughnuts.

Smothered Pork Steaks

1/4 cup butter
4 small onions, finely chopped
4 cooked-ham slices, diced
2 white-bread slices
2 tablespoons ketchup
2 tablespoons chopped mixed herbs
8 thin pork-loin fillets
Salt and white pepper
2 cups hot beef stock or broth
1/4 cup half and half
2 tablespoons all-purpose flour

Melt butter in a large skillet. Add onions and ham; sauté until onions are transparent. Set aside. Remove crust from bread; use for another purpose. Crumble bread. In a large bowl, combine crumbled bread, sautéed onion mixture, ketchup and herbs. Preheat oven to 400F (205C). Grease a medium casserole; set aside. Arrange pork fillets on a flat surface. Sprinkle each with salt and white pepper. Spread filling evenly over fillets. Roll each fillet; tie securely with kitchen string or secure with wooden picks or metal skewers. Arrange pork rolls in greased casserole. Add hot stock or broth. Cover and bake 40 minutes. Remove cooked pork rolls from dish; remove string or skewers. Keep pork rolls warm. In a small bowl, stir half and half into flour, making a smooth paste. Stir in about 1/4 cup cooking liquid from casserole. Stir into remaining cooking liquid. Return pork rolls to sauce. Bake, uncovered, 10 minutes. Makes 4 servings.

Carpet-Bag Steak

1 tablespoon butter
1 cup finely sliced mushrooms
5 oz. fresh ham, finely chopped
1 tablespoon finely chopped parsley
1 small onion, finely chopped
1-1/2 cups fresh breadcrumbs
Grated peel of 1/2 lemon
1 egg, beaten
1/2 teaspoon salt
1/8 teaspoon white pepper
1 (1-3/4-lb.) beef top sirloin, 2-1/2 inches thick
1/4 cup vegetable oil

Melt butter in a large skillet. Add mushrooms, ham, parsley and onion. Simmer until ham is cooked through. Stir in breadcrumbs, lemon peel, egg, salt and white pepper. Cut a deep horizontal slit or pocket in beef; fill loosely with mushroom mixture. Secure cut edges with wooden picks or metal skewers. Heat oil in a large skillet. Over medium heat, brown beef on both sides in hot oil. Reduce heat to low; cook 10 to 15 minutes on each side. Cut in slices to serve. Makes 4 servings.

Colonial Gouse

2 lambs' kidneys
1 cooking apple, peeled, chopped
1 medium tomato, peeled, chopped
4 cups crumbled bread or fresh breadcrumbs
2 teaspoons chopped fresh parsley
2 teaspoons chopped fresh sage
2 teaspoons chopped fresh thyme
Salt and white pepper
1 egg, beaten
3 or 4 bacon slices, chopped
1 onion, finely chopped
1 (4-1/2-lb.) boneless lamb shoulder
2 tablespoons butter, melted
1 cup beef stock or broth

Soak kidneys in cold water to cover 30 minutes; core and chop kidneys. Preheat oven to 400F (205C). In a large bowl, combine chopped kidneys, apple, tomato, bread or breadcrumbs, parsley, sage, thyme, 1 teaspoon salt, 1/4 teaspoon white pepper, egg, bacon and onion. Season lamb with 1/2 teaspoon salt and 1/8 teaspoon white pepper. Spread filling over lamb. Starting at narrow end, roll up lamb; tie with kitchen string or secure with skewers. Brush with melted butter. Place roast on a rack in a shallow roasting pan. Roast 2 to 2-1/2 hours or until tender, basting frequently with stock or broth. Stir any remaining stock or broth into drippings in pan; pour through a strainer. Serve roast on a platter. Serve sauce separately. Makes 8 servings.

Baked Lettuce

Water
4 heads iceberg lettuce
5 tablespoons butter
1/4 cup all-purpose flour
2 cups milk
1 teaspoon salt
1/8 teaspoon red (cayenne) pepper
3/4 cup dry breadcrumbs
3/4 cup chopped walnuts

Bring 2 quarts water to a boil in a large pot. Quarter heads of lettuce. Blanch lettuce in boiling water 30 seconds; drain on paper towels. Discard water. Place blanched lettuce in same pot. Add cold water to cover. Bring water to a boil; simmer 5 minutes or until lettuce is tender. Pour into a colander to drain; press out excess water. Melt 3 tablespoons butter in a large saucepan. Stir in flour until smooth. Gradually stir in milk. Stirring constantly, simmer 5 minutes; season with salt and red pepper. Preheat oven to 450F (230C). Butter a large casserole. Arrange cooked lettuce in buttered dish; pour sauce over top. Sprinkle with breadcrumbs and nuts; dot with remaining butter. Bake 15 minutes or until golden brown. Serve with steak or chops. Makes 8 servings.

Roast Venison or Reindeer

DYRESTEG

1 (2- to 3-1/2-lb.) venison,
  reindeer or beef tenderloin
Salt and white pepper
1 teaspoon chopped parsley
Pinch of dried leaf thyme
8 to 10 thin bacon slices
1/4 cup butter
1/4 cup vegetable oil
1 tablespoon all-purpose flour
2 cups hot beef stock or broth
1 cup whipping cream
1 teaspoon soy sauce
1 tablespoon red-currant jelly
2 oz. Norwegian gjetost cheese,
  diced

Preheat oven to 325F (165C). Remove thin white membrane from meat; place meat on a large piece of heavy foil. Rub meat with salt, white pepper, parsley and thyme; cover with bacon. Wrap meat airtight in foil. Place on a baking sheet; place on lowest rack in oven. Roast 1 hour. Fold back foil. Increase heat to 400F (205C); roast 40 to 50 minutes longer. About 10 minutes before end of roasting time, melt butter in a large saucepan; stir in oil. Stir in flour until smooth. Stirring constantly, gradually add stock or broth; bring to a boil. Add meat juices from foil. Stir in cream, soy sauce, jelly and a little salt. Stir cheese into sauce; do not boil. Slice meat; arrange on a deep platter. Spoon sauce over meat. Makes 6 to 8 servings.

Cod with Egg Sauce
TORSK MED EGGESAUS

Water
Salt
1 small onion
1 tablespoon white-wine vinegar
5 whole peppercorns
4 (7-oz.) cod fillets
1 medium tomato
1/2 cup butter
2 hard-cooked eggs, finely chopped
1 tablespoon chopped fresh parsley
1 tablespoon chopped fresh chives
Pepper
1 tablespoon butter
2 carrots, thinly sliced
Juice of 1 lemon
Lemon slices
Fresh dill

In a fish kettle or roasting pan, pour water to a 4-inch depth.
Add 1 teaspoon salt, onion, vinegar and peppercorns; bring to a
boil. Reduce heat so water simmers. Add fish; poach 5 to 7 minutes, skimming foam from surface until surface is clear. Use a
wide spatula to lift fish from cooking liquid; drain. Place on a
platter; keep warm. Reserve 6 tablespoons cooking liquid.
To make sauce, peel tomato; remove and discard seeds. Chop
tomato. Melt 1/2 cup butter in a medium saucepan. Stir in
reserved fish stock, chopped tomato, eggs, parsley and chives.
Season with salt and pepper. Gently stir over medium heat until
heated through. Serve sauce separately.
To complete, melt 1 tablespoon butter in a medium skillet. Add
carrots; sauté until crisp-tender. Do not brown. Sprinkle lemon
juice over sautéed carrots; arrange over cod. Garnish with
lemon slices and dill. Makes 4 servings.

Lamb & Cabbage Casserole
FÅR I KÅL

6 tablespoons butter
1-1/2 lbs. lean lamb, cut in cubes
1 tablespoon all-purpose flour
1-1/2 lbs. cabbage, chopped
1 large potato, peeled, sliced
Salt
5 whole peppercorns
1 bay leaf
1 cup beef stock or broth
1 tablespoon chopped parsley

Melt butter in a large stovetop casserole. Add lamb; sprinkle
with flour. Turning constantly, brown meat; remove from dish.
Add cabbage to dish; sauté 3 to 5 minutes. Spoon cabbage into a
large bowl. Seasoning each layer with salt, alternate layers of
browned lamb, sautéed cabbage and potato slices in casserole,
ending with a layer of cabbage. Tie peppercorns and bay leaf in a
cloth bag; place in casserole. Add stock or broth. Cover and
cook over low heat 1-1/2 to 2 hours or until lamb is tender.
Remove spice bag. Garnish with parsley. Makes 4 to 6 servings.

Chick-Pea Soup with Spinach
POTAJE DE GARBANZO CON ACELGA

1 cup dried chick peas or garbanzo beans
Water
2 medium tomatoes
1 onion, cut in quarters
4 garlic cloves, cut in halves
1 teaspoon sweet paprika
1 teaspoon salt
1 bay leaf
1-1/2 lbs. spinach
2 tablespoons olive oil
2 tablespoons white wine
2 tablespoons chopped parsley

Soak peas or beans in cold water to cover 12 hours; drain well. In a large saucepan, combine soaked peas or beans and 3-1/2 cups water; bring to a boil. Add whole tomatoes, onion, garlic, paprika, salt and bay leaf. Cover and cook over low heat 1-1/4 hours. Clean spinach; place damp spinach in a large saucepan. Do not add water. Cover and cook 2 minutes. Drain well; chop spinach. Remove onion quarters, tomatoes, garlic and 1 tablespoon cooked peas or beans from saucepan. Discard tomato peels. Press mixture through a sieve or puree in a blender or food processor. Heat oil in a small skillet; add pureed mixture. Cook 2 to 3 minutes; return to saucepan. Stir in wine and chopped cooked spinach; simmer 10 minutes. Remove bay leaf. Pour into a tureen or serve in individual bowls. Garnish with parsley. Makes 4 servings.

Sweet-Corn & Meat Patties
BORI-BORI

1/2 lb. ground lean beef
1/2 lb. ground lean lamb
1 teaspoon salt
1/8 teaspoon white pepper
1/2 teaspoon red (cayenne) pepper
2 eggs, slightly beaten
1-1/2 cups canned whole-kernel corn, drained
1/4 to 1/2 cup fresh breadcrumbs
2 tablespoons olive oil

In a large bowl, combine beef, lamb, salt, white pepper, red pepper, eggs and corn. Add enough breadcrumbs to give a firm texture. Shape meat mixture into 4 thick patties. Heat oil in a large skillet. Add meat patties; cook over medium heat 3 to 4 minutes on each side or until cooked through. Makes 4 servings.

Cook's Tip

These meat patties are delicious served with fried bananas and a thick sauce made of pureed tomatoes, a little pureed potato and salt and pepper to taste.

Potatoes with Pepper Sauce
PAPAS A LA HUANCAÍNA

1 onion, cut in thin rings
Juice of 1 lemon
Salt and black pepper
1 teaspoon chili powder
8 small potatoes, peeled
Water
1 (8-oz.) pkg. cream cheese, room temperature
1/3 cup half and half
1 teaspoon ground turmeric
1 celery stalk, finely chopped
1 green bell pepper, finely chopped
1 fresh yellow or red chili
2 hard-cooked eggs, cut in wedges
8 green or ripe olives
Lettuce leaves

Place onion rings in a large deep bowl. In a small bowl, combine lemon juice, 1/2 teaspoon salt, 1/8 teaspoon black pepper and chili powder; pour mixture over onion rings. Cover and let stand 30 minutes. In a medium saucepan, cook whole potatoes in boiling salted water about 20 minutes. Potatoes should not become too soft. In a small saucepan, stir together cream cheese, half and half and turmeric. Stir in celery and green pepper. Cook over low heat, stirring constantly, until heated through. To handle fresh chili, cover your hands with rubber or plastic gloves; after handling, do not touch your face or eyes. Cut chili in thin strips; discard seeds. Drain onion rings and cooked potatoes; arrange potatoes in a serving bowl. Pour warm cheese sauce over potatoes; arrange yellow- or red-chili strips and marinated onion rings over potatoes. Garnish with egg wedges, olives and lettuce. Makes 4 servings.

Potato with Shrimp & Corn
CAUSA A LA LIMEÑA

Water
Salt
5 or 6 medium potatoes, peeled, cut in halves
4 ears of corn
1/2 cup butter
8 jumbo shrimp, shelled, deveined
1 small fresh yellow or red chili
1 onion, grated
2 tablespoons lemon juice
1 small fresh yellow or red chili
1/8 teaspoon red (cayenne) pepper
2 hard-cooked eggs, cut in halves lengthwise
6 to 8 ripe olives

In a medium saucepan, bring 2 cups water to a boil; add 1/2 teaspoon salt and potatoes. Cook potatoes 25 to 30 minutes or until soft. Cut each ear of corn into 4 pieces. In a large saucepan, bring 2 quarts water to a boil. Add 3/4 teaspoon salt and corn pieces. Cook 15 to 20 minutes; drain. Melt 3 tablespoons butter in a medium skillet; add shrimp and chili. Cook over low heat, turning once; keep warm. In a large bowl, combine onion, lemon juice and red pepper. Drain potatoes; mash thoroughly. Gradually stir onion sauce and remaining butter into mashed potatoes. Spoon potato mixture into a serving dish. Arrange cooked corn and shrimp on top. Discard chili. Garnish with egg halves and olives. Makes 4 servings.

Marinated-Fish Salad
KILAW

1-3/4 lbs. firm fish fillets, cut in 3/4-inch pieces
Water
1 teaspoon salt
Juice of 2 or 3 limes or lemons
1 onion, cut in thin rings
1 tablespoon finely chopped fresh gingerroot
1/2 teaspoon black pepper
1 garlic clove, chopped
1-1/2 cups grated fresh or packaged unsweetened coconut
6 tablespoons milk
1/8 teaspoon ground turmeric
1 head iceberg or leaf lettuce
1 medium onion, finely chopped
1/2 cup thinly sliced green bell pepper
1/2 cup shredded cucumber
4 medium tomatoes, peeled, chopped
1 tablespoon finely chopped cilantro or parsley

Place fish in a large saucepan. Cover with water; bring to a gentle boil. Simmer 5 minutes. Drain; rinse with cold water. Pour drained fish into a large deep non-metal bowl. Sprinkle with salt and lime or lemon juice. Scatter onion rings over fish. Sprinkle with gingerroot and black pepper. Cover with foil; refrigerate 8 to 12 hours. In a blender or food processor, puree garlic, coconut, milk and turmeric. Cover and let stand in a cool place 1 hour. Line a salad bowl with lettuce leaves. Line a sieve with muslin or cheesecloth. Strain coconut mixture through lined sieve, reserving coconut milk. Squeeze coconut to remove all milk; discard coconut mixture. Stir coconut milk, chopped onion, green pepper, cucumber and tomatoes into marinated fish. Spoon mixture into lettuce-lined bowl. Garnish with cilantro or parsley. Makes 4 servings.

Lumpia-Stuffed Wrappers
LUMPIA LABONG

5 tablespoons vegetable oil
2 garlic cloves, finely chopped
1 medium onion, finely chopped
1 cup diced cooked pork
3/4 cup peeled cooked shrimp
1 (8-oz.) can bamboo shoots, cut in julienne strips
2 cups shredded Chinese cabbage
1/2 teaspoon salt
1 cup fresh or canned bean sprouts
1/2 (18-oz.) pkg. Philippine lumpia wrappers or spring-roll wrappers
1 head iceberg or leaf lettuce

Lumpia Sauce:
1/4 cup cornstarch
1/3 cup packed brown sugar
1/2 cup soy sauce
1-1/2 cups water

Prepare sauce. Heat 2 tablespoons oil in a wok or large skillet. Add garlic and onion; sauté until transparent. Add pork, shrimp, bamboo shoots, cabbage and salt. Stir-fry 2 to 3 minutes. Stir in bean sprouts; keep warm. Keep wrappers covered until used. Top each wrapper with a lettuce leaf and 1 to 2 tablespoons filling; fold wrapper over stem-end of lettuce. Roll wrapper and filling, with some of lettuce and filling extending from open end of wrapper. Arrange filled wrappers on a platter. Serve with Lumpia Sauce. Makes 4 to 6 servings.
To make sauce, combine all sauce ingredients in a small saucepan. Stir over medium heat until slightly thickened.

Cook's Tip
Lumpia wrappers are available in Oriental specialty-food stores.

Barley & Vegetable Soup
KRUPNIK

1/2 cup pearl barley
5-1/2 cups beef stock or broth
2 tablespoons vegetable oil
2 onions, finely chopped
1/4 cup sliced mushrooms
1 carrot, finely chopped
1 parsnip, finely chopped
2 potatoes, peeled, finely chopped
3 celery-leaf sprigs, chopped
1 bay leaf
Salt and pepper
Chopped dill or parsley

In a medium saucepan, combine barley and 3-1/2 cups stock or broth. Bring to a boil; reduce heat and simmer 5 minutes. Heat oil in a large saucepan. Add onions; sauté until transparent. Add barley with liquid, remaining stock or broth, mushrooms, carrot, parsnip, potatoes, celery leaves and bay leaf. Cover and simmer 30 minutes. Remove and discard bay leaf; season with salt and pepper. Pour into a tureen or serve in individual bowls. Garnish with dill or parsley. Makes 4 servings.

Sour-Rye Soup
ŻUR

Water
2-1/4 cups rye flour
Crust of 1 whole-wheat-bread slice
2 tablespoons dried mushrooms
1 onion, finely chopped
1 carrot, chopped
1 turnip, chopped
1 garlic clove
2 small potatoes, peeled, cut in 1/2-inch cubes
2 bacon slices, chopped
4 Polish sausages or 6 oz. salami, sliced
1/2 teaspoon salt

Begin making *kvass* 3 days ahead. To make *kvass,* the sour mixture, bring 4 cups water to a boil; stir in flour. Add enough water to make a thin mixture; cool slightly. Stir in 1 cup warm water and bread crust. Pour mixture into a glass or stoneware jar. Cover with cheesecloth; let stand 3 days at room temperature. Mixture will turn to *kvass* and develop a sour aroma. Soak mushrooms in 1/4 cup water, 2 hours or until softened; drain. In a large pot, bring 3-1/2 cups water to a boil. Add drained mushrooms, onion, carrot and turnip. Cover and cook 30 minutes. Strain and reserve cooking liquid. Chop mushrooms; return to cooking liquid. Add 1-1/2 to 2-1/2 cups kvass, depending on how sour you want the soup to be. Squeeze garlic through a garlic press into soup. Simmer soup 15 minutes longer. Add potatoes; cook 15 minutes longer. In a small skillet, fry bacon until crisp; add bacon and drippings to soup. Add sausage or salami. Cook until heated through. Stir in salt. Pour into a tureen or serve in individual bowls. Makes 4 servings.

Cabbage & Meat Stew

BIGOS

3 tablespoons lard
1 onion, finely chopped
2 cooking apples, peeled, diced
3 medium tomatoes, peeled, cut in wedges
8 oz. cabbage, shredded
1 lb. sauerkraut
2 bacon slices, diced
1/2 lb. boneless beef round steak, cut in 1-inch cubes
1/2 lb. boneless lean pork, cut in 1-inch cubes
1/2 lb. boneless venison or lean lamb, cut in 1-inch cubes
2 Polish sausages or 3 oz. salami, sliced
1 cup beef stock or broth
1 cup red wine
1 teaspoon sugar
1 teaspoon salt
1/8 teaspoon pepper
1 tablespoon sweet paprika
1 bay leaf
5 allspice berries

Preheat oven to 350F (175C). Melt lard in a large stovetop casserole. Add onion and apples; sauté until onion is transparent. Add tomatoes, cabbage and sauerkraut. Stir well; set aside. In a large skillet, fry bacon; set cooked bacon aside. Brown meat in bacon drippings. Stir browned meat and sausage or salami into cabbage mixture. Stir stock or broth and wine into remaining bacon drippings; then stir liquids into stew. Stir in sugar, salt, pepper, paprika, bay leaf and allspice berries. Cover and bake 1-1/2 hours. Remove cover; bake 30 minutes longer or until meats are tender. Remove and discard bay leaf. Serve hot. Makes 6 servings.

Glazed Pork Roast

PIECZONY SCHAB

1 teaspoon salt
1/8 teaspoon pepper
1 (3-lb.) boneless pork-loin roast
10 whole cloves

Applesauce:
5 cooking apples, peeled, diced
1/2 cup sugar
1 (3-inch) cinnamon stick
1 tablespoon lemon juice
1 cup water

Preheat oven to 350F (175C). Rub salt and pepper into pork; press cloves into pork at equal intervals. Place pork, fat-side up, on a rack in a roasting pan. Roast in center of oven 1-1/2 hours, turning occasionally. Prepare applesauce. Coat pork generously with applesauce. Without turning again, roast 30 minutes longer. Applesauce will form a golden-brown glaze over pork. Turn off oven; leave roast in oven 10 minutes longer. Carve pork into thick slices. Serve with additional applesauce or cooked plums and a sauerkraut salad. Makes 4 servings.
To make applesauce, in a medium saucepan, combine apples, sugar, cinnamon stick, lemon juice and water. Cook over medium heat 10 minutes. Remove cinnamon stick. Press mixture through a sieve or puree in a blender or food processor. Set aside to cool.

Poland

Poppy Roll
ZAWIJANIEC MAKOWY

1/4 cup warm water (110F, 45C)
1 (1/4-oz.) pkg. active dry yeast (1 tablespoon)
1 cup warm milk (110F, 45C)
1/4 teaspoon salt
1/2 cup plus 2 tablespoons butter, melted
1/3 cup sugar
2 eggs
3-1/2 to 3-3/4 cups all-purpose flour

Filling:
1/4 cup cornstarch
2 tablespoons sugar
2 cups milk
1/4 teaspoon vanilla extract
1 tablespoon honey
3/4 cup ground poppy seeds (11 oz.)
2 tablespoons finely chopped candied fruit
1 teaspoon ground cinnamon

In a large bowl, combine water and yeast. Let stand 5 minutes. Stir in milk, salt and 1/2 cup butter. Beat in sugar, eggs and 1-1/2 cups flour. Cover; let rise 30 minutes. Stir in enough remaining flour to make a medium-soft dough. Knead until smooth. Cover; let rise until doubled.
To make filling, in a saucepan, combine cornstarch and sugar. Stir in 2 to 3 tablespoons milk and vanilla, making a paste. Slowly stir in remaining milk. Stir in honey; cook until thickened. Stir in poppy seeds, candied fruit and cinnamon; cool.
To complete, punch down; roll to a 14'' x 12'' rectangle. Spread filling over dough to within 1/2 inch of edges. Roll up from a long side. Place, seam-side down, on a greased baking sheet. Cover; let rise until doubled. Preheat oven to 375F (190C). Cut slashes about 1 inch apart through top layer. Brush top with 2 tablespoons butter. Bake 50 to 60 minutes. Makes 1 large roll.

Walnut Sponge Cake
TORT ORZECAOWY

5 eggs, separated
1/2 cup granulated sugar
1/2 teaspoon vanilla extract
3-3/4 cups finely ground walnuts
2 tablespoons vanilla-cookie crumbs

Icing:
3 tablespoons cornstarch
1/3 cup granulated sugar
2 cups milk
1 teaspoon vanilla extract
1 cup plus 2 tablespoons butter, room temperature
1 cup powdered sugar
2 egg yolks
1 cup coarsely chopped walnuts
Whipped cream and chocolate buttons

Preheat oven to 350F (175C). Grease and flour a round 9-inch cake pan or springform pan. Beat egg whites until stiff. In a large bowl, combine egg yolks, sugar and vanilla; beat until creamy. Fold in beaten egg whites. Fold in nuts and cookie crumbs, 1 tablespoon at a time. Spoon into prepared pan. Bake 30 to 35 minutes or until cake tests done; cool.
To make icing, combine cornstarch and granulated sugar in a saucepan. Stir in milk. Stirring constantly, cook until slightly thickened. Stir in vanilla; set aside to cool. In a medium bowl, cream butter and powdered sugar; beat in egg yolks, 1 at a time. Fold in cornstarch mixture, 1 tablespoon at a time. Refrigerate until firm enough to spread.
To complete, slice cake horizontally into 3 layers. Cover each layer with icing. Stack iced layers. Spread remaining icing on side of cake. Sprinkle top and side with nuts. Garnish with whipped cream and chocolate buttons. Makes 1 (9-inch) cake.

Chestnut Soup
SOPA DE CASTANHAS

1 lb. chestnuts
2-1/2 cups beef or vegetable stock or broth
4 white-bread slices
Pinch of salt
Pinch of white pepper
Pinch of sugar
1 tablespoon butter

Preheat oven to 475F (245C). Cut a cross in pointed end of each chestnut. Spread chestnuts on a baking sheet; roast 20 minutes or until shells split. Peel chestnuts; place in a medium saucepan. Add stock or broth; bring to a boil. Boil 40 minutes. Remove 8 chestnuts; finely dice and set aside for garnish. Press remaining chestnuts through a sieve or puree in a blender or food processor, adding some stock or broth, if needed. Pour puree into remaining stock or broth in pan. Cut crusts from bread; use crusts for another purpose. Tear bread into small pieces. Stir bread pieces into soup; cook over medium heat 3 to 4 minutes. Season with salt, white pepper and sugar. Stir in butter until melted. Pour into a tureen or serve in individual bowls. Garnish with reserved diced chestnuts. Makes 4 servings.

Cook's Tip
Rather than roasting chestnuts in the oven, boil them in water 20 minutes.

Green-Cabbage Soup
CALDO VERDE

8 oz. cabbage or other greens
4 oz. chorizo or salami, sliced
Water
1 teaspoon salt
3 medium potatoes, peeled, sliced
2 tablespoons olive oil
1/8 teaspoon pepper

Clean cabbage or greens. Roll up each leaf; cut into thin slices. Place chorizo or salami in a medium saucepan; add hot water to cover. Bring to a boil; simmer 15 minutes. Drain; set aside to cool. In a large saucepan, bring 2 quarts water to a boil. Add salt and potatoes; cook 20 minutes or until potatoes are tender. Use a slotted spoon to remove cooked potatoes; reserve cooking liquid. Mash potatoes. Return mashed potatoes to cooking liquid. Stir in sliced cabbage or greens, cooked chorizo or salami, oil and pepper. Cover and cook 10 minutes or until heated through. Serve with crusty French bread. Makes 4 servings.

Shrimp Croquettes
CROQUETES DE CAMARÃO

1-1/4 lbs. fresh shrimp
Salt
Water
3 tablespoons butter
1/4 cup all-purpose flour
2 egg yolks, beaten
White pepper
1 egg, beaten
3 cups dry breadcrumbs
1-1/2 cups olive oil or vegetable oil

Place shrimp in a large saucepan. Add 1 teaspoon salt and water to cover. Bring to a boil; boil 5 minutes. Use a slotted spoon to remove shrimp from water; reserve cooking water. Cool, peel and devein shrimp. Return shrimp trimmings to cooking water; boil 10 minutes. Strain and reserve cooking water; discard trimmings. Finely chop cooled shrimp; set aside. Melt butter in a small saucepan. Stir in flour until mixture is smooth. Gradually beat in 1/2 cup reserved cooking liquid; bring to a boil over low heat. Vigorously stir in egg yolks; cook 2 minutes, stirring constantly. Stir in chopped shrimp; season with salt and white pepper. Heat through quickly; set aside to cool. Shape cooled mixture into small balls. Roll balls in beaten egg, then in breadcrumbs. In a medium saucepan, heat oil to 365F (240C) or until a 1-inch cube of bread turns golden brown in 60 seconds. Fry croquettes in hot oil until crisp and browned on all sides; drain on paper towels. Serve croquettes hot. Makes 4 servings.

Dried-Cod Bake
BACALHAU À GOMES DE SÁ

2 lbs. dried cod
Water
1-1/2 cups milk
1/4 to 1/2 cup olive oil or vegetable oil
4 onions, sliced
6 medium potatoes, cooked, peeled, sliced
Salt and pepper
1 tablespoon butter, melted
10 green olives, chopped
1 tablespoon chopped parsley
1 hard-cooked egg, cut in wedges
1 parsley sprig

Soak cod in cold water to cover 12 hours, changing water frequently; drain. Cover soaked cod with boiling water; soak 15 minutes. Drain; remove fins, skin and bones. Flake fish into small pieces; place flaked fish in a deep bowl. Heat milk; pour over flaked fish. Soak 1 hour. Preheat oven to 475F (245C). Heat oil in a large stovetop casserole. Add onions; sauté until transparent. Spread sautéed onions evenly over bottom of casserole. Use a slotted spoon to remove cod pieces from milk; reserve milk. Arrange alternate layers of potatoes and cod over onions, sprinkling each layer with salt and pepper. Top layer should be potatoes. Spoon 1 to 2 tablespoons reserved milk in which cod was soaked over top. Drizzle butter over top. Bake 20 minutes. Sprinkle olives and chopped parsley over top. Garnish with egg wedges and a parsley sprig. Makes 6 servings.

Pork & Mussels

AMEIJOAS A MARINHEIRA
COM CARNE DE
PORCO FRITA

2 lbs. fresh mussels
Salt and white pepper
1 (1-lb.) pork-loin roast
1 tablespoon lard, melted
4 medium tomatoes
3 tablespoons vegetable oil
2 onions, finely chopped
1 garlic clove
1 tablespoon all-purpose flour
1 cup white wine
1 tablespoon chopped parsley
1/2 teaspoon dried leaf thyme
1/2 teaspoon dried leaf basil
1 basil sprig

Soak mussels 2 hours in several changes of salted water. Scrape shells clean; pull out and cut off beards. Rinse mussels in cold water. Meanwhile, preheat oven to 425F (220C). Rub salt and white pepper into pork roast. Place pork in a large roasting pan. Pour lard over pork; roast 60 minutes. Peel tomatoes; remove and discard seeds. Chop tomatoes; set aside. Heat oil in a large saucepan. Add onions and garlic; sauté until transparent. Remove and discard garlic. Add chopped tomatoes; cook until soft. In a small bowl, combine flour and a little wine; set aside. Add remaining wine to tomato mixture; bring to a gentle boil. Add cleaned mussels. Cover and cook over high heat 10 minutes or until shells open. Discard any shells that do not open. Set aside 5 cooked mussels in their shells; remove remaining mussels from shells. Stir flour mixture, parsley, thyme, 1/2 teaspoon basil and a little salt into sauce. Bring mixture to a boil. Dice roast pork; stir diced pork and shelled mussels into sauce. Heat through but do not boil. Spoon into a serving bowl. Arrange reserved mussels in their shells on top of sauce. Garnish with basil sprig. Makes 4 servings.

Braised Beans
(top)
FEIJÃO VERDE À MINHOTA

3 tablespoons olive oil
1-1/2 lbs. fresh green beans, chopped
5 small tomatoes, peeled, chopped
2 onions, sliced vertically in strips
Water
Salt and white pepper
1 tablespoon all-purpose flour
Dash of white-wine vinegar
1 tablespoon chopped parsley

Heat oil in a large skillet. Add beans, tomatoes and onions; cook until tender. Add about 2 tablespoons water, salt and white pepper. Cover; simmer 30 minutes, adding water as needed. In a small bowl, blend flour with a little water; stir into bean mixture. Cook until thickened. Stir in vinegar. Spoon into a serving dish. Garnish with parsley. Makes 4 servings.

Beans in Onion Sauce
(bottom)
FEIJÃO VERDE GUISADO

2 tablespoons olive oil
4 onions, finely chopped
2 tablespoons chopped parsley
1 lb. fresh green beans, cut in 2-inch pieces
Salt and white pepper
Water
Dash of white-wine vinegar
2 tablespoons dry breadcrumbs browned in 1 tablespoon butter

Heat oil in a large skillet. Add onions and parsley; sauté until soft. Press through a sieve or puree in a blender or food processor; return to skillet. Add beans, salt, white pepper and enough water to cover beans. Simmer 30 minutes; add vinegar. Spoon into a serving dish. Sprinkle breadcrumbs over bean mixture. Makes 4 servings.

Oven-Baked Rice
ARROS DE FORNO

1 qt. water
Salt
1-3/4 cups uncooked long-grain white rice
2 tablespoons lard
2 onions, finely chopped
2 carrots, finely chopped
1 cup chopped ham
8 oz. chorizo or salami, thinly sliced
2 tablespoons chopped parsley
1 tablespoon olive oil

Bring water to a boil in a large saucepan. Stir in salt and rice. Cook 10 minutes over medium heat. Preheat oven to 400F (205C). Melt lard in a large stovetop casserole. Add onions and carrots; sauté until onion is transparent. Add ham, chorizo or salami and parsley. Stirring frequently, cook until lightly browned. Stir in rice and any remaining cooking water; sprinkle oil over top. Bake 15 to 20 minutes or until rice is tender. Serve with a salad. Makes 4 servings.

Transylvanian Layered Casserole

1/2 cup uncooked long-grain white rice
Water
Salt
8 oz. bacon slices, diced
1 lb. pork loin, diced
2 onions, finely chopped
1 garlic clove, finely chopped
1 tablespoon paprika
4 frankfurters, sliced
1-1/2 lbs. sauerkraut, drained
6 tablespoons milk
6 tablespoons dairy sour cream
1 teaspoon paprika

Cook rice in boiling salted water 5 minutes. Drain; set aside. Preheat oven to 350F (175C). In a large saucepan, cook bacon. Use a slotted spoon to place cooked bacon into a large bowl. Remove all but 2 tablespoons drippings from saucepan. Add pork to saucepan. Cook until browned on all sides; sprinkle with salt. Use a slotted spoon to place browned pork in bowl with cooked bacon. Add onions and garlic to saucepan; sauté until golden brown. Stir in 1 tablespoon paprika; spoon onion mixture into bowl with cooked meat. Fry frankfurter pieces in saucepan; place in bowl with other cooked meat. Stir 1 cup water into drippings in saucepan; then stir water and drippings into cooked meats. Arrange alternate layers of sauerkraut, meat mixture and cooked rice in a large casserole. In a small bowl, combine milk, sour cream, 1 teaspoon paprika and 1/2 teaspoon salt; pour over casserole. Bake 30 minutes. Add 6 tablespoons hot water; bake 30 minutes longer. Makes 4 to 6 servings.

Baked Zucchini
DOVLĂCEI CU BRENZĂ

6 to 8 small zucchini
Salt
Water
2 tablespoons fresh breadcrumbs
3/4 cup shredded Swiss or Emmentaler cheese (3 oz.)
1/4 cup butter, cut in pieces
2 tablespoons finely chopped parsley
Pepper
1 teaspoon sugar
2 cups whipping cream

Place zucchini in a medium saucepan; add 2 teaspoons salt and water to cover. Partially cover pan; cook over medium heat 10 to 15 minutes or until zucchini is tender but not soft. Drain, cut cooked zucchini into halves lengthwise. Preheat oven to 350F (175C). Butter a large casserole; sprinkle with 1 tablespoon breadcrumbs. Arrange zucchini halves, cut-side up, in prepared dish. Sprinkle with cheese; dot with butter. Sprinkle with parsley, salt and pepper Bake in center of oven 30 to 40 minutes or until golden brown. Stir sugar into whipping cream; serve with baked zucchini. Makes 6 to 8 servings.

Hors d'Oeuvres Table

SAKUSSKA

The hors d'oeuvres table, or *sakusska,* dates from Czarist Russia. Its small delicacies were intended to revive guests arriving after a long coach or sled ride. It also filled the time before the evening meal was served. For us, the sakusska symbolizes legendary Russian hospitality. Apart from the recipes given here, the table would also include small meat pasties, caviar, marinated mushrooms, assorted salads, highly seasoned buckwheat groats, various breads, pickled cucumbers and chilled vodka.

Liver Pâté

PASCHTET

1/4 cup vegetable oil
1 lb. calves' liver, finely chopped
1/2 cup plus 2 tablespoons butter
1 medium carrot, coarsely chopped
3 medium onions, coarsely chopped
1 tablespoon chopped parsley
Salt
1/4 teaspoon pepper
1/8 teaspoon ground nutmeg

Heat oil in a large skillet. Add liver; cook over medium heat 10 to 15 minutes until done but not overcooked. Drain on paper towels; set aside. Melt 2 tablespoons butter in skillet. Add carrot and onions; cook over low heat 15 to 20 minutes or until tender. Using a blender or food processor, process cooked liver, cooked carrot and onions, parsley, 1/2 teaspoon salt, pepper and nutmeg until finely chopped. Add remaining 1/2 cup butter; process until completely smooth. Season to taste. Spoon into a mold; cover and refrigerate 10 hours. To serve, turn out onto a plate or platter. Garnish as desired. Serve with crackers or toast triangles. Makes 3-1/2 to 4 cups.

Fish in Aspic

OSSETRINA SALIWNAJA

1 (10-oz.) can condensed chicken broth
Water
Mixed fresh herbs, tied with string
1 large carrot
1 onion, chopped
1 bay leaf
4 black peppercorns
3 tablespoons red-wine vinegar
1/2 to 3/4 lb. halibut or other white fish
1 (1/4-oz.) envelope unflavored gelatin (1 tablespoon)
2 egg whites
Several dill sprigs

In a large saucepan, combine broth, broth can of water, mixed herbs, whole carrot, onion, bay leaf, peppercorns and vinegar. Bring to a boil. Reduce heat; simmer 15 to 20 minutes or until carrot is tender. Strain cooking liquid, reserving liquid and other ingredients. Slice carrot; cut in decorative shapes, if desired. Set aside. Bring strained liquid to a boil; add fish. Poach 8 minutes. Remove poached fish; reserve liquid. Cut fish into small pieces; refrigerate until needed.
To make aspic, soften gelatin in 2 tablespoons cold water. Line a sieve with muslin or 3 layers of cheesecloth; set aside. In a small bowl, beat egg whites until stiff. Bring cooking liquid to a boil; stir in softened gelatin and beaten egg whites. When liquid begins to foam, remove from heat; strain through lined sieve. Cool aspic to room temperature; do not refrigerate.
To complete, spray 8 individual molds with non-stick aerosol. Arrange carrot slices in molds; add a few small dill sprigs to each mold. Pour aspic 1/4 inch deep in each mold; refrigerate until set. Top with pieces of fish; fill molds with aspic. Refrigerate until set. To serve, turn out onto a platter or onto individual plates. Makes 8 servings.

Borscht
BORSCHTSCH

5-1/2 cups water
Salt
1 lb. boneless beef round, finely chopped
1/2 lb. boneless pork, finely chopped
2 tablespoons lard
1 onion, finely chopped
1 lb. beets, peeled, cut in strips
2 tablespoons red-wine vinegar
Pinch of sugar
1 lb. cabbage, shredded
1 large carrot, grated
1/4 celeriac or 2 celery stalks, finely chopped
1 tablespoon lemon juice
1 bay leaf
12 bacon slices, diced
1/3 cup dairy sour cream
1 tablespoon chopped parsley

In a large saucepan, bring water and 2 teaspoons salt to a boil. Add beef and pork; cover and cook 1 hour and 10 minutes or until tender. Remove meat; set aside to cool. Reserve cooking liquid. Melt lard in a large saucepan. Add onion; sauté until transparent. Add beets, vinegar, 1/2 teaspoon salt and sugar. Stir in 1 cup reserved cooking liquid. Cover and simmer 50 minutes. Combine cabbage, carrot and celeriac or celery; sprinkle with lemon juice. Add to beet mixture; add bay leaf, cooled meat and bacon. Simmer 25 minutes longer. Remove and discard bay leaf. Pour into a tureen or serve in individual bowls. Garnish with a dollop of sour cream; sprinkle with parsley. Makes 6 servings.

Siberian Ravioli
SIBIRSKIJE PELJMENI

3 cups all-purpose flour
Salt
2 eggs, slightly beaten
Water
1 lb. ground beef
1 medium onion, finely chopped
1/4 teaspoon pepper
1 egg yolk, beaten
4 cups chicken stock or broth
2 to 4 cups beef stock or broth
Chopped fresh dill

Stir together flour and 1/4 teaspoon salt. Stir in 2 eggs and 6 to 8 tablespoons warm water, making a smooth dough. Wrap in plastic wrap; let stand 20 minutes. Knead dough until smooth; set aside. In a large bowl, combine beef, onion, 3 tablespoons ice-cold water, 1 teaspoon salt and pepper. Divide dough into 4 equal pieces. On a lightly floured surface, roll out dough, 1 piece at a time, until 1/16 inch thick. Cut dough into 1-1/2- to 2-inch circles. Brush edges of circles with egg yolk. Place 1/2 teaspoon meat mixture on each dough circle. Fold dough over filling; crimp edges with a fork. Arrange ravioli, not touching, on floured surface; let stand 10 minutes to dry slightly. Pour chicken and beef broth or stock into a large pot; bring to a boil. Add ravioli, a few at a time; keep liquid boiling. Reduce heat; simmer ravioli, uncovered, 10 minutes. Pour ravioli and cooking liquid into a tureen or serve in individual bowls. Garnish with dill. Makes about 200 ravioli.

Variation

While ravioli stands to dry, add sliced carrots and onion rings to hot broth; bring to a boil. Continue as directed above.

Blini with Salmon

BLINI

2 teaspoons active dry yeast
2 cups warm water (110F, 45C)
2 cups warm milk (110F, 45C)
1-1/2 cups buckwheat flour
2 eggs, separated
1 teaspoon sugar
1/4 teaspoon salt
2 tablespoons butter, melted
1 cup all-purpose flour
Vegetable oil
1 cup dairy sour cream or 1/2 cup butter, melted
4 oz. smoked salmon, thinly sliced, or 1 (2 oz.) jar caviar
2 hard-cooked eggs, chopped

In a large bowl, dissolve yeast in water. Add 1 cup milk. Stir in 3/4 cup buckwheat flour. Let rise in a warm place, free from drafts, until doubled in bulk, 2 to 3 hours. In a small bowl, beat egg yolks. Stir in sugar, salt, 2 tablespoons butter and remaining milk. Stir into raised yeast mixture. Stir in remaining buckwheat flour and all-purpose flour; beat until smooth. In a medium bowl, beat egg whites until stiff but not dry. Fold into yeast mixture; cover and let stand 45 minutes. Heat 1 to 2 teaspoons oil in a large skillet. Spoon 1/4 cup batter into skillet; spread to a 4-inch circle. Cook on both sides until lightly browned. Dip cooked blini in sour cream or melted butter. Immediately place a slice of smoked salmon or a little caviar and a little hard-cooked egg on coated blini. Roll and place on a platter or serve as shown. Blini are eaten with the fingers. Makes 24 to 28 (4-inch) blini.

Braised Liver

TSCHARENAJA TEL JATSCHJA PETSCHONKA

3 tablespoons butter
1-3/4 lbs. sliced calves' liver
1/2 teaspoon salt
1/2 teaspoon dried leaf oregano
6 to 8 bacon slices
1-1/2 to 2 cups hot beef stock or broth
2 teaspoons all-purpose flour
1 cup dairy sour cream

Melt butter in a large skillet. Add liver; brown on both sides. Season with salt and oregano. Arrange bacon on liver. Add 1-1/2 cups stock or broth. Cover and simmer 30 minutes. Add more stock or broth, as needed. Remove liver and bacon; place on a warm platter. Whisk flour into sour cream; stir into stock or broth in pan. Cook until thickened, stirring constantly. Pour sauce over liver. Serve with mashed potatoes. Makes 4 servings.

Variation

Add 2 tablespoons caviar to the cream sauce.

Cook's Tip

In Russia, the whole liver is soaked in 2 cups milk for 1 hour. It is then *larded* or has long strips of fat bacon threaded through it. The liver is sliced after it is cooked.

Uzbek Pilaf
PLOW PO USBEZKI

1/4 cup vegetable oil
1 lb. boneless lamb, cut in 3/4-inch cubes
1 onion, finely chopped
3 large carrots, coarsely chopped
2-1/2 cups beef stock or broth
1-1/2 cups uncooked long-grain white rice
1/2 teaspoon salt
1/8 teaspoon white pepper
3 medium tomatoes, peeled, sliced

Heat oil in a large skillet. Add lamb; sauté until browned. Add onion; sauté 5 minutes. Add carrots and 1 cup stock or broth. Bring to a boil; reduce heat and simmer 30 minutes. Stir rice into lamb mixture; simmer 5 minutes longer. Add remaining stock or broth. Cook 15 to 20 minutes or until rice and lamb are tender. Add salt and white pepper. Spoon into a serving dish. Arrange sliced tomatoes over top. Serve with radishes and yogurt. Makes 4 servings.

Variation

Turkmenian Pilaf: Add 1 tablespoon each soaked raisins and prunes to pilaf before serving.

Chicken Caucasia-Style
TSCHACHOCHBILI

1/4 cup vegetable oil
1 (2- to 3-lb.) chicken, cut in quarters
2 onions, finely chopped
1 carrot, finely chopped
1 small celeriac or 3 celery stalks, finely chopped
1 small cucumber, peeled, finely chopped
1/4 lb. pumpkin or squash, peeled, finely chopped
1 teaspoon salt
1/8 teaspoon pepper
1 bay leaf
Pinch of ground fennel seeds
3-1/2 cups water
6 tablespoons uncooked long-grain white rice
1 large pickled cucumber, diced
1/4 cup dairy sour cream

Preheat oven to 350F (175C). Heat oil in a large stovetop casserole. Add chicken quarters; cook until browned on all sides. Remove chicken quarters. Add onions, carrot, celeriac or celery, cucumber and pumpkin or squash; sauté about 5 minutes. Stir salt, pepper, bay leaf, fennel, water and rice into onion mixture. Add browned chicken quarters. Cover and bake 1-1/2 hours or until chicken and vegetables are tender. Before serving, remove bay leaf; stir in pickle and sour cream. Serve on a platter or in a serving bowl. Makes 4 servings.

Cabbage Pastie
KULEBJAKA

3 tablespoons butter
3 onions, finely chopped
2 lbs. cabbage, shredded, blanch 5 minutes in hot water
1 cup water
3 hard-cooked eggs, chopped
3 tablespoons chopped dill
2 tablespoons chopped parsley
White pepper
1/4 teaspoon sugar

Pastry:
3/4 cup plus 2 tablespoons butter, chilled
2-3/4 cups all-purpose flour
6 tablespoons dairy sour cream
1 egg, beaten
1 egg yolk, beaten

To make filling, preheat oven to 350F (175C). Melt butter in a stovetop casserole. Add onions; sauté until golden. Add blanched cabbage and water. Cover; bake 30 to 40 minutes. When cabbage is tender, drain; cool. Stir in hard-cooked eggs, dill, parsley, salt, white pepper and sugar.
To make pastry, in a medium bowl, use a pastry blender or fork to cut in butter. Stir in sour cream and whole egg; shape into a ball. Refrigerate 15 minutes.
To complete, roll out 1/2 of chilled pastry into an oval slightly less than 1/4 inch thick. Place on a greased baking sheet. Roll out remaining pastry into a slightly larger oval; cover and set aside. Increase heat to 425F (220C). Spoon cabbage mixture over pastry base; cover with top pastry. Fold bottom pastry over top pastry. Pinch together to seal edges; flute or decorate as desired. Cut a hole in top pastry; decorate with leftover pastry. Brush with egg yolk. Refrigerate 15 minutes; bake 30 minutes or until golden brown. Makes 8 to 10 servings.

Cheese Tarts
WATRUSCHKI

Pastry:
2-1/2 cups all-purpose flour
1/2 teaspoon baking powder
1/2 teaspoon salt
6 tablespoons butter, chilled
1 egg, beaten
1/4 cup plus 3 tablespoons dairy sour cream
1 egg yolk, beaten

Filling:
1 lb. large-curd cottage cheese (2 cups)
2 tablespoons dairy sour cream
2 eggs, beaten
1/2 teaspoon salt
1/8 teaspoon white pepper
1 teaspoon sugar

To make pastry, in a medium bowl, stir together flour, baking powder and salt. Use a pastry blender or fork to cut in butter. Stir in egg and sour cream; shape into a ball. Wrap in plastic wrap; refrigerate 45 minutes.
To make filling, in a large sieve, gently rinse cottage cheese to remove cream; drain 5 minutes. Press drained cottage cheese through sieve into a large bowl; stir in sour cream, eggs, salt, white pepper and sugar. Refrigerate 45 minutes.
To complete, preheat oven to 400F (205C). Lightly grease 2 large baking sheets; set aside. On a lightly floured surface, roll out pastry 1/8 inch thick. Cut 6 (5-inch) and 6 (4-inch) rounds. Arrange 5-inch rounds on greased baking sheets. Top each with 2 tablespoons cheese mixture; cover each with a 4-inch round. Brush edges of 5-inch rounds with egg yolk; fold edges as shown. Brush tops of tarts with egg yolk. Bake 20 minutes or until golden brown. Makes 6 tarts.

Paskha

PASSCHA

3 (12-oz.) pkgs. large-curd
  cream-style cottage cheese
  (4-1/2 cups)
1/2 cup unsalted butter, room
  temperature
Generous pinch of salt
5 eggs, beaten
1 cup dairy sour cream
1 cup raisins
1-1/2 cups sugar
Grated peel of 1 lemon
3/4 cup chopped blanched almonds
1 tablespoon finely chopped
  candied orange peel
1 tablespoon finely chopped
  candied lemon peel

Decorations:
Candied cherries
Blanched almonds
Candied orange and lemon peel
Angelica strips

Line a colander with muslin or several layers of cheesecloth; place over a large bowl. Drain cheese in lined colander in refrigerator 3 hours. Cheese should be as dry as possible. Stir butter until creamy. In a large saucepan, combine creamed butter, salt, eggs, sour cream and drained cheese. Stir constantly over low heat until warm; do not boil. Remove from heat; stir until cool. Wash and dry raisins. Fold washed raisins, sugar, lemon peel, chopped almonds and chopped candied peels into cheese mixture. Use wet muslin or 2 layers of wet cheesecloth to line a paskha mold or a tall flower pot with a hole in the base. Spoon mixture into mold; press down firmly. Fold ends of cloth over top of mixture. Place a small plate on top; place another weight on plate. Place mold in a pie dish; refrigerate 12 hours or overnight. To serve, turn out onto a serving plate; remove cloth. Decorate with candied cherries, blanched almonds, candied peels and angelica strips. Makes 16 to 20 servings.

Variation

Use chopped mixed candied fruits in place of candied peels.

Cook's Tip

Paskha is traditionally eaten in Russia at Easter. The Russian letters XB on the side translate to *Christ has risen.*

Fried Shrimp

8 fresh or frozen jumbo shrimp
1/2 teaspoon salt
1 egg white
2 tablespoons cornstarch
Vegetable oil for deep-frying
1 tablespoon soy sauce
1 tablespoon chicken stock or broth
4 garlic cloves, cut in thin slices
1 oz. fresh gingerroot, cut in thin slices
3 dried green chilies, crushed

Thaw frozen shrimp. Peel and devein shrimp; cut each into 3 pieces. Sprinkle with salt; set aside. In a small bowl, beat egg white with cornstarch. Dip shrimp pieces in egg-white mixture until completely coated. Heat oil in a wok or large skillet to 350F (175C) or until a 1-inch cube of bread turns golden brown in 65 seconds. Stirring constantly, cook coated shrimp, a few pieces at a time, in hot oil, 3 to 5 minutes or until golden. Drain on paper towels; keep warm. Heat soy sauce and stock or broth in a small saucepan. Stir in garlic, gingerroot and chilies. Bring to a boil. Place drained shrimp on a platter. Immediately pour mixture over shrimp. Serve as an appetizer or side dish. Makes 4 to 6 servings.

Fried Noodles

Water
Salt
1 lb. egg noodles
1 fresh red chili
7 oz. boneless lean pork
3 tablespoons vegetable oil
1 garlic clove, finely chopped
1 oz. fresh gingerroot, finely chopped
2 cups fresh or canned bean sprouts, drained
1 (4-oz.) can sliced bamboo shoots, drained
2 green onions, sliced
3 tablespoons soy sauce
Pepper

Cook noodles in boiling, salted water, 4 to 5 minutes or until tender but firm to the bite; drain well. To handle fresh chilies, cover your hands with rubber or plastic gloves; after handling, do not touch your face or eyes. Slice chili; remove and discard seeds and pith. Cut pork into 2'' x 1/4'' strips. Heat oil in a wok or deep skillet. Stir-fry garlic and gingerroot 2 to 3 minutes. Add pork strips; stir-fry 2 minutes. Add sliced chili, bean sprouts, bamboo shoots and green onions; stir-fry 3 minutes. Add cooked noodles; stir-fry 3 minutes. Season with soy sauce, salt and pepper. Spoon into a serving dish. Serve with additional soy sauce, if desired. Makes 4 servings.

Salmon & Pork

LAULAU

7 oz. smoked salmon, thinly sliced
1-1/2 lbs. boneless lean pork
1-1/2 lbs. fresh spinach
Salt
Freshly ground pepper
Lemon slices

Cut salmon into 3/4-inch-wide strips. Cut pork into 2-inch squares about 3/4 inch thick. Clean spinach; drain well. Cut as many 8-1/2-inch squares of foil as you have pork squares. In the center of each foil piece, place a thick layer of spinach and 1 square of pork. Season with pepper. If salmon is mild-flavored, sprinkle a little salt over meat. Arrange salmon strips over pork. Fold foil to make airtight packages. Bring a large saucepan of water to a boil. Add foil packages; boil 20 minutes. If necessary, add more boiling water. Open foil packages and spoon contents onto plate. Garnish with lemon slices. Serve with sweet potatoes. Makes 4 servings.

Fijian Baked Fish

2 cups milk
1 cup half and half
1-1/2 cups grated fresh or packaged unsweetened coconut
1-3/4 lbs. cod or haddock fillets
Juice of 1 lemon
Salt and white pepper

Sauce:
2 fresh green chilies
1/2 cup canned coconut milk or Coconut Milk, page 7
1 lemon, peeled, chopped
1/2 onion, chopped
Salt

In a medium saucepan, combine milk, half and half and coconut. Bring to a boil; reduce heat and simmer 10 minutes. Set aside to cool slightly. Preheat oven to 375F (190C). Generously butter a shallow baking dish. Arrange fish in buttered dish. Sprinkle lemon juice over fish; season with salt and white pepper. Spoon slightly cooled coconut mixture over top. Bake 30 to 40 minutes or until fish flakes easily.

To make sauce, prepare chilies. To handle fresh chilies, cover your hands with rubber or plastic gloves; after handling, do not touch your face or eyes. Cut chilies in halves; remove and discard seeds and pith. Chop chilies. Stir together chopped chilies, coconut milk, lemon and onion. Add salt to taste. Serve over baked fish. Makes 4 servings.

Beef Kabobs with Pineapple
TERIYAKI

1 (12-oz.) can pineapple chunks
1 garlic clove, finely chopped
6 tablespoons soy sauce
1 teaspoon ground ginger or 1 tablespoon grated fresh gingerroot
1 lb. beef sirloin steak, cut in 3/4-inch cubes
12 pimiento-stuffed green olives
Vegetable oil
Salt

Drain pineapple, reserving juice in a small bowl; set pineapple aside. Stir garlic, soy sauce and ginger or gingerroot into pineapple juice. Place beef cubes in a large bowl. Pour pineapple-juice mixture over beef. Cover and refrigerate 1 hour. Preheat barbecue grill or broiler. Drain beef, reserving marinade. Thread marinated beef cubes onto metal or wooden skewers, alternating with pineapple chunks. Thread an olive on each skewer. Brush kabobs with oil; brush oil on grill. Broil or grill 10 to 12 minutes or to desired doneness, turning occasionally and brushing with reserved marinade. Season with salt. Serve with cooked rice. Makes 4 servings.

Cook's Tip

These kabobs taste even better made with fresh pineapple.

Pumpkin Pudding
PUMPKIN PILHI

1 (29-oz.) can pumpkin or 3 cups cooked fresh pumpkin
2 (7-3/4-oz.) cans coconut milk or Coconut Milk, page 7
3/4 cup sugar
2 to 4 tablespoons all-purpose flour
1 teaspoon salt
1/4 teaspoon ground allspice
1 tablespoon butter
1/4 cup grated coconut

Preheat oven to 375F (190C). Generously butter a 10-inch quiche or flan dish; set aside. In a blender or food processor, puree pumpkin; add coconut milk, sugar, flour, salt and allspice. Turn motor on and off 2 or 3 times to blend thoroughly. Pour pumpkin mixture into buttered dish; smooth top. Dot with butter. Sprinkle coconut over top. Bake 1 hour or until a knife inserted off-center comes out clean. When coconut begins to brown, cover with foil. Serve with fried meat or poultry. Makes 6 to 8 servings.

Variations

Substitute 3/4 cup packed brown sugar for granulated sugar.
For a pumpkin dish with pumpkin-pie flavor, add 1/2 teaspoon ground ginger, 1/4 teaspoon ground cloves and 1 teaspoon ground cinnamon.

Semolina Soup with Almonds
SOPA CREMA DE SÉMOLA CON ALMENDRAS

1/3 cup toasted blanched almonds
Salt
1/4 cup semolina, farina or regular Cream of Wheat cereal
1 tablespoon butter
3 cups beef or vegetable stock or broth
3 egg yolks
1/2 cup half and half
Freshly ground white pepper

Crush almonds with a mortar and pestle or process in a blender or food processor. Heat crushed almonds and a pinch of salt in a stovetop casserole, stirring constantly. Stir in semolina, farina or Cream of Wheat. Continue cooking 2 to 3 minutes. Add butter; heat until melted. Gradually stir in stock or broth. Bring to a boil over low heat, stirring frequently. Cook 10 minutes. In a medium bowl, beat egg yolks. Stir in half and half; season with salt and pepper. Stir about 5 tablespoons hot soup into egg-yolk mixture. Stir egg-yolk mixture into remaining hot soup. Cook, stirring constantly, until thickened. Pour into a tureen or serve in individual bowls. Sprinkle with white pepper. Serve immediately. Makes 4 servings.

Cream of Mussel Soup
CREMA DE ALMEJAS

4 medium tomatoes
2 tablespoons butter
4 shallots, finely chopped
2 cups fish or vegetable stock or broth
Pinch of saffron threads
1 teaspoon hot water
2 tablespoons cornstarch
1/2 cup milk
1 (14-oz.) jar mussels
2 egg yolks
1/2 cup half and half
Pinch of white pepper
1 tablespoon chopped fresh rosemary
1 teaspoon chopped fresh lemon balm

Peel and quarter tomatoes; remove and discard seeds. Melt butter in a large saucepan. Add shallots; sauté until transparent. Add stock or broth and tomato quarters. Cover and simmer 10 minutes. In a small bowl, combine saffron and hot water; let stand 5 minutes. Stir cornstarch into saffron mixture. Gradually stir in milk. Stir mixture into tomato mixture. Bring to a simmer, stirring constantly. Add mussels and any liquid that has accumulated; heat through. In a small bowl, beat together egg yolks, half and half and white pepper. Stir about 1/3 cup liquid from tomato mixture into egg-yolk mixture. Stir egg-yolk mixture into remaining tomato mixture until slightly thickened. Pour into a tureen or serve in individual bowls. Sprinkle with rosemary and lemon balm. Makes 4 servings.

Vegetable Soup
SOPA JULIANA

2 tablespoons olive oil
4 green onions, cut in strips
4 cups beef stock or broth
1/2 head cabbage, shredded
1 green bell pepper, cut in strips
2 medium carrots, peeled, sliced
2 medium potatoes, peeled, finely chopped
4 medium tomatoes
2 cups fresh or frozen green peas
2 tablespoons chopped parsley

Heat oil in a large saucepan. Add green onions; sauté until transparent. Add stock or broth; bring to a boil. Add cabbage, green peppers, carrots and potatoes. Cover and simmer 20 minutes. Peel and quarter tomatoes; remove and discard seeds. Add tomato quarters and peas to soup. Simmer 8 to 10 minutes. Pour into a tureen or serve in individual bowls. Garnish with parsley. Makes 4 servings.

Madrid Garlic Soup
SOPA DE AJO A LA MADRILEÑO

6 to 8 thin white-bread slices
4 garlic cloves
Salt
2 tablespoons olive oil
1 tablespoon sweet paprika
3 cups water
4 eggs
2 tablespoons chopped chives

Remove crusts from bread; set bread aside. Use crusts for another purpose. Crush garlic with a little salt. Heat oil in a large saucepan. Stir in garlic-salt mixture. Add bread; lightly brown on both sides, turning carefully. Sprinkle paprika over bread. Add water; bring to a boil. Reduce heat; simmer 15 minutes. Remove from heat. Crack 1 egg into a ladle. Carefully lower egg into hot mixture. Repeat with remaining eggs. Return pan to heat; simmer 2 to 3 minutes or until egg whites are set. Remove eggs from soup. Pour soup into a tureen or serve in individual bowls. Arrange eggs over soup in tureen or, top individual servings with eggs. Garnish with chives. Makes 4 servings.

Eggs Flamenco
HUEVOS A LA FLAMENCA

4 cherry tomatoes
5 tablespoons olive oil
1 onion, finely chopped
2 garlic cloves, finely chopped
1 red bell pepper, cut in strips
1 cup fresh or frozen green peas
6 oz. fresh green beans, cut in 2-inch pieces
Salt and white pepper
Pinch of red (cayenne) pepper
8 oz. chorizo or salami, thinly sliced
4 to 8 fresh side-pork slices, cut in strips
4 eggs

Peel tomatoes; remove and discard seeds. Chop tomatoes. Heat oil in a stovetop casserole. Add onion and garlic; sauté until browned. Add chopped tomatoes, red bell pepper, peas and beans. Season with salt, white pepper and cayenne pepper. Cover and simmer 15 minutes. Preheat oven to 400F (205C). Reserve 4 chorizo or salami slices. Stir remaining chorizo or salami and side pork into vegetables. Using a small ladle, make 4 indentations in vegetable mixture. Place an egg in each indentation. Cover each egg with a reserved slice of chorizo or salami. Place casserole in center of oven. Bake until egg whites are firm and heated through. Serve from casserole or, spoon onto 4 plates. Arrange eggs over casserole or, top individual servings with eggs. Makes 4 servings.

Empanadillas
EMPANADILLAS

1 (1-1/4-lb.) pkg. frozen puff pastry, thawed (2 sheets)
2 tablespoons olive oil
1/2 medium onion, finely chopped
2 bacon slices, finely chopped
9 oz. diced cooked lamb (about 1 cup)
1/2 teaspoon salt
1/2 teaspoon paprika
1 tablespoon chopped chives
1 egg, slightly beaten
1 egg yolk, beaten

Thaw pastry. Heat oil in a large skillet. Add onion and bacon; sauté about 4 minutes. Add lamb; cook about 5 minutes, stirring frequently. Season with salt and paprika. Stirring rapidly, add chives and whole egg. On a lightly floured surface, roll out each thawed pastry sheet until 12'' x 12''. Cut each sheet into 9 (4-inch) squares. Spoon meat mixture evenly onto pastry squares. Fold corner-to-corner over filling, making triangles. Use a fork to crimp edges firmly together. Arrange triangles on 2 ungreased baking sheets. Preheat oven to 400F (205C). Let empanadillas stand 15 minutes, then brush each with egg yolk. Bake 20 to 25 minutes. Serve hot or cold. Makes 18 empanadillas.

Paella

PAELLA

1 lb. fresh mussels
Water
Salt
1/8 teaspoon saffron threads
1 cup olive oil
1 (3-lb.) chicken, cut in pieces
Pepper
2 onions, finely chopped
3 garlic cloves, finely chopped
1-1/2 cups uncooked long-grain white rice
1 qt. beef stock or broth
8 oz. whitefish fillets, skinned, chopped
8 oz. peeled cooked shrimp
1 cup fresh or frozen green peas
6 tomatoes, peeled, cut in wedges
1/2 cup dry white wine
8 oz. chorizo or salami, sliced
15 pimiento-stuffed green olives, cut in halves
Lemon wedges

Soak mussels 2 hours in several changes of salted water. Scrape shells clean; pull out and cut off beards. Rinse mussels in cold water. In a large saucepan, cover cleaned mussels with water. Bring to a boil; boil vigorously 10 minutes or until shells open. Discard any shells that do not open. Strain mussels; set aside. In a small bowl, soak saffron in 1 teaspoon hot water 5 minutes. Heat 3/4 cup oil in a large deep skillet or paella pan. Add chicken pieces; cook until browned on all sides. Season with salt and pepper. Add onions, garlic and rice; sauté until onions are transparent. Add stock or broth; stir in soaked saffron. Simmer 10 minutes. Carefully stir in cooked mussels, fish, shrimp, peas and tomatoes. Add wine; simmer 10 minutes longer. Add more stock, broth, wine or water if liquid evaporates before rice is cooked. If rice is too moist, boil until liquid is mostly evaporated. Heat remaining 1/4 cup oil in a small skillet. Add chorizo or salami; cook until browned and crisp. Spoon rice mixture into a serving dish or platter. Sprinkle olives over paella; top with fried chorizo or salami. Garnish with lemon wedges. Makes 6 servings.

Variation

Baby squid are delicious in paella. Vary the shellfish to include cockles, whelks, crayfish and even lobster. Substitute pork pieces or tiny sausages for chorizo. Vegetables may include green beans, red and green bell peppers, zucchini and artichoke hearts.

Cook's Tip

Paella varies according to what foods are available. Essential ingredients are rice and saffron. Other ingredients may be added, if desired.

Basque Hot-Pot
MINESTRA A LA VISCAINA

1 small head cauliflower
2 tomatoes
3 tablespoons olive oil
1 (2-lb.) chicken, skinned, boned, cut in large pieces
1/2 lb. boneless veal, cut in 1-inch cubes
1 onion, finely chopped
3 leeks, sliced
1 carrot, sliced
1 tablespoon all-purpose flour
1-1/2 cups beef stock or broth
1/3 cup white wine
Salt and white pepper
12 small new potatoes, peeled
8 artichoke hearts, cut in halves
2 hard-cooked eggs, sliced
1 tablespoon chopped parsley

Break cauliflower into flowerets. Steam flowerets 30 minutes; set aside. Peel tomatoes; remove and discard seeds. Chop tomatoes; set aside. Heat oil in a deep skillet. Add chicken and veal; cook until browned on all sides. Drain on paper towels. Add onion, leeks and carrot to oil in pan. Sprinkle with flour; cook until onion is soft. Stir in chopped tomatoes, stock or broth and wine. Season with salt and white pepper; cook 15 minutes. Press cooked vegetables through a sieve or puree in a blender or food processor; return puree to skillet. Add cooked chicken, veal and potatoes. Cover and cook 30 minutes. Add steamed cauliflower and artichoke hearts; heat through. Spoon into a large dish. To serve, garnish with egg slices and parsley. Makes 4 servings.

Catalan Chicken
POLLO A LA CATALANA

8 chicken legs with thighs attached
1/2 teaspoon salt
1 tablespoon sweet paprika
6 tablespoons olive oil
2 onions, finely chopped
4 garlic cloves, crushed
1 bay leaf, crumbled
2 dried mild green chilies, crushed
2 dried mushrooms, chopped
1/2 cup dry red wine
2 tablespoons half and half
About 1 tablespoon red-wine vinegar
1 tablespoon honey
Soy sauce
Pinch of red (cayenne) pepper
1/4 cup roasted peanuts, coarsely chopped

Make several cuts in each chicken piece; rub with salt and paprika. Let stand 15 minutes. Heat oil in a large saucepan. Add chicken pieces; brown on all sides. Drain on paper towels. Add onions and garlic to oil in pan; sauté until golden brown. Return browned chicken pieces to pan. Add bay leaf, chilies, mushrooms, wine, half and half and 1 tablespoon vinegar. Cover and cook over low heat 20 minutes. Remove and discard chicken skin. Place skinned chicken in a serving dish; keep warm. Pour off any fat from pan drippings; strain remaining drippings. Stir in honey; bring to a vigorous boil. Boil until sauce becomes creamy. Season with soy sauce, red pepper and a few drops vinegar, if desired. Pour sauce over chicken. Garnish with peanuts. Serve immediately. Makes 4 servings.

Seafood Curry

MALU CURRY

1 lb. crabmeat or peeled cooked shrimp
3 fresh red chilies
3 tablespoons vegetable oil
1 onion, finely chopped
2 garlic cloves, finely chopped
2 tablespoons medium-hot curry powder
1 oz. fresh gingerroot, grated
2 (7-3/4-oz.) cans coconut milk or 2 cups Coconut Milk, page 7
1/2 leek, cut in 1/2-inch slices
1 lb. cod fillets, cut in pieces
Citronella leaves, if desired
2 medium tomatoes, peeled, cut in wedges
Juice of 1 lime or lemon
Water

Break crabmeat or shrimp into pieces; set aside. To handle fresh chilies, cover your hands with rubber or plastic gloves; after handling, do not touch your face or eyes. Cut chilies open lengthwise; remove seeds and pith. Chop chilies. Heat oil in a large skillet. Add onion and garlic; sauté until golden. Stir in chopped chilies, curry powder and gingerroot. Stirring constantly, cook 2 to 3 minutes. Stir in coconut milk and leek. Simmer 10 minutes. Add crabmeat or shrimp, cod and citronella leaves, if desired. Cook 10 minutes over low heat, shaking pan occasionally to prevent burning. Add tomatoes; cook 5 minutes longer. Season with lime or lemon juice; add enough water to moisten ingredients, if necessary. Makes 6 servings.

Cook's Tips

Ground curry powder begins to lose its flavor and fragrance after a few months. Buy your curry powder in small amounts and use within one year.

Curry powder is not a single spice, but a blend of many spices. The spices included in the curry depend on the manufacturer. The flavor may be very peppery or mild. In India, housewives often grind the various spices daily, adding their own favorite spices.

Curry refers to any dish that is seasoned with curry powder. Many foods can be curried. There are different ways to prepare curries, but the meat, fish or poultry is usually simmered slowly in stock or broth that is seasoned with curry powder. Onions, vegetables and hard-cooked eggs are often added. Coconut milk or yogurt may also be added. The curry is served with rice, couscous, fruit, vegetables, chutney, coconut or chapatis. See page 110 for Chapatis recipe.

Pepper Curry
HARAK MAS CURRY

1 (2-1/4-lb.) beef-round steak, sliced 1/2 inch thick
2 teaspoons salt
2 teaspoons pepper
2 tablespoons vegetable oil
2 tablespoons butter
2 onions, finely chopped
4 garlic cloves, crushed
2 tablespoons medium-hot curry powder
2 oz. fresh gingerroot, thinly sliced
Juice of 1/2 lime or lemon
2 (7-3/4-oz.) cans coconut milk or 2 cups Coconut Milk, page 7
Citronella leaves, if desired
1 (8-oz.) can sliced bamboo shoots, drained
2 tablespoons shredded unsweetened coconut

Place beef in a deep bowl. In a small bowl, stir together salt, pepper and oil; pour mixture over beef. Cover and marinate 30 minutes. Melt butter in a large skillet. Add onions and garlic; sauté until golden. Stir in curry powder; cook 2 minutes. Add gingerroot, lime or lemon juice and coconut milk. Simmer 10 minutes. Pour curry sauce into a medium saucepan; keep warm. Add beef to skillet; cook over high heat with no added fat until browned. Add to curry sauce with a few citronella leaves, if desired. Simmer 5 minutes. Stir in bamboo shoots. Cook 3 to 5 minutes longer. Spoon onto a platter; garnish with coconut. Serve hot. Makes 6 servings.

Molded Coconut Mousse
VATTALAPPAM

1/2 cup packed brown sugar
1/4 teaspoon ground cardamom
1/4 teaspoon ground mace
1/4 teaspoon ground cloves
1/4 cup dark corn syrup
1/4 cup water
4 eggs
1-1/2 cups plus 2 tablespoons Coconut Milk, page 7
3/4 cup unsalted cashews

Preheat oven to 325F (165C). Lightly oil 8 individual heatproof molds; set aside. In a medium saucepan, combine brown sugar, cardamom, mace and cloves; blend well. Stir in corn syrup and water; bring to a boil. Simmer until sugar is dissolved; cool slightly. In a medium bowl, beat eggs thoroughly; stir in coconut milk. Stir in sugar mixture. Sprinkle cashews evenly in bottoms of oiled molds. Pour milk mixture over cashews. Place a large shallow baking pan in center of oven. Pour hot water to a 1-inch depth in pan. Place filled molds in hot water. Hot water should come half-way up sides of molds. Bake 1 hour. Remove from oven; set aside to cool. When cold, turn out each mousse onto a dessert plate. Turn cashew-side up. Makes 8 servings.

Split Peas with Pork

ÄRTER MED FLÄSK

2 cups dried yellow split peas
3-1/2 cups water
1 onion, coarsely chopped
1 carrot, coarsely chopped
1 teaspoon dried leaf marjoram
1/2 teaspoon dried leaf thyme
Salt
1 lb. fresh salt pork

Combine split peas and water in a large saucepan. Bring to a boil over medium heat. Remove from heat; cover and let stand 1 hour. Skim to remove any skins from top of water. Add onion, carrot, marjoram, thyme and a little salt. Leave salt pork in 1 piece; add to saucepan. Cook 1-1/2 hours. Season to taste. Remove and slice salt pork. Serve with black bread and mustard. Makes 6 servings.

Jansson's Temptation

JANSSONS FRESTELSE

5 medium potatoes
3 tablespoons butter
2 large onions, cut in thin rings
White pepper
1 (3-oz.) can Swedish anchovy fillets
1 cup half and half
2 tablespoons dry breadcrumbs
2 teaspoons finely chopped parsley

Preheat oven to 400F (205C). Butter a large casserole; set aside. Peel and slice potatoes; cut slices into thin strips. Melt 2 tablespoons butter in a large skillet. Add onion rings; sauté until transparent. Spread 1/2 of the potato strips in bottom of buttered dish. Sprinkle with white pepper. Scatter sautéed onion rings over top; season with white pepper. Top with anchovies and remaining potatoes; season with white pepper. Pour half and half over casserole. Sprinkle breadcrumbs over top; dot with remaining tablespoon butter. Place in center of oven; bake 45 minutes or until breadcrumbs are browned and potatoes are tender. To serve, garnish with parsley. Makes 4 to 6 servings.

Cook's Tip

Swedish anchovies are larger, moister and less salty than other anchovies. They are available in gourmet stores and Scandinavian specialty stores.

Swedish Meatballs
SVENSKA KÖTTBULLAR

1 soft dinner roll or 2 white-bread slices
1/4 cup warm water
1 small red onion, finely chopped
1 teaspoon salt
1 teaspoon ground allspice
1 egg yolk
1 lb. lean ground beef
1/4 cup butter

In a small bowl, soften bread in water. Drain water from bread; squeeze to remove as much water as possible. In a large bowl, combine moistened bread, onion, salt, allspice and egg yolk. Add beef; blend thoroughly, beating with an electric beater or by hand until smooth. Dampen your hands with water. Use your hands to shape beef mixture into 1-inch balls. Melt butter in a large skillet. Over medium heat, brown meatballs, a few at a time, on all sides. Serve immediately with mashed potatoes and cloudberry or whole-cranberry sauce. Makes 4 servings.

Cook's Tip

For a tasty meatball dip, beat together 1 cup dairy sour cream, 2 teaspoons Dijon-style mustard, 1 teaspoon onion salt, 1 teaspoon lemon juice, 1/4 teaspoon salt and 1/8 teaspoon white pepper.

Beef Patties à la Lindstrom
BIFF À LA LINDSTRÖM

6 tablespoons butter
2 onions, finely chopped
1 (8-oz.) can beets
1 lb. ground beef
3 tablespoons drained capers
6 tablespoons half and half
1 egg, slightly beaten
1 to 2 teaspoons salt
1/2 teaspoon pepper

Melt 2 tablespoons butter in a large skillet. Add onions; sauté until transparent. Drain beets, reserving juice; finely chop beets. In a large bowl, combine sautéed onions, chopped beets, 6 tablespoons reserved beet juice, ground beef, capers, half and half, egg, salt and pepper. Shape mixture into 4 flat patties. Melt remaining 4 tablespoons butter in skillet; cook patties 3 to 4 minutes on each side until browned on outside but pink inside. Makes 4 servings.

Variation

Cut toasted white bread into rounds. Generously spread beef mixture over 1 side of each toast round. Bake in a 450F (230C) oven 5 to 6 minutes. Serve hot.

Sweet Beans
BRUNA BÖNOR

2 cups dried pinto beans, Swedish brown beans or kidney beans
Water
1 to 2 teaspoons salt
1/3 cup wine vinegar
1/3 cup dark corn syrup
1 tablespoon brown sugar

In a large saucepan, soak beans in water to cover 12 hours; cook beans in soaking water over low heat 1 hour, leaving lid slightly ajar. Stir in salt, vinegar, corn syrup and brown sugar. Cook 1 hour longer or until beans are tender. Add a little water occasionally, if necessary. Sauce will have consistency of a thick stew but beans will not be mushy. Makes 4 servings.

Variation

Add a fully cooked sausage during final 15 minutes of cooking time. Or, serve beans with cooked bacon.

Dilled Shellfish
KRÄFTOR

3 lbs. live crayfish, frozen rock or slipper lobster, or shrimp in shells
4 qts. water
2 tablespoons salt
1 leek, white part only, chopped
1 qt. tightly packed fresh dill heads and stems
Fresh dill sprigs

Wash crayfish, lobster or shrimp in cold water. In a large pot, combine water, salt, leek and 1 quart dill. Bring to a boil; reduce heat and simmer 10 minutes. Add crayfish, lobster or shrimp. Bring to a boil again. Remove from heat; let stand 15 minutes. Pour off excess liquid, leaving only enough to cover seafood. Refrigerate until chilled. Drain off liquid. Arrange chilled seafood on a platter. Garnish with dill sprigs. Serve with toasted white bread and butter or melted butter and lemon wedges. Makes 4 servings.

Cook's Tip

Crayfish are considered a great delicacy in Sweden. They can only be caught from midnight on August 7th until the end of September. During this time, open-air crayfish parties are a popular form of entertainment.

Swedish Pancakes

PLÄTTAR

2 eggs
1 cup milk
1/4 cup half and half
2/3 cup all-purpose flour
2 teaspoons baking powder
2 tablespoons sugar
1/2 teaspoon salt
3 tablespoons butter, melted

In a medium bowl, beat eggs; stir in milk and half and half. Stir together flour, baking powder, sugar and salt; sprinkle over egg mixture. Gently stir in until batter is smooth. Stir in butter. Let stand 1 hour. Stir batter thoroughly. Preheat a plättar pan or a 6-inch cast-iron skillet. Grease cups of plättar pan or grease skillet. Spoon 2 rounded tablespoons batter into each cup or onto skillet; cook about 1 minute on each side until golden brown. Repeat with remaining batter. Serve with stewed fruit, lingonberry jam or other jam or jelly and sour cream. Makes 4 servings.

Variation

Make 8-inch pancakes. Layer several pancakes with thick lingonberry, bilberry or blackberry jam between them. When cool, frost stack with whipped cream.

Zurich Veal with Rôsti

ZÜRCHER
KALBS-GESCHNETZELTES

1 tablespoon all-purpose flour
1 tablespoon butter
1/4 cup vegetable oil
1-1/2 lbs. boneless veal, thinly
   sliced
1 onion, finely chopped
3/4 lb. mushrooms, thinly sliced
1/2 cup dry white wine
1 cup half and half
1 teaspoon salt
1/8 teaspoon white pepper

Rôsti:
3 medium potatoes
About 2 tablespoons lard

In a small bowl, use a pastry blender or fork to combine flour and butter; set aside. Heat oil in a large skillet. Brown veal, a few pieces at a time, in hot oil. Remove browned veal from skillet; place in a sieve over a medium bowl to drain. Add onion to oil in skillet; sauté until transparent. Add mushrooms; sauté until tender. Add wine and half and half; stir in flour mixture. Simmer 3 to 4 minutes, stirring constantly, until slightly thickened. Season with salt and white pepper. Stir in drippings from veal; stir in veal. Heat through.

To make rôsti, boil or bake potatoes until about half-cooked. Slice hot potatoes. Melt lard in a large skillet. Add potato slices. Cook until potatoes soften and form a potato cake with a golden crust. Serve veal mixture with rôsti, and a green or cucumber salad. Makes 4 servings.

Bread & Cheese Pudding
RAMEQUIN

10 oz. Emmentaler or Swiss cheese
1 (1-lb.) loaf white bread, thinly sliced
3 eggs
1 cup milk
1/2 teaspoon salt
Pinch of white pepper
Pinch of grated nutmeg

Preheat oven to 400F (205C). Butter a 13" x 9" baking dish; set aside. Cut cheese into slices slightly larger than bread slices. In a medium bowl, beat eggs; beat in milk, salt, white pepper and nutmeg. In buttered dish, arrange alternate slices of bread and cheese, slightly overlapping. Pour egg mixture over bread and cheese. Bake 30 minutes or until top is browned and crisp. Serve with a fresh green salad. Makes 4 servings.

Cook's Tip

This is a good way to use leftover bread. Vary the recipe by substituting other types of cheese.

Savory Pancakes
PANNEQUETS

1-1/2 cups all-purpose flour
1 cup milk
6 tablespoons white wine
5 tablespoons vegetable oil
6 tablespoons water
4 eggs
1/2 teaspoon salt

Filling:
1-1/4 cups grated Emmentaler or Swiss cheese (5 oz.)
1 cup grated Gruyère cheese (4 oz.)
1/2 cup plus 2 tablespoons white wine
Pinch of white pepper
Pinch of ground nutmeg

Sauce:
2 tablespoons butter
1 tablespoon all-purpose flour
1 (13-oz.) can evaporated milk
1-1/4 cups grated Emmentaler or Swiss cheese (5 oz.)
2 tablespoons kirsch or other cherry-flavored liqueur
Pinch of white pepper

In a medium bowl, beat together flour, milk, wine, 2 tablespoons oil, water, eggs and salt. Cover; let stand 1 hour. Fry batter in remaining 3 tablespoons oil. Pancakes will be thin.
To make filling, combine filling ingredients. Butter a large baking dish. Fill pancakes with cheese mixture; roll up or fold into fourths. Arrange pancakes in buttered dish, slightly overlapping. Preheat oven to 475F (245C).
To make sauce, melt butter in a medium skillet. Stir in flour until browned. Gradually stir in milk. Stir in cheese, liqueur and white pepper. Pour sauce over filled pancakes; bake 20 minutes. Serve with a lettuce and tomato salad. Makes 4 servings.

Cheese Fondue
FONDUE NEUCHÂTELOISE

1 garlic clove, cut in half
1-1/2 cups white wine
12 oz. Gruyère cheese, diced
12 oz. Emmentaler cheese, diced
1 teaspoon cornstarch
3 tablespoons kirsch or other cherry-flavored liqueur
Pinch of grated nutmeg
Pinch of white pepper
1 or 2 (1-lb.) loaves white bread, unsliced

Rub inside fondue pot with garlic halves. Finely chop garlic; sprinkle in pot. Add wine; heat until wine is slightly warm. Add cheeses; melt over medium heat, stirring constantly. Do not let cheese mixture boil. In a small bowl, combine cornstarch and liqueur; stir into cheese mixture. Season with nutmeg and white pepper. Place pot over an alcohol burner or a small candle. Stir occasionally; do not let mixture boil. Cut bread into 1-1/2-inch cubes. Each guest pierces a bread cube with a fondue fork and dips it into fondue, letting bread soak up as much cheese as possible. A cheese crust will form at the bottom of the pot. Cheese crust at bottom of pot is considered a great delicacy. When fondue is used down to crust, lift out and divide among guests. Makes 4 servings.

Cook's Tips

Each Swiss canton has its own cheese-fondue recipe, using local cheeses. Depending on availability, vary your fondue with other Swiss cheeses. French bread is excellent with fondue—small slices have a lot of crust and are especially easy to pierce with a fondue fork.

For a drink, serve the same wine as was used in the fondue. Or, serve hot black tea and kirsch. Traditionally, anyone who loses a piece of bread in the fondue must provide the host with a bottle of wine!

Another Swiss national dish is beef fondue. Fill the pot with hot oil. Guests skewer small pieces of tender beef on their forks, then cook it in hot oil. French bread and an assortment of salads and sauces are traditionally served with beef. Horseradish sauce, mustard pickles, ripe olives and thinly sliced onion rings are all popular accompaniments.

Apple Tarts
APFELTÖRTCHEN

1/2 (1-1/4-lb.) pkg. frozen puff pastry (1 sheet)
6 apples
1/2 cup apricot jam
1 to 2 tablespoons water
1 egg yolk, beaten
2 tablespoons toasted flaked almonds

Thaw pastry. On a lightly floured surface, roll out until 16" x 12". Cut into 12 (4-inch) squares. Cover with a dry cloth; set aside. Peel apples; cut in halves lengthwise. Remove cores; cut lengthwise incisions almost all the way through each apple half, 1/16 to 1/8 inch apart. Do not cut all the way through. In a small saucepan, stir jam over low heat until melted. Stir in water, 1 teaspoon at a time, to make a thick puree. Place 1 apple half on each square of pastry. Roll up edges slightly, folding in corners, as shown. Brush egg yolk over pastry. Brush apples with warmed jam mixture. Arrange tarts on an ungreased baking sheet; let stand 15 minutes. Preheat oven to 400F (205C). Bake tarts 20 to 30 minutes or until pastry is golden brown. Cool tarts, then brush with remaining jam mixture. Sprinkle evenly with almonds. Makes 12 tarts.

Prune Tartlets
PAPETTE-TÖRTCHEN

Filling:
1-1/2 lbs. pitted prunes (2 lbs. unpitted)
2-1/3 cups golden raisins
Water
1-1/4 cups sugar

Pastry:
4-1/4 cups all-purpose flour
1-1/2 cups butter
1/4 teaspoon salt
1/2 cup water
1 egg
1 egg yolk, beaten

To make filling, in separate bowls, soak prunes and raisins in water to cover 12 hours. Drain fruit; remove pits from prunes, if necessary. Chop prunes. In a large saucepan, combine chopped prunes, raisins, sugar and water to cover. Simmer 1 hour or until thickened. Cool, stirring frequently.
To make pastry, sift flour into a large bowl. Dot with butter. Use a pastry blender or fork to cut butter into flour until mixture resembles coarse crumbs. Make a well in center of flour mixture. Place salt, 1/2 cup water and whole egg into well; beat together slightly. Using a fork, gradually stir in flour mixture to make a smooth dough. Wrap and refrigerate 1 hour.
To complete, preheat oven to 450F (230C). On a lightly floured surface, roll out pastry. Use to line 12 tartlet molds or 2 (8- or 9-inch) pie pans. Fill each evenly with prune mixture. Roll and cut pastry trimmings into thin strips; arrange in a lattice pattern as shown. Brush egg yolk over lattice top. Bake in center of oven 20 to 25 minutes. Makes 12 tartlets or 2 (8- or 9-inch) pies.

Switzerland

Swiss Pastry Shell
MÜRBETEIGKUCHEN

2-1/2 cups all-purpose flour
Pinch of salt
1/2 cup butter, chilled
2 tablespoons lard, chilled
About 3 tablespoons water
1 tablespoon butter, melted

Sift flour and salt into a medium bowl. Use a pastry blender or fork to cut 1/2 cup butter and lard into flour until mixture resembles coarse crumbs. Sprinkle with water. Use a fork to stir in water, making a firm dough. Wrap dough and refrigerate 1 hour. Preheat oven to 400F (205C). On a lightly floured surface, roll out dough until 1/8 inch thick. Use to line a 9- or 10-inch flan or quiche pan. Brush dough with melted butter. Line with foil, being sure no air pockets remain. Bake 10 minutes. Remove foil; bake 5 to 8 minutes longer. Set aside to cool. Makes 1 (9- or 10-inch) pastry shell.

Apple Flan
(right)
APFELWÄHE

1 baked Swiss Pastry Shell, opposite
5 medium cooking apples
3/4 cup sugar
1 egg
1/2 cup half and half
2 tablespoons all-purpose flour
1 tablespoon apple brandy
1 tablespoon water
1/2 cup apricot jam

Prepare pastry shell. Preheat oven to 400F (205C). In a bowl, toss sliced apples with 1/2 cup sugar. Arrange in pastry shell. Bake 20 minutes. In a medium bowl, beat egg. Beat in half and half, remaining 1/4 cup sugar, flour and brandy; pour over partially baked apples. Bake 20 minutes or until custard sets. In a small saucepan, stir water into jam; stir over low heat until melted. Press through a sieve or puree in a blender or food processor; brush over apple flan. Makes 1 (9- or 10-inch) flan.

Cheese Flan
(left)
KÄSEWÄHE

1 baked Swiss Pastry Shell, above
2 tablespoons vegetable oil
1 onion, finely chopped
1/8 teaspoon red (cayenne) pepper
1-1/4 cups grated Emmentaler cheese (5 oz.)
1-1/4 cups grated Gruyère cheese (5 oz.)
2 eggs
1/2 cup milk
1 tablespoon all-purpose flour
1/2 cup half and half
1/4 teaspoon salt
Pinch of grated nutmeg

Prepare pastry shell. Preheat oven to 350F (175C). Heat oil in a skillet. Add onion; sauté until soft. Sprinkle with red pepper; set aside. Toss cheeses together. Sprinkle 1/2 of cheeses in baked pastry shell. Sprinkle with sautéed onion. Top with remaining cheeses. In a small bowl, beat eggs. Stir in milk, flour, half and half, salt and nutmeg; pour over cheese mixture. Bake 10 minutes; increase heat to 425F (220C). Bake 15 minutes longer or until a knife inserted off-center comes out clean. Makes 1 (9- or 10-inch) flan.

Iced-Fruit Salad
CHOZHAFFE

3 oz. dried apricots
3 oz. pitted prunes
3 oz. dried figs
3 oz. dried pear or apple rings
3 tablespoons raisins
Cold water
2 tablespoons whole blanched
　almonds
2 tablespoons pistachios
2 tablespoons pine nuts
Pinch of ground cardamom
Pinch of ground cinnamon
1/4 cup grenadine
1/4 cup rose water
Small ice cubes

In a medium bowl, cover dried fruits with cold water. Cover and refrigerate 24 hours; drain well. In a large bowl, combine drained fruit and nuts. In a small bowl, combine cardamom, cinnamon, grenadine and rose water; pour over fruit and nuts. Cover and refrigerate at least 2 hours. To serve, stir in ice cubes. Makes 6 servings.

Cook's Tip

Eastern desserts are often sweet. If preferred, add juice of 1 lemon for a less sweet, but refreshing salad.

Shrimp Soup
KAENG CHUED

4 oz. fresh or frozen peeled, cooked, baby shrimp
2 (7-3/4-oz.) cans coconut milk or 2 cups Coconut Milk, page 7
4 shallots, fincly chopped
1 garlic clove, finely chopped
1 teaspoon ground coriander
1 tablespoon soy sauce
1 tablespoon sugar
1/8 teaspoon red (cayenne) pepper
10 whole peppercorns
Grated peel of 1 lemon
1-1/2 teaspoons butter
1 white-bread slice, toasted, cut in cubes

Thaw frozen shrimp. In a medium saucepan, combine coconut milk, shallots, garlic, coriander, soy sauce, sugar, red pepper, peppercorns and lemon peel. Bring mixture to a boil. Add shrimp; heat through. Melt butter in a medium skillet. Sauté bread cubes in butter until golden. Pour soup into a tureen or serve in individual bowls. Sprinkle bread cubes over soup. Makes 4 servings.

Hot Rice & Pork
KHAO PHAT

1/4 cup vegetable oil
1 large onion, finely chopped
1 garllc clove, crushed
1/2 lb. boneless pork, cut in thin strips
7 oz. fresh or frozen peeled, cooked shrimp
2 cups cooked long-grain white rice
2 tomatoes, peeled, diced
2 teaspoons chili sauce
Salt
1 teaspoon shrimp paste
3 eggs, slightly beaten
6 to 8 green onions, finely chopped
1 tablespoon chopped cilantro or parsley

Heat oil in a wok or large skillet. Add 1 chopped onion and garlic; sauté until onion is transparent. Add pork; cook until browned. Add shrimp; cook 3 to 4 minutes, stirring occasionally. Stir in rice, tomatoes, chili sauce, 1 teaspoon salt and shrimp paste; heat through. Stir eggs into rice mixture; cook until set. Stir in green onions. Spoon into a large dish or serve in individual dishes. Sprinkle with cilantro or parsley. Makes 4 servings.

Cook's Tip

This peppery dish can be made with meat, fish, shrimp or vegetables, but always includes eggs.

Couscous with Stewed Beef

KUSKI BIL LHAM

Couscous:
1 lb. couscous
1 teaspoon salt
1 cup water
2 teaspoons olive oil

Stew:
3 medium potatoes, peeled
2 carrots
2 beets, peeled
1 small cabbage
2 large tomatoes, peeled
3 medium zucchini
1/2 lb. pumpkin, peeled
6 tablespoons vegetable oil
1 lb. boneless beef-round steak, cut in 3/4-inch cubes
2 onions, finely chopped
1 teaspoon salt
1/2 teaspoon red (cayenne) pepper
1/2 teaspoon ground cumin
1/8 teaspoon ground allspice
Water
1 (14-oz.) can chick peas or garbanzo beans, drained

To start couscous, spread couscous on a board or work surface. Dissolve salt in water; sprinkle salt-water mixture and olive oil over couscous. Rub couscous between the palms of your hands to make small balls. Cover and let stand to swell.

To make stew, cut potatoes, carrots, beets, cabbage, tomatoes, zucchini and pumpkin into 2-inch pieces. Heat vegetable oil in a large, deep saucepan. Add beef cubes and onions; cook 10 minutes, stirring frequently. Add salt, red pepper, cumin, allspice and 6 tablespoons water. Cover pan; simmer beef mixture 30 minutes, stirring frequently. Add prepared vegetables, peas or beans and water to cover.

To cook couscous, line a steamer with muslin or several layers of cheesecloth. Place steamer in pan over stew. Use damp cheesecloth or muslin to seal any space left between steamer and side of pan. Rub a handful of couscous between your palms; let couscous kernels fall into lined steamer. As soon as it begins to steam, add a second handful. Continue until all couscous has been crumbled into steamer. Steam 20 minutes; pour or spoon steamed couscous onto a platter. Spread out; set aside to dry. Remove cooked beef and vegetables from saucepan; keep warm. Return dry couscous to steamer. Steam 10 to 15 minutes over stew liquid or until couscous is tender but still holds its shape. Spoon couscous onto a large platter; keep warm. Return beef and vegetables to liquid; heat through. Strain off liquid; arrange hot beef and vegetables around couscous. Keep hot. Boil liquid until reduced; serve separately. Makes 6 servings.

Tunisia

Orange Doughnuts with Honey

YO-YO

Doughnuts:
4 eggs
1/4 cup vegetable oil
1/4 cup orange juice
Grated peel of 1 orange
1/4 cup sugar
3 cups all-purpose flour
2 teaspoons baking powder

Honey Syrup:
1 cup sugar
3/4 cup water
Juice of 1/2 lemon
1/2 cup honey
Oil for deep frying

To make doughnuts, in a medium bowl, beat eggs. Stir in oil, orange juice, orange peel and sugar. In a large bowl, stir together flour and baking powder. Stir into egg mixture, 1 tablespoon at a time, making a soft dough. Cover; let stand 30 minutes.
To make syrup, in a medium saucepan, combine sugar, water and lemon juice. Stir over medium heat until sugar dissolves. Bring to a boil; boil gently 5 minutes. Stir in honey; boil 5 minutes longer. Set aside; keep warm.
To complete, heat oil to 350F (180C) or until a 1-inch cube of bread turns golden brown in 65 seconds. Divide dough into 10 equal pieces. Shape each piece into a ball. Press on each ball to flatten slightly. Press your thumbs through center of each flattened ball, making a 1-inch hole. Fry 2 doughnuts at a time in hot oil, 2 to 3 minutes on each side. Drain on paper towels; keep warm. Using a wooden skewer, prick cooked doughnuts in 6 or 7 places. Dip pricked doughnuts in warm syrup. Serve immediately. Makes 10 doughnuts.

Almond & Sesame Pastry

SAMSA

1 (1-1/4-lb.) pkg. frozen puff pastry
3-1/2 cups sliced almonds
3 cups sesame seeds
1-1/2 cups sugar
1 egg yolk, slightly beaten
1 cup water
Juice of 1 lemon
1 tablespoon rose water

Thaw pastry. Preheat oven to 350F (175C). Sprinkle almonds and sesame seeds onto a baking sheet. Lightly brown in oven 15 to 20 minutes, stirring occasionally. In a blender or food processor, process browned almonds and sesame seeds about 1/3 at a time until finely ground. In a medium bowl, combine ground almond mixture and 1/2 cup sugar; set aside. On a lightly floured surface, roll out thawed pastry; cut into 5 (10-inch) circles. Rinse a 10-inch springform pan with cold water. Place 1 pastry circle in bottom of wet pan; sprinkle with 1/4 of the almond mixture. Top with another pastry circle. Continue layering pastry circles and almond mixture, ending with a pastry circle. Brush egg yolk over top pastry; cut cake into 12 wedges. Bake 30 minutes; reduce heat to 300F (150C). Bake 20 to 30 minutes longer or until golden brown. In a small saucepan, combine remaining 1 cup sugar and water. Bring to a boil. Stirring constantly, boil 5 minutes. Stir in lemon juice and rose water. Cool syrup slightly. With cake still in pan, pour warm syrup over hot cake. Serve warm. Makes 12 servings.

Variation

Substitute 2 packages frozen patty shells or 1 double-crust pie pastry for frozen puff pastry. Also see Puff Pastry, page 8.

Fish in Olive Oil
ZEYTIN YAĞI ILE KIZARTILMIS BALIK

1 (2-1/4-lb.) whole perch, pike, sea bream or sunfish
2 garlic cloves
Salt
6 tablespoons olive oil
2 large onions, cut in rings
2 green bell peppers, cut in strips
2 or 3 medium tomatoes, peeled, sliced
1 parsley sprig, chopped
3 tablespoons tomato paste
Water
Pinch of black pepper
12 ripe olives

Clean fish; rinse in cold water. Pat dry with paper towels. Crush garlic with a little salt. Heat oil in a large skillet. Add cleaned fish; cook 2 minutes on each side. Remove from skillet; set aside. Sauté onions in skillet until golden brown. Add pepper strips; cook until tender. Stir in garlic-salt mixture; add tomatoes and parsley. In a small bowl, combine tomato paste and 1 cup water; stir into tomato mixture. Season with salt and black pepper; simmer 10 minutes. Return fish to skillet; add water to cover. Simmer 10 to 15 minutes or until fish flakes easily and vegetables are tender. Arrange fish and vegetables in a shallow serving bowl; garnish with olives. Refrigerate 30 minutes or until chilled. Serve cold. Makes 2 servings.

Baked Cabbage & Lamb
LAHANA FIRINDA

1/4 cup butter
2 onions, finely chopped
12 oz. lean ground lamb
1 large cabbage, shredded
1/2 teaspoon salt
1 teaspoon red (cayenne) pepper
2 tablespoons fresh breadcrumbs
1 teaspoon tomato paste
1 cup beef stock or broth
3 oz. feta cheese, crumbled
2 eggs
1 cup milk

Melt butter in a large saucepan. Add onions; sauté until slightly browned. Add lamb; cook 5 minutes, stirring to break up meat. Stir in cabbage, salt and red pepper; simmer 30 minutes. Butter a large shallow casserole; sprinkle breadcrumbs over bottom and sides. Spoon cabbage mixture into prepared casserole. In a small bowl, stir tomato paste into stock or broth; pour over cabbage mixture. Cook over medium heat until most of the liquid has evaporated; set aside to cool slightly. Preheat oven to 350F (175C). Sprinkle cheese over cabbage mixture. In a small bowl, beat eggs; beat in milk. Pour over casserole. Bake 45 minutes. Makes 4 to 6 servings.

Stuffed Eggplant
IMAM BAYILDI

4 medium eggplants
3 garlic cloves
Salt
5 tablespoons olive oil
3 onions, cut in rings
3 medium tomatoes, peeled, chopped
1 bay leaf
1 (3-inch) cinnamon stick
1/8 teaspoon sugar
1 tablespoon chopped parsley
2 tablespoons chopped almonds

Preheat oven to 400F (205C). Butter 2 large shallow baking dishes; set aside. Bake eggplants on oven rack 15 minutes, turning frequently. Remove from oven. Reduce heat to 350F (175C). Peel eggplants; cut in halves. Remove eggplant flesh leaving a 3/4-inch shell; chop flesh. Crush garlic with 1/2 teaspoon salt. Heat 2 tablespoons oil in a large skillet. Add onions; sauté 5 minutes. Add garlic-salt mixture and tomatoes. Cover and cook 5 minutes. Add bay leaf, cinnamon stick, sugar, 1 teaspoon salt, parsley and chopped eggplant. Cook 10 minutes. Remove bay leaf and cinnamon stick; stir in almonds. Arrange eggplant shells in buttered dishes. Spoon tomato mixture into each eggplant shell. Sprinkle with remaining oil. Bake 15 to 20 minutes or until cooked through. Makes 6 to 8 servings.

Pan-Fried Aubergine & Lamb
PATLICAN KEBABI

2 small eggplants, cut in cubes
Salt
1 garlic clove
3 tablespoons butter
3 tablespoons sesame oil or sunflower oil
1-1/2 lbs. boneless lamb, cut in 3/4-inch cubes
3 onions, coarsely chopped
2 large tomatoes, peeled, chopped
Pepper
5-1/2 cups hot beef stock or broth

In a medium bowl, sprinkle eggplant cubes with 1 tablespoon salt; let stand 30 minutes. Crush garlic with 1/4 teaspoon salt. Rinse eggplant with cold water; drain on paper towels. Heat butter and oil in a large skillet. Add drained eggplant; sauté until golden brown. Drain on paper towels. Add lamb to fat remaining in skillet; brown lamb over high heat. Use a slotted spoon to remove lamb; place in a large saucepan. In skillet, sauté onions in remaining fat until golden. Add tomatoes and garlic-salt mixture; cook 5 minutes. Add to browned lamb. Season with salt and pepper. Add stock or broth to lamb mixture. Cover and simmer 30 minutes. Add browned eggplant; simmer 30 minutes longer or until eggplant is tender. To serve, spoon into a large bowl. Makes 4 to 6 servings.

Lamb Pilaf
KARIŞIK PİLAV

Salt
Water
1 lb. uncooked long-grain white rice (2-1/2 cups)
4 oz. lambs' or calves' kidneys
3 tablespoons butter
4 oz. lambs' or calves' liver, chopped
1/4 cup olive oil
2 onions, chopped
8 oz. lean lamb, chopped
2-1/2 cups hot beef stock or broth
2 tablespoons pine nuts
1/8 teaspoon ground cinnamon
1 teaspoon allspice berries
2 tablespoons currants
1 teaspoon sugar
1 tablespoon tomato paste
Pepper
3 tablespoons finely chopped dill or 1-1/2 tablespoons dill weed

In a large deep bowl, dissolve 1 teaspoon salt in 5 cups warm water. Stir in rice. Let stand until water is cool; drain well. Soak kidneys in cold water to cover 30 minutes. Drain kidneys; pat dry with paper towels. Chop kidneys, removing any ligaments and fat. Melt butter in a large saucepan. Add chopped kidneys and liver. Cook 5 minutes; set aside. Heat oil in a large skillet. Add onions; sauté until transparent. Add lamb; cook 5 minutes over high heat. Add soaked rice; sauté until transparent. Stir in stock or broth, pine nuts, cinnamon, allspice berries, currants, sugar, tomato paste, salt and pepper. Simmer until most of the liquid has evaporated. Stir in cooked liver and kidneys with any fat from pan. Add dill. Cover and cook 20 minutes longer or until rice is tender. Spoon into a serving dish; serve hot. Makes 8 to 10 servings.

Chicken Pilaf Istanbul-Style
ISTANBUL-PİLÂVI

Salt
Water
1 lb. uncooked long-grain white rice (2-1/2 cups)
6 tablespoons vegetable oil
1/8 teaspoon saffron threads
2 cups hot chicken stock or broth
3 oz. chicken livers, chopped
1 boneless chicken breast, chopped
1/4 cup whole blanched almonds
1 cup fresh or frozen green peas

In a large deep bowl, dissolve 1/4 teaspoon salt in 2 cups warm water. Stir in rice. Let stand until cool and water is absorbed. Heat oil in a large saucepan. Add soaked rice; sauté 10 minutes. In a small bowl, soak saffron in 1 teaspoon hot water 5 minutes. Stir saffron mixture and stock or broth into rice. Stir in liver, chicken breast, almonds, peas and 1/2 teaspoon salt. Bring to a boil; stir constantly over medium heat until most of the liquid evaporates. Cover; cook over low heat 20 minutes or until rice is tender. Spoon into a serving dish; serve hot. Makes 8 to 10 servings.

Turkey

Lamb Kabob with Yogurt

YOĞORTLU KEBAB

1 large onion, grated
Salt
1-1/2 lbs. boneless lamb, cut in
1/2-inch cubes
2 tablespoons olive oil
4 brown-bread slices, about 2/3
inch thick
5 tablespoons butter, room
temperature
5 tomatoes, peeled, chopped
1 (8-oz.) carton plain yogurt
(1 cup)

In a large bowl, combine onion and 1 teaspoon salt. Cover and let stand 15 minutes. Puree onion mixture in a blender or food processor. Place lamb in a deep bowl; pour onion puree and oil over lamb. Cover and refrigerate 1 hour. Set oven at lowest temperature setting; leave door ajar. Cut crusts from bread; use crusts for another purpose. Toast bread lightly. Stir butter until creamy; spread over bread. Cut toasted bread into cubes; place in a heatproof bowl. Place in oven to keep warm. Preheat barbecue grill or broiler; oil grill and 4 metal or wooden skewers. Drain marinated lamb cubes. Thread lamb cubes onto oiled skewers, leaving about 1/2 inch between each cube. Grill or broil 10 to 15 minutes, turning several times. Meanwhile, place tomatoes in a large skillet. Cook over low heat, stirring constantly. Stir yogurt; season with salt. Arrange bread cubes on 4 plates. Place 1 kabob on bread cubes on each plate. Spoon tomatoes and yogurt over top. Makes 4 servings.

Shrimp Cocktail

1/4 cup mayonnaise
1/4 cup half and half
1/2 teaspoon Worcestershire sauce
1/2 teaspoon sugar
1/2 teaspoon lemon juice
1/4 teaspoon salt
1 teaspoon dry mustard
1 teaspoon anchovy paste
Lettuce leaves
1/4 cup sliced ripe olives
1-1/4 lbs. peeled cooked shrimp
6 lemon slices

In a medium bowl, beat together mayonnaise, half and half, Worcestershire sauce, sugar, lemon juice, salt, mustard and anchovy paste. Set aside to let flavors blend. Line 4 cocktail glasses with lettuce leaves. Arrange olives and shrimp in lettuce-lined glasses. Spoon mayonnaise dressing over shrimp. Garnish with lemon slices. Makes 6 servings.

Variation

Substitute lightly whipped cream for mayonnaise and half and half. Add 1 or 2 tablespoons drained canned crushed pineapple or chopped fresh orange segments.

Picnic Macaroni Salad

1 cup mayonnaise
2 tablespoons white-wine vinegar
1-1/2 teaspoons sugar
2 teaspoons prepared mustard
1/8 teaspoon celery seeds
1 teaspoon salt
1/8 teaspoon black pepper
8 oz. elbow or salad macaroni, cooked, drained, cooled
2 green onions, thinly sliced
1 cup finely chopped celery
1/2 cup cooked green peas
1/2 green bell pepper, sliced

In a small bowl, combine mayonnaise, vinegar, sugar, mustard, celery seeds, salt and black pepper. In a large bowl, combine macaroni, green onions, celery and peas. Pour mayonnaise mixture over macaroni mixture; toss to blend. Serve immediately or, cover and refrigerate until ready to serve. Garnish with green-pepper slices. If used on a picnic, carry in a chilled ice chest. Makes 8 to 10 servings.

Variation

Add 1 cup (4 ounces) diced Cheddar cheese when peas are added.

Coleslaw

1 small cabbage, shredded
4 bacon slices, cooked crisp, crumbled
1/2 onion, finely chopped
1 small carrot, shredded
1/4 cup mayonnaise
2 tablespoons white-wine vinegar
1/2 teaspoon sugar
1 teaspoon salt
1/8 teaspoon freshly ground white pepper

Place cabbage in a large serving bowl. Add bacon, onion and carrot. In a small bowl, stir together mayonnaise, vinegar, sugar, salt and white pepper. Fold dressing into cabbage. Cover and let stand 15 minutes. Makes 4 to 6 servings.

Variations

Sweet Slaw: Stir in 1 grated apple and 1/4 cup finely chopped celery. If apple is sweet, add extra vinegar. Sprinkle with 1/3 cup coarsely chopped walnuts. Omit onion.

Sweet-&-Sour Slaw: Add 1/2 cup drained canned pineapple tidbits or crushed pineapple. Omit onion.

Southern-Style Corn Soufflé

10 bacon slices, cut in halves
1/4 cup butter
1 small onion, finely chopped
3 tablespoons all-purpose flour
1/3 cup milk
1 teaspoon salt
1/4 teaspoon dry mustard
1/4 teaspoon red (cayenne) pepper
1/4 teaspoon sugar
1 egg yolk
3 white-bread slices, cut in small cubes
1 (17-oz.) can whole-kernel corn, drained
1/2 cup finely shredded Monterey Jack cheese (2 oz.)
1 cup fresh breadcrumbs

Preheat oven to 400F (205C). In a medium skillet, fry bacon until crisp. Place cooked bacon and drippings in a 1- to 1-1/2-quart baking dish; set aside. Melt 2 tablespoons butter in skillet. Add onion; sauté until transparent. Stir in flour until moistened; stir in milk. Season with salt, mustard, red pepper and sugar. Stirring constantly, simmer about 5 minutes. In a small bowl, beat egg yolk. Stir in about 1/4 cup hot sauce. Stir egg-yolk mixture into remaining sauce; set aside. Melt 1 tablespoon butter in a small saucepan. Add bread cubes; sauté until golden brown. Stir corn and sautéed bread cubes into sauce. Pour over bacon in baking dish. Combine cheese and breadcrumbs; sprinkle over soufflé. Dot with remaining butter. Bake 20 minutes or until top is lightly browned. Makes 4 servings.

All-American Meatloaf

1-1/2 lbs. ground beef
1/2 lb. ground pork
1 onion, finely chopped
1/2 cup fresh breadcrumbs
1 teaspoon salt
1/8 teaspoon white pepper
1 egg, slightly beaten
About 1 cup tomato juice
4 canned pineapple rings
1 tablespoon butter

Preheat oven to 350F (175C). In a large bowl, combine beef and pork. Stir in onion, breadcrumbs, salt, white pepper and egg. Stir in enough tomato juice to make a firm loaf. Shape mixture into a loaf; place on a rack in a roasting pan. Or, pack mixture into a 9'' x 5'' loaf pan. Bake on bottom oven rack 1 to 1-1/2 hours. About 20 minutes before end of cooking time, arrange pineapple rings over top of meatloaf; dot with butter. Continue cooking until pineapple begins to brown and loaf is cooked through. Makes 6 servings.

Variation

Omit pineapple rings. Brush top of unbaked loaf with ketchup, tomato sauce or canned condensed tomato soup. About 20 minutes before end of cooking time, arrange 5 bacon slices over top of meatloaf. Bake until bacon is crisp.

Ham & Sweet Potatoes

1 (1-3/4-lb.) fully cooked ham
1 cup hot water
4 sweet potatoes, peeled, cut in quarters
1 orange, peeled, sliced
2 tablespoons butter
1/4 cup packed brown sugar
1 tablespoon lemon juice

Preheat oven to 325F (165C). Place ham in a baking dish with a tight-fitting lid. Pour water around ham. Arrange sweet potatoes and orange slices alternately around ham. Dot ham with butter; sprinkle with brown sugar and lemon juice. Cover and bake on bottom oven rack 1 hour. Baste ham and potatoes 2 or 3 times with pan drippings. Makes 6 to 8 servings.

Variation

Substitute pineapple slices or apple slices for orange slices.

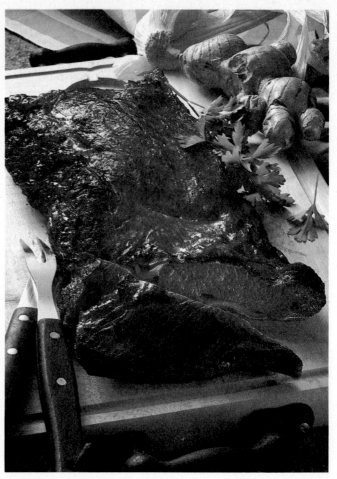

Baked Spareribs

4-1/2 lbs. fresh pork spareribs, cut in pieces
Salt and pepper

Barbecue Sauce:
1 tablespoon lard or vegetable shortening
1 onion, finely chopped
1/4 cup ketchup
5 tablespoons water
3 tablespoons Worcestershire sauce
2 tablespoons vinegar
1/4 cup lemon juice
2 teaspoons prepared mustard
2 tablespoons brown sugar
1 teaspoon dried leaf basil
1/2 teaspoon chili powder

Prepare Barbecue Sauce; keep hot. Preheat oven to 450F
(230C). Season spareribs with salt and pepper; arrange on a rack
in a shallow baking pan. Brush with barbecue sauce. Bake
spareribs 30 minutes. Reduce heat to 350F (175C). Bake 1 hour
longer, brushing frequently with sauce. To serve, arrange baked
spareribs on a platter. Makes 8 servings.
To make sauce, melt lard or shortening in a medium saucepan.
Add onion; sauté until transparent. Stir in remaining sauce
ingredients. Cover and simmer 30 minutes.

Texas Grilled Steak

1 garlic clove, crushed
1 cup soy sauce
1/2 teaspoon grated fresh gingerroot
2 tablespoons dry sherry
3/4 cup sugar
1 (3-lb.) beef top-round or sirloin steak

In a small bowl, combine garlic, soy sauce, gingerroot, sherry
and sugar; stir until sugar dissolves. Place beef in a large shallow
dish. Pour soy mixture over beef. Cover and refrigerate at least
2 hours, turning frequently and spooning marinade over beef.
Preheat barbecue grill or broiler. Drain beef, reserving
marinade. Place beef on grill or under broiler. Cook on each
side to desired doneness. Brush once or twice during cooking
with reserved marinade. To serve, thinly slice beef across the
grain. Makes 8 servings.

Cook's Tip

The longer beef marinates, the more tender and flavorful it becomes.
Store remaining marinade in refrigerator; use within 2 weeks.

Louisiana Jambalaya

1 (2-1/2- to 3-lb.) chicken, cut in pieces
3/4 lb. fully cooked ham, cut in 3/4-inch cubes
About 1 cup vegetable oil
2 onions, finely chopped
2 tomatoes, peeled, finely chopped
1 green bell pepper, finely chopped
1/2 teaspoon saffron threads
1 teaspoon hot water
1 cup hot chicken stock or broth
1/2 teaspoon dried leaf thyme
1/8 teaspoon red (cayenne) pepper
1/2 teaspoon salt
1 cup uncooked long-grain white rice
1 cup fresh or frozen green peas
2 large smoked sausages, sliced
3/4 to 1 lb. cooked lobster, finely chopped

Place chicken and ham in a deep bowl. Pour 1 cup oil over chicken and ham. Cover and refrigerate 2 hours. Pour chicken mixture into a large skillet. Cook over medium heat about 10 minutes, adding more oil if necessary. Add onions; cook until transparent. Add tomatoes and green pepper. Cover and cook 30 minutes. In a small bowl, soak saffron in hot water 5 minutes. Stir saffron mixture, stock or broth, thyme, red pepper, salt and rice into chicken mixture. Cover and simmer 20 minutes or until rice is tender. Stir in peas, sausages and lobster; heat through. Spoon into a large serving bowl or platter. Makes 8 servings.

Crispy Fried Chicken

Vegetable oil for deep-frying
Salt
1 (3-lb.) chicken, cut in pieces

Batter:
2/3 cup all-purpose flour
1 teaspoon baking powder
2 eggs
1/4 teaspoon salt
6 to 7 tablespoons milk

Prepare batter; set aside. Pour oil 2 inches deep into a large, heavy saucepan or skillet. Heat oil to 350F (175C) or until a 1-inch cube of bread turns golden brown in 65 seconds. Rub salt over chicken; dip pieces in batter, coating completely. Place 3 or 4 coated pieces at a time in hot oil. Avoid crowding or chicken will not brown evenly. Fry, turning with tongs, until evenly browned and cooked through, 25 to 30 minutes for dark meat, 15 to 20 minutes for white meat. To test for doneness, remove 1 piece from oil. Pierce meat near bone with point of a knife. Meat should be white but still moist. As each piece is cooked, remove from fat using tongs or a slotted spoon; drain on paper towels. Repeat until all pieces are fried. Arrange fried chicken on a platter. Serve with a green-tomato or corn salad. Makes 8 servings.

To make batter, sift flour and baking powder into a medium bowl. In a small bowl, beat eggs with salt. Gradually beat in 6 tablespoons milk. Stir egg mixture into flour mixture, making a smooth batter. Add remaining milk if necessary.

Thanksgiving Stuffed Turkey

1 (11- to 13-lb.) turkey with giblets
Salt and white pepper
Vegetable oil
Giblet broth or water
2 tablespoons cornstarch

Stuffing:
2 (1-lb.) loaves day-old white bread
1 lb. veal or pork sausage
1 onion, finely chopped
4 celery stalks, finely chopped
2 eggs, beaten
1/2 cup butter, melted
1/4 cup chopped parsley
1 teaspoon dried leaf thyme
1/4 teaspoon dried leaf marjoram
1/4 teaspoon rubbed sage
1 teaspoon salt
1/4 teaspoon white pepper

Remove giblets from turkey. Prepare stuffing, using giblets. Preheat oven to 325F (165C). Remove excess fat from turkey. Rub inside turkey with salt and white pepper. Spoon stuffing lightly into neck cavity. Pull neck skin over stuffing; fasten to back with small skewers. Place turkey, neck-side down, in a large bowl. Lightly stuff turkey. Close cavity by folding skin over stuffing; fasten with skewers. Place turkey breast-side up. Lift wings toward neck and fold under the back. Tie tail and ends of drumsticks together with kitchen string. Rub turkey with oil. Place breast-side up on a rack in a shallow roasting pan. Season with salt. Insert a meat thermometer in center of inner-thigh muscle, if desired. Cover turkey loosely with foil; roast 3-1/2 hours, brushing lightly with oil every 20 to 30 minutes. Remove foil. Roast 1 to 2 hours longer or until thermometer registers 180F to 185F (80C to 85C) or until juices run clear when a knife is inserted between thigh and breast. Place turkey on a platter; cover with foil. Let stand 20 to 30 minutes before carving.

To make stuffing, in a medium saucepan, cover turkey giblets with water. Cook over medium-high heat until tender. Drain, reserving giblets and broth. Cut bread into small cubes; chop cooked giblets, using only half of liver, if desired. In a large bowl, combine chopped giblets, bread cubes, remaining stuffing ingredients and enough reserved broth to dampen bread cubes.

To make gravy, skim fat from pan drippings. Stir 1/2 cup reserved giblet broth into drippings; season with salt and white pepper. Boil 15 minutes to reduce liquid. In a small bowl, combine 1/4 cup water and cornstarch. Stir cornstarch mixture into reduced drippings. Cook, stirring constantly, until thickened. Serve gravy with sliced turkey. Makes 8 to 10 servings.

Cook's Tip

If turkey is frozen, allow time to thaw. An 11- to 13-lb. turkey takes 36 to 48 hours to thaw in the refrigerator.

Boston Baked Beans

1 lb. dried pea beans, small white beans or navy beans
Water
1-1/2 teaspoons salt
1 teaspoon dry mustard
1/2 cup molasses
1/4 cup packed brown sugar
1 onion, finely chopped or sliced
1/4 lb. fresh lean salt pork, cut in 3/4-inch slices
Pepper

Soak beans in cold water to cover 12 hours; drain well. In a large saucepan, bring beans and 6 cups water to a boil. Cover and simmer 15 minutes. Drain, reserving cooking liquid; place drained beans in a 2- or 3-quart bean pot or casserole with a tight-fitting lid. Preheat oven to 325F (165C). In a small bowl, combine salt and mustard. Stir in molasses, brown sugar and 1 cup reserved cooking liquid. Stir molasses mixture and onion into beans. Arrange salt pork over beans. Add enough reserved cooking liquid to cover beans. Cover and bake on bottom oven rack 4 to 5 hours. Stir occasionally during cooking, adding more reserved cooking liquid when necessary to keep beans covered with liquid. About 30 minutes before end of cooking time, remove lid to let some liquid evaporate, if desired. Sprinkle with freshly ground pepper. Makes 6 servings.

Variation

Substitute bacon for salt pork.

Dinner Casserole Loaf

3/4 cup warm water (110F, 45C)
1/2 teaspoon sugar
1 (1/4-oz.) envelope active dry yeast (1 tablespoon)
1 cup ricotta cheese or cottage cheese (8 oz.)
1 egg, beaten
1 teaspoon salt
1/3 cup vegetable oil
1/2 teaspoon celery seeds
1/4 teaspoon celery salt
1 teaspoon dried leaf rosemary, crushed
3/4 teaspoon dried leaf basil, crushed
1/4 cup finely chopped onion
2-1/2 to 3 cups all-purpose flour
1/4 teaspoon celery seeds

Generously grease a deep, round 1-1/2-quart casserole with straight sides; set aside. In a large bowl, combine water, sugar and yeast; let stand 5 minutes or until foamy. In a small saucepan, heat cheese until warmed through; stir until smooth. Set aside to cool slightly. Stir in egg, salt, oil, 1/2 teaspoon celery seeds, celery salt, rosemary, basil and onion. Stir cheese mixture into yeast mixture until blended. Stir in 2-1/2 cups flour until blended. Add enough remaining flour to make a soft dough. Turn out dough onto a lightly floured surface. Knead gently about 5 minutes. Dough will be very soft, but not sticky. Place in greased casserole, turning to grease all sides. Sprinkle with 1/4 teaspoon celery seeds. Cover and let rise in a warm place until doubled in bulk, about 45 minutes. Preheat oven to 425F (220C). Bake 10 minutes. Reduce heat to 350F (175C). Bake 15 to 20 minutes longer or until loaf is golden brown and sounds hollow when tapped on the bottom. Turn out of casserole onto a rack. Cool right-side up 10 to 15 minutes before cutting with a serrated knife. Makes 1 large loaf.

Light & Crisp Waffles

1 cup all-purpose flour
1 tablespoon baking powder
Pinch of salt
2 teaspoons sugar
2 eggs, separated
3 tablespoons butter, melted
About 6 tablespoons milk
1/3 cup half and half
Maple syrup

Preheat a waffle iron according to manufacturer's directions. In a medium bowl, stir together flour, baking powder, salt and sugar. In another medium bowl, beat egg yolks; stir in butter, 6 tablespoons milk and half and half. Beat in flour mixture until batter is smooth, thick and creamy. If necessary, add a little more milk. In a small bowl, beat egg whites until stiff but not dry. Fold into batter. Spoon some of the batter onto each section of hot waffle iron. Close iron and keep closed until waffles are golden brown on both sides. Repeat with remaining batter. Warm maple syrup; serve with waffles. Makes 4 servings.

Cook's Tip

If you do not have a waffle iron, fry batter on a griddle, making small pancakes.

Cranberry-Nut Bread

2 cups all-purpose flour
1-1/2 teaspoons baking powder
1/2 teaspoon baking soda
1 cup sugar
1/2 teaspoon salt
2 tablespoons butter, melted
1 tablespoon grated orange peel
1/2 cup plus 2 tablespoons orange juice
1 egg, beaten
1/2 cup chopped walnuts
1 cup finely chopped fresh cranberries

Grease a 9'' x 5'' loaf pan; set aside. Preheat oven to 350F (175C). In a large bowl, stir together flour, baking powder, baking soda, sugar and salt. In a medium bowl, combine butter, orange peel, orange juice and egg. Stir into dry ingredients only until moistened. Fold in nuts and cranberries. Spoon into greased pan. Bake 70 minutes or until a wooden pick inserted in center comes out clean and top is golden brown. Remove from pan; cool on a rack. Makes 1 loaf.

Cook's Tip

Recipe can be doubled or tripled.

Down-Home Apple Pie

Flaky Pie Pastry, page 8
3/4 cup sugar
2 tablespoons all-purpose flour
1/4 teaspoon salt
1/2 teaspoon ground cinnamon
1/8 teaspoon ground nutmeg
6 to 7 cups thinly sliced, peeled apples (about 3 lbs.)
2 tablespoons butter, shaved

Prepare pastry; gently ease bottom pastry into a 9-inch pie pan. Trim edge 1/2 inch larger than pan. Preheat oven to 375F (190C). In a large bowl, stir together sugar, flour, salt, cinnamon and nutmeg; stir in apples. Toss to coat evenly. Spoon into bottom pastry. Dot with butter. Place top pastry over apple filling. Trim edge 1 inch larger than pan. Fold upper crust under lower crust, making a raised edge; flute edge. Cover pie with foil, carefully covering fluted edge. Bake 25 minutes; remove foil. Bake 25 to 30 minutes longer or until crust is golden brown. Serve warm. Makes 1 (9-inch) pie.

Variation

Add 1/3 cup raisins to sugar mixture.

Cook's Tip

Although many dishes in the United States had their origins in other countries, some foods are typically *American*. Apple pie and ice cream are two of these.

Apple trees are found in every state of the Union. Legend tells of a man named John who wandered throughout the Middle West in the United States planting apple seeds. But it is not just legend. John Chapman, a pioneer nurseryman, began collecting apple seeds in western Pennsylvania. He soon began a trek westward, planting apple nurseries. He sold and gave seedlings to pioneers. His cheerfulness and his quaint appearance—long flowing hair, bare feet, ragged trousers, cooking-pot hat and burlap vest—gave rise to stories and poems about *Johnny Appleseed*. There are many apple orchards today that began from John Chapman's seedlings.

Cooking apples are available all year round. They include McIntosh, Northern Spy, Winesap, Granny Smith, Jonathan, Newtown Pippin and Rome Beauty. Golden Delicious can also be used. Beacon, Cortland, Gravenstein, Lodi and Wealthy are juicy and fairly sweet, making them excellent for applesauce.

Cranberry & Cream-Cheese Bombe

2 cups fresh cranberries
1-1/2 cups sugar
2 (8-oz.) pkgs. cream cheese, room temperature
1-3/4 cups whipping cream
2 tablespoons honey
2 tablespoons ground almonds

Reserve a few cranberries for garnish. Finely chop remaining cranberries or puree in a blender or food processor. Stir in 3/4 cup sugar. In a medium bowl, beat cheese with remaining 3/4 cup sugar. In another medium bowl, whip cream until stiff peaks form; reserve 1 cup whipped cream. Fold remaining whipped cream and pureed cranberries into cheese mixture. Pour honey into a medium bowl or blancmange mold, turning until inside is completely coated with honey. Sprinkle almonds into honey-coated bowl or mold, covering side completely. Spoon cheese mixture into bowl or mold; freeze 4 to 5 hours. To serve, dip bowl or mold quickly in hot water. Invert onto a serving platter. Garnish with reserved whipped cream and cranberries. Makes 6 to 8 servings.

Celebration Mocha Cake

1/2 cup vegetable shortening
1 cup lightly packed brown sugar
3 eggs, separated
1 teaspoon vanilla extract
2-1/3 cups all-purpose or cake flour
1/2 cup unsweetened cocoa powder
1-1/2 teaspoons baking soda
1/2 teaspoon salt
1-1/3 cups strong-brewed coffee
3/4 cup granulated sugar

Frosting:
1/4 cup butter, room temperature
2-1/2 cups powdered sugar
2 tablespoons unsweetened cocoa powder
1 teaspoon vanilla extract
2 tablespoons hot strong-brewed coffee
Chocolate flakes or grated chocolate

Preheat oven to 350F (175C). Grease and flour 2 round 9-inch cake pans; set aside. In a large bowl, beat shortening until creamy; beat in brown sugar until fluffy. Beat in egg yolks 1 at a time; stir in vanilla. In a medium bowl, stir together flour, cocoa powder, baking soda and salt. Alternately stir flour mixture and coffee into brown-sugar mixture, beginning and ending with flour mixture. In a medium bowl, beat egg whites until soft peaks form. Gradually beat in granulated sugar until stiff but not dry. Fold into batter. Pour batter evenly into prepared pans. Bake 35 to 40 minutes or until a pick inserted in center comes out clean. Cool on a rack.
To make frosting, in a medium bowl, cream butter. Gradually beat in powdered sugar, cocoa powder, vanilla and coffee until smooth. Frost layers; place one on top of other. Frost side of cake. Sprinkle top with chocolate. Makes 1 (2-layer) 9-inch cake.

Cherry-Vanilla Ice Cream

Ice Cream:
2 eggs
1-1/4 cups sugar
2 cups half and half
1 teaspoon vanilla extract
1 cup whipping cream
1 (16-oz.) jar maraschino cherries

Topping:
2 to 3 tablespoons all-purpose flour
Pinch of salt
1 cup water
Juice from cherries
1/4 teaspoon cherry flavoring
3 to 4 drops red food coloring, if
  desired

To make ice cream, in a large bowl, beat eggs until thick and lemon colored. Beat in sugar until light and airy. Gently beat in half and half, vanilla and whipping cream. Pour into ice cream canister. Freeze in an ice-cream maker according to manufacturer's directions. Drain cherries, reserving liquid for topping; coarsely chop cherries. When ice cream is partially frozen, remove lid and add chopped cherries. Continue freezing until firm.

To make topping, in a small bowl, combine flour and salt; stir to blend. Stir in 2 to 4 tablespoons water until mixture is smooth. In a small saucepan, combine cherry juice, flour mixture and remaining water. Stir over medium-high heat until mixture thickens slightly. Stir in cherry flavoring and red food coloring, if desired. Stirring constantly, cook about 1 minute longer. Makes about 2 quarts ice cream and about 1-1/2 cups topping.

Fifteen-Minute Soup
SOPA DE CUARTO DE HORA

1 lb. cod or haddock fillets, cut in small pieces
1 teaspoon lemon juice
3-1/2 cups water
1/2 bay leaf
1 teaspoon salt
1 cup fresh or frozen green peas
2 tablespoons vegetable oil
1 onion, finely chopped
1 medium tomato
1/4 cup cooked rice
5 oz. peeled cooked shrimp
24 freshly opened oysters
1 white-bread slice, cut in cubes
1 tablespoon chopped parsley

Sprinkle fish with lemon juice. In a medium saucepan, bring water, bay leaf and salt to a boil. Add fish pieces and peas. Simmer 6 minutes. Meanwhile, heat 1 tablespoon oil in a medium skillet. Add onion; sauté until transparent. Peel tomato; remove and discard seeds. Chop tomato. Add tomato to onion; cook until soft. Stir onion mixture, rice and shrimp into fish mixture. Add oysters, in their shells, and any oyster liquid. Heat remaining 1 tablespoon oil in a skillet; sauté bread cubes in hot oil until golden brown. Remove and discard bay leaf. Pour soup into a tureen or serve in individual bowls. Sprinkle with browned bread cubes and parsley. Makes 4 servings.

Steak with Olives
LOMO DE VACA CON ACEITUNAS

4 medium tomatoes
2 tablespoons all-purpose flour
1 teaspoon salt
1/8 teaspoon white pepper
4 (6- to 8-oz.) beef top-loin or sirloin steaks
1/4 cup olive oil
1 onion, finely chopped
4 garlic cloves, finely chopped
1 cup white wine
20 pitted ripe olives, coarsely chopped
2 hard-cooked eggs, chopped
2 tablespoons chopped parsley

Preheat oven to 400F (205C). Peel tomatoes; remove and discard seeds. Chop tomatoes. In a small bowl, combine flour, salt and white pepper; coat beef with flour mixture. Heat oil in a large skillet. Add beef; brown on both sides. Place browned beef in a large casserole. Add onion to oil remaining in skillet; sauté until transparent. Add garlic and chopped tomatoes; sauté 3 to 4 minutes. Stir in wine. Pour onion mixture over beef; sprinkle with olives. Bake 10 minutes or until beef is tender. Arrange cooked beef in a serving dish; pour sauce over top. Sprinkle with eggs and parsley. Makes 4 servings.

Cornmeal Pasties

HALLACAS

Corn husks or waxed paper and foil
1/2 lb. boneless pork
Water
Salt
1-1/2 tablespoons olive oil
1 onion, finely chopped
1/2 lb. boneless chicken thighs or breasts, chopped
2 garlic cloves, finely chopped
1 green bell pepper, finely chopped
2 tomatoes, peeled, chopped
5 pimiento-stuffed green olives, sliced
1 tablespoon chopped parsley
1 tablespoon capers
1/2 tablespoon vinegar
1/2 tablespoon sugar
2 tablespoons raisins
1/8 teaspoon chili powder
Black pepper

Cornmeal dough:
Water
Salt
1-1/3 cups yellow cornmeal
2 tablespoons butter
1 egg

If corn husks are used, pasties will be smaller. Place corn husks in a large shallow pan; cover with hot water. Soak at least 1 hour; then dry thoroughly before using. To use waxed paper and foil, cut 12 to 15 (10-inch) squares of each.
To make filling, in a large saucepan, cover pork with lightly salted water. Bring to a boil; boil 30 minutes. Heat oil in a large skillet. Add onion; sauté until transparent. Stir in chicken, garlic, green pepper, olives, parsley, capers, vinegar, sugar, raisins, chili powder, black pepper and salt. Cover and cook 20 minutes. Finely dice cooked pork; stir into chicken mixture. Cook 5 to 10 minutes longer.
To make cornmeal dough, in a large saucepan, bring 2 cups water and 1/2 teaspoon salt to a boil. Slowly stir in cornmeal. Stirring constantly, simmer until slightly thickened. Stir in butter. Continue stirring over medium heat until mixture thickens. Remove from heat; beat in egg. Cover and set aside until cooled slightly.
To complete with waxed paper and foil, spoon about 2 tablespoons cornmeal dough on each piece of waxed paper. Use your fingers to spread dough to 7'' x 6'' rectangles. Place 3 to 4 tablespoons meat filling on each rectangle of dough. Fold waxed paper over filling so dough surrounds filling; press edges of dough to seal. Wrap each packet airtight with foil.
To complete with soaked, dried corn husks, place a spoonful of dough in center of each husk. Spread slightly, leaving a 1/2-inch margin of husk around dough. Place a little filling on dough; spread slightly. Top with a little dough. Fold sides of husk over dough and filling, enclosing completely. Fold pointed end of husk under, keeping seam on outside.
To cook, stand foil-wrapped packets or filled husks on folded ends in a large steamer or metal colander. In a large pot, place steamer or colander over boiling water. Cover and steam pasties 1 hour. Makes 12 to 15 foil-wrapped pasties or 20 to 30 corn-husk-wrapped pasties.

Variation

To make 1 large pastie, arrange layers of cornmeal dough and filling in a greased casserole, beginning and ending with dough. Cover with a lid or foil. Place casserole in a shallow baking pan. Add 1 inch water to outer pan. Bake 1 hour in preheated 350F (175C) oven.

Rice with Bananas

ARROZ CON BANANAS

1/4 teaspoon saffron threads
1 to 2 teaspoons hot water
2 cups hot cooked long-grain white rice
4 bananas
1 tablespoon vegetable oil
Pinch of salt
Pinch of red (cayenne) pepper
2 tablespoons chopped parsley

Preheat oven to 300F (150C). Dissolve saffron in hot water 5 minutes; stir into rice. Spoon rice into a heatproof serving bowl or shallow casserole. Place in oven to dry slightly. Peel bananas; cut in halves lengthwise. Heat oil in a large skillet; fry bananas until golden brown on both sides. Season with salt and red pepper. Sprinkle chopped parsley over rice; arrange fried bananas on top. Makes 4 servings.

Vegetable Stew with Corn

LORCO

4 ears of corn
5 tomatoes, peeled, cut in wedges
10 bacon slices, diced
2 tablespoons olive oil
2 onions, finely chopped
1 cup fresh or frozen green peas
1 lb. fresh pumpkin, peeled, chopped
1 green bell pepper, chopped
1 red bell pepper, chopped
4 potatoes, peeled, chopped
1 garlic clove, crushed
1/2 teaspoon dried leaf marjoram
1 teaspoon salt
1/8 teaspoon black pepper
About 1 cup water
1/2 cup shredded Cheddar cheese (2 oz.)
1 tablespoon chopped parsley

Cut corn into thick slices. Remove and discard seeds from tomatoes. Set cut corn and tomatoes aside. In a deep skillet, cook bacon until crisp. Add oil; when hot, add onions. Sauté until transparent. Stir in corn pieces, peas, pumpkin, green and red peppers, potatoes, garlic, marjoram, salt, black pepper and 1 cup water. Cover and simmer 25 to 30 minutes, adding a little water occasionally to prevent drying. Spoon into a large serving bowl. Sprinkle with cheese and parsley. Makes 4 to 6 servings.

Spring Rolls with Hot Sauce

CHA GIO/NUOC MAM

Spring Rolls:
2 oz. Chinese transparent noodles
Water
1 (4-oz.) can crabmeat or 4 oz. peeled cooked shrimp
1 small onion, finely chopped
3 green onions, finely chopped
1/4 lb. lean ground pork
1/4 teaspoon salt
Pinch of pepper
1 teaspoon shrimp paste
1 teaspoon chopped parsley
10 egg-roll skins
Vegetable oil for deep-frying

Hot Dipping Sauce:
1 lemon
4 dried red chilies, crushed
2 garlic cloves, chopped
1 teaspoon sugar
1 tablespoon red-wine vinegar
1 tablespoon water
1 tablespoon shrimp paste
1 tablespoon oyster sauce

To make rolls, soak noodles in hot water 10 minutes to soften; drain well. Cut noodles in 1-1/4-inch pieces. Chop crabmeat or shrimp. In a large bowl, combine soaked-noodle pieces, chopped crab or shrimp, onions, pork, salt, pepper, shrimp paste and parsley. Keep egg-roll skins covered until used. Place 2 heaping tablespoons filling on each egg-roll skin; press down slightly. Fold long sides of skin over filling. Roll up, starting at a short edge. Moisten outer edge of skin; firmly press edge to roll to seal. Pour oil into a wok or deep skillet. Heat oil to 350F (175C) or until a 1-inch cube of bread turns golden brown in 65 seconds. Fry 5 rolls at a time in hot fat, 7 to 8 minutes or until golden. Drain on paper towels.

To make sauce, peel lemon, removing all white pith. Chop lemon. Puree lemon, chilies, garlic, sugar, vinegar, water, shrimp paste and oyster sauce in a blender or food processor. Serve egg rolls with sauce, bean sprouts and pieces of cucumber wrapped in lettuce leaves. Makes 10 rolls.

Cook's Tip

In Vietnam, these rolls are held with the fingers and dipped in the sauce.

Fish Soup with Pineapple

CAN MANG CHUA THOM

1/2 fresh pineapple
2/3 lb. perch, pike, sea bream or sunfish fillets
1-1/2 teaspoons tamarind pulp, if desired
Water
2 tablespoons vegetable oil
1 (8-oz.) can sliced bamboo shoots, drained
1 teaspoon sugar
1/2 teaspoon salt
1/8 teaspoon ground ginger
1/8 teaspoon white pepper
1-1/2 teaspoons Hot Dipping Sauce, page 211
Juice of 1/2 lime or lemon
1-1/2 teaspoons chopped fresh mint

Peel pineapple; remove woody center and *eyes*. Cut pineapple into chunks. Cut fish into 1/4-inch pieces. If used, boil tamarind pulp in 6 tablespoons water until liquid is reduced by half. Strain tamarind liquid; discard pulp. Heat oil in a wok or large skillet. Add pineapple chunks and bamboo shoots; sauté 3 to 4 minutes. Sprinkle with sugar; stir in tamarind liquid, if used. In a large saucepan, bring 1 cup water and 1/4 teaspoon salt to a boil. Add fish pieces; season with ginger, white pepper, Hot Dipping Sauce and lime or lemon juice. Add sautéed bamboo shoots and pineapple chunks; simmer 2 to 3 minutes. To serve, spoon into a large bowl; sprinkle with mint. Makes 4 servings.

Pork with Shrimp

MANG XAO THIY HEO

2 tablespoons vegetable oil
10 to 12 green onions, white part only, chopped
2 or 3 dried red chilies, crushed
12 oz. lean pork, thinly sliced
5 oz. pork liver, thinly sliced
1 (8-oz.) can sliced bamboo shoots, drained
8 oz. peeled cooked shrimp
1 teaspoon salt
Pinch of white pepper
2 medium tomatoes, peeled, diced
1 teaspoon cornstarch
2 tablespoons water
1-1/2 teaspoons Hot Dipping Sauce, page 211
1 teaspoon shrimp paste
1-1/2 teaspoons chopped cilantro leaves or parsley

Heat oil in a wok or large skillet. Add onions and chilies; sauté 3 minutes. Add pork and liver; cook 2 minutes. Stir in bamboo shoots and shrimp. Season with salt and white pepper. Add tomatoes; cook 2 minutes longer. In a small bowl, combine cornstarch and water; stir into pork mixture. Stir in Hot Dipping Sauce and shrimp paste. Stirring constantly, cook until thickened. Spoon into a serving dish. Sprinkle with cilantro or parsley. Makes 4 servings.

Lamb Paprika
DJUVEČ SA JAGNJEČIM MÉSOM

7 tablespoons vegetable oil
2 medium onions, cut in rings
1 large eggplant, chopped
8 oz. fresh pumpkin, peeled, chopped
4 green bell peppers, chopped
1-1/2 lbs. boneless lamb, thinly sliced
1 cup uncooked long-grain white rice
Salt and black pepper
1 tablespoon sweet paprika
1 cup water
4 medium tomatoes, sliced

Preheat oven to 350F (175C). Lightly oil a large baking dish; set aside. Heat 6 tablespoons oil in a large saucepan. Add onions; sauté until transparent. Stir in eggplant, pumpkin, green peppers and lamb. Cover and cook 10 minutes. Add rice; season with salt, black pepper and paprika. Stir in water. Spoon lamb mixture into oiled dish. Top with tomatoes. Cover and bake 1-1/2 hours. Serve with a green salad or beet salad. Makes 4 to 6 servings.

Zucchini Moussaka
MÚSAKA OD TIKVICA SA SIROM

2-1/4 lbs. zucchini
Salt
6 eggs
1 tablespoon all-purpose flour
5 tablespoons vegetable oil
2 cups milk
2 cups diced cooked ham
1 (1-lb.) carton lowfat cottage cheese or ricotta cheese (2 cups)

Peel zucchini, if desired. Cut zucchini lengthwise into 1/4-inch slices. Sprinkle with salt; place in a sieve. Let drain 10 minutes. Pat zucchini dry with paper towels. In a small bowl, beat 2 eggs. Dip each zucchini slice in flour, then in beaten egg. Heat oil in a large skillet. Fry coated zucchini slices in hot oil, a few slices at a time, until golden brown on both sides. Drain on paper towels. Preheat oven to 400F (205C). Butter a large baking dish; set aside. In a medium bowl, beat remaining 4 eggs plus any egg left from dipping zucchini; stir in milk. In a large bowl, stir ham into cottage cheese or ricotta cheese. Stir in about 1/3 of the egg mixture or enough to make a thick mixture. Arrange a layer of coated zucchini slices over bottom of buttered dish. Top with some of the cheese mixture. Alternate layering zucchini slices and cheese mixture, ending with a layer of zucchini. Pour remaining egg mixture over top. Bake 40 minutes or until zucchini is tender. Makes 4 to 6 servings.

Yugoslavian Goulash
SATARAŠ

6 tablespoons vegetable shortening
8 oz. beef cubes for stew
8 oz. boneless lamb, cut in cubes
8 oz. boneless pork, cut in cubes
3 onions, coarsely chopped
2 garlic cloves, crushed
1 tablespoon sweet paprika
About 1 cup water
1 teaspoon salt
1 teaspoon caraway seeds
5 medium tomatoes, peeled, chopped
3 green bell peppers, chopped
1 cup dairy sour cream

Melt shortening in a large saucepan. Add beef, lamb and pork; brown over high heat, stirring constantly. Add onions and garlic; cook 3 to 4 minutes. Sprinkle with paprika; stir in water, salt and caraway seeds. Cover and simmer 45 minutes over low heat, adding more water as necessary. Stir in tomatoes and green peppers. Cook 20 to 30 minutes. Reserve about 2 tablespoons sour cream for garnish. Stir remaining sour cream into goulash. Spoon into a serving bowl; top with reserved sour cream. Serve with cooked rice. Makes 4 to 6 servings.

Lamb Kabob
ŠIŠ ĆEVAP

2-1/4 lbs. boneless lamb
Salt and black pepper
1 tablespoon sweet paprika
3 green bell peppers, cut in large squares
3 large tomatoes, cut in wedges
2 onions, cut in thick slices
3 tablespoons vegetable oil

Preheat barbecue grill or broiler. Season lamb with salt, black pepper and paprika. Oil a large spit or 4 to 6 metal or wooden skewers. Slide pieces of seasoned lamb, green peppers, tomato and onion onto spit or each skewer, until all ingredients are used. Brush lightly with oil. Grill or broil 15 to 20 minutes, turning occasionally. If using an electric grill, reduce cooking time to 10 to 15 minutes. Remove cooked meat and vegetables from spit or skewers. Arrange in a serving dish. Serve with finely chopped onion and chili peppers. Makes 4 to 6 servings.

Ground-Meat Patties
PLJESKAVICA

12 oz. ground lean pork
12 oz. ground lean lamb
3 onions, finely chopped
2 garlic cloves, crushed
1 large green bell pepper, chopped
1 teaspoon salt
1/2 teaspoon black pepper
1/2 teaspoon dried leaf oregano
1 tablespoon chopped parsley
3 tablespoons vegetable oil
4 medium tomatoes
2 onions

In a large bowl, combine pork, lamb, chopped onions, garlic, green pepper, salt, black pepper, oregano and parsley; blend thoroughly. Shape mixture into flat patties about 6 inches in diameter. Cover and refrigerate 2 hours. Preheat barbecue grill or broiler; oil rack. Grill or broil patties 3 to 5 minutes on each side, brushing often with oil. Cut tomatoes and whole onions in halves; heat on grill or broiler 5 minutes. Serve with meat patties. Makes 4 servings.

Cook's Tip

In Yugoslavia, these meat cakes are served with a salad of cooked white beans, diced green and red peppers and sliced onion. The salad is served with a dressing of olive oil, white-wine vinegar, salt, pepper, crushed garlic and a little fresh or dried leaf oregano.

Meat Rolls & Meat Kabobs
ĆEVAPČIĆI/RAŽNJIĆI

Ground-Meat Rolls:
8 oz. finely ground veal
8 oz. finely ground pork
8 oz. finely ground lamb
3 garlic cloves, crushed
2 teaspoons salt
1/2 teaspoon white pepper
2 tablespoons vegetable oil

Meat Kabobs:
4 onions
1 lb. boneless veal, cut in 1-inch cubes
1 lb. lean boneless pork
6 tablespoons vegetable oil
1 teaspoon salt

To make rolls, in a large bowl, combine veal, pork, lamb, garlic, salt and white pepper. Shape mixture to resemble short sausages. Cover and refrigerate 3 to 4 hours. Preheat barbecue grill or broiler. Brush meat rolls with oil; grill or broil until browned and crisp. Serve with chopped onion. Makes 4 to 6 servings.
To make kabobs, finely chop 2 onions; cut remaining 2 onions into thin rings. Place veal, pork, onion rings and oil in a large bowl. Cover and refrigerate 3 to 4 hours, stirring occasionally. Discard onion rings and oil. Thread marinated meat onto 4 wood or metal skewers. Grill or broil until browned and crisp, turning frequently; season with salt. Serve with chopped onions. Makes 4 to 6 servings.

Foreign Title Index

Foreign Title Index

Index

Index

Index

Index

8.427081302974